THE INNOCENTS

A Photographic Essay of Vietnamese Children During the War

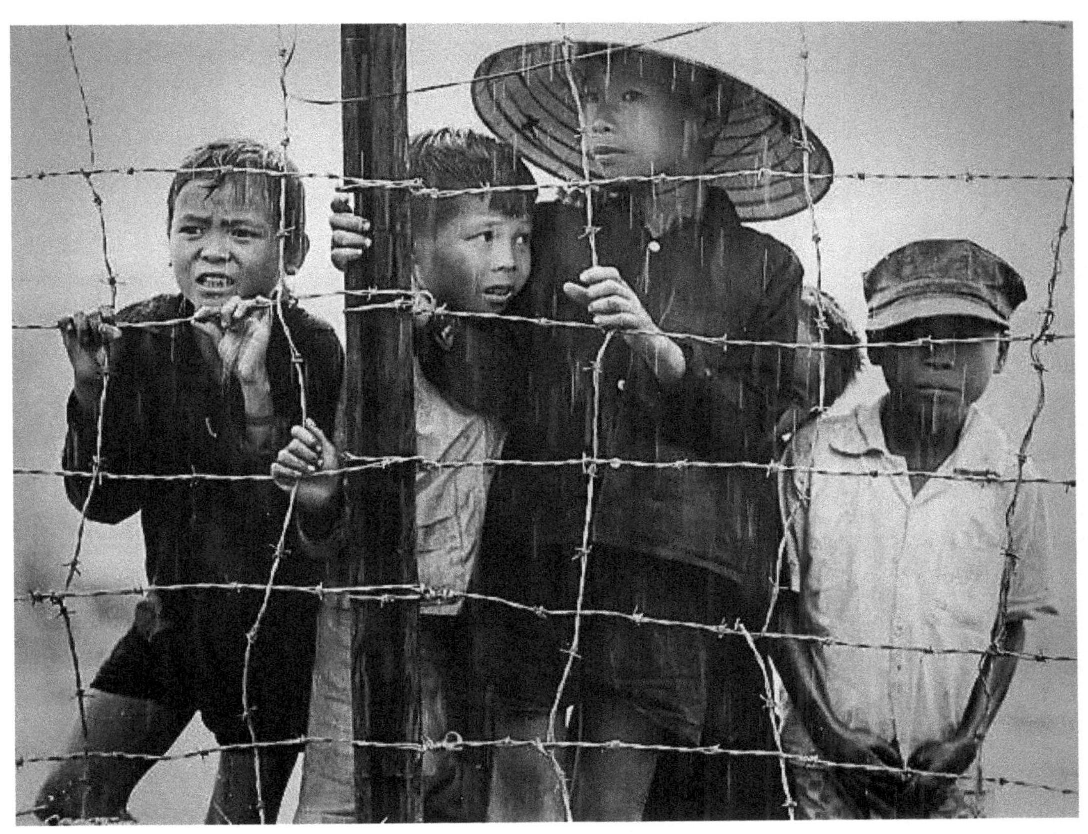

By
Bedford Chandler

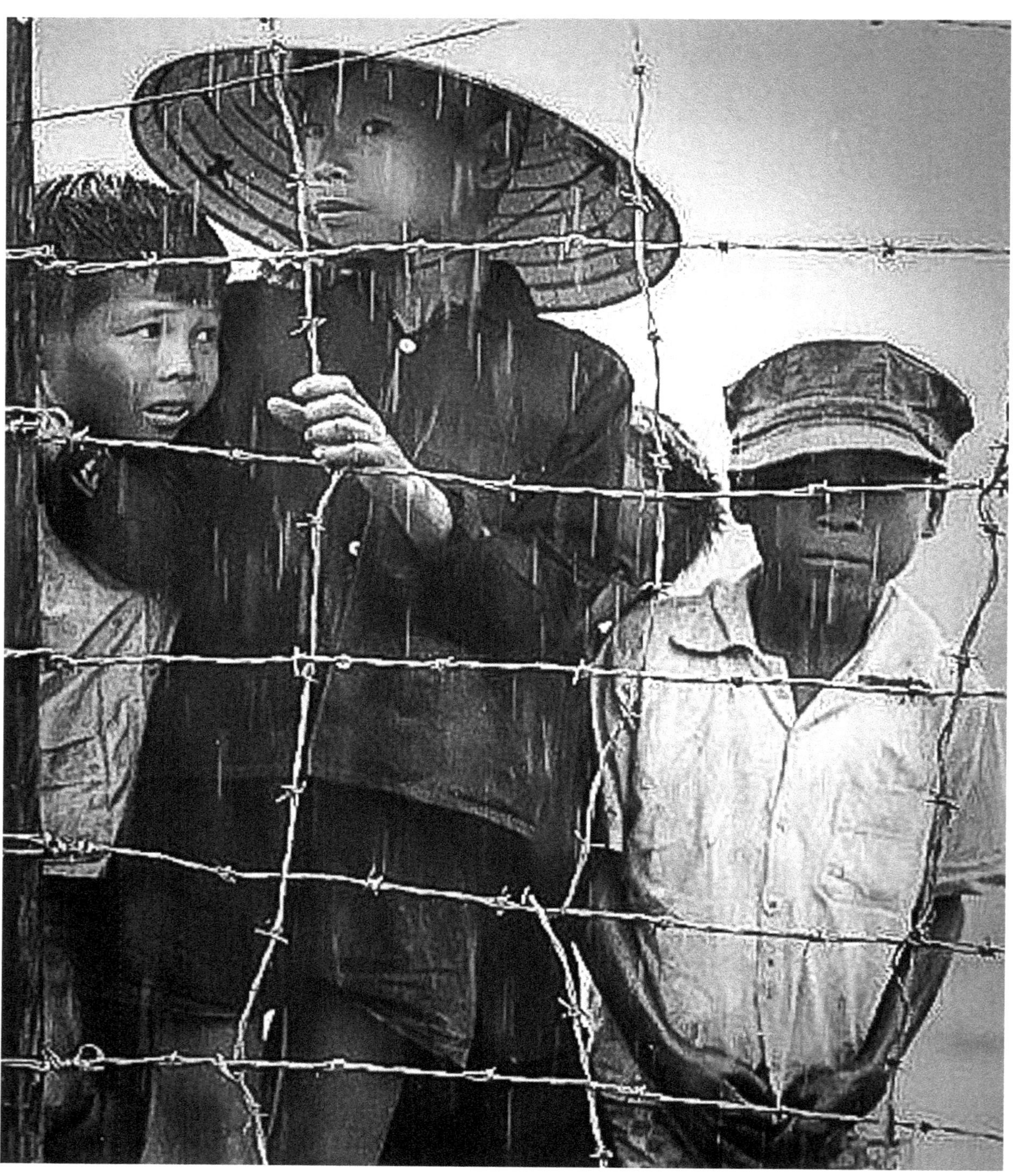

ISBN: 978-1-916770-77-5

Dedication

For the children of Vietnam and the world who have been victimized by the calamity of war. My wife Stephanie, whose tireless support and encouragement were vital for the completion of this book. My children's children, and all children, that they may be spared.

Acknowledgment

Carol Sterbenze, who advised, assisted, and encouraged me in formulating a path forward. Stan Ledington and John Buffington who assisted me with the technical aspects of digital formatting. The numerous friends who gave me insight, impartial enlightenment, and vital guidance.

Table of Contents

Introduction

As a Navy Corpsman I cared for wounded Marines in Viet Nam. When possible during combat operations in the field or from field medical units, I provided medical care to the local Vietnamese population in hamlets and villages. Medical care for the Vietnamese was practically non-existent in rural areas and the living conditions were primitive. The reality of what I saw so influenced me that I felt an ethical and humane need to commit as much time as possible to the Vietnamese people. After one year of caring primarily for battle casualties, I asked for, and was tasked, with the responsibility for civil affairs within my unit's tactical area of operations. For the following two years I ventured regularly into hamlets and villages providing care to the Vietnamese people.

The poignant images of children in this book were taken by me at the height of U.S. involvement in the war during the years of 1966-69. These images reveal the anguish, terror, bewilderment, and happiness of children born into a war that affected their everyday lives. Those who greeted me on jungle trails, happy, frightened… wary. Bare footed, often balancing a little brother or sister on their hip, holding out a hand for anything that we might give them. The children standing apart, fearful, harboring memories of horrific things endured or witnessed. At the time I knew little of their life realities. It was to come to me fitfully with time, as they confronted me in the hamlets and villages with disease, illness, and injury.

Today, 56 years after I began that journey, the images continue to penetrate with a power and emotion captured in the moment...the innocents continue to haunt me.

Overview

This book is about the Vietnamese children that I encountered during my three years in Viet Nam. Images of the children portrayed herein were taken in a variety of locations and situations that existed at the time I was exposed to them. What were normal everyday events to me at that time are now, in retrospect, abnormal.

Extreme poverty among the peasantry made their lives a hand to mouth existence. In the absence of war, it had been the norm since antiquity. Vietnamese in rural areas lived a simple agrarian lifestyle where village and family were all that mattered in life. Cycles of life within the family flowed with harvests, famine, death and births. Ethical systems within the culture sustained life and purpose. War, given birth by colonial and ideological conflict, changed the fabric of all that existed within the hamlets and villages of Viet Nam.

The war was a battle for the allegiance and control of the people. Children were the innocent casualties in this process. It is in this context that I entered their lives, hoping and assuming that I would have a positive impact providing medical care.

The Author

Bedford Chandler was born in Norfolk, Virginia in 1944, and lived in multiple states before completing his primary education in El Paso, Texas where he began secondary education at Texas Western College (UTEP). Bedford received specialty training with the United States Navy and served as a Medical Corpsman with the Marine Corps in Viet Nam for 3 Years. After completing his military service, Bedford attended and graduated from the University of Washington's Physician Assistant Program (Medex) in 1972. He provided medical care to under- served populations in Washington State and Alaska for 43 years. He assisted the University of Hawaii in establishing the Physician Assistant Program in Guyana, South America. When possible, Bedford continued his education with Schiller College, Madrid, Spain, Central Washington University, Ellensburg, Washington, Kennedy Western University, and Yakima Valley Community College, Yakima, Washington. Bedford has continued his journey with photographic excellence and exhibits his images in galleries, online, and solo exhibits. He has five children, seven grandchildren, and lives in Idaho and Alaska with his wife Stephanie

Phouc Ly Hamlet

Located west of Da Nang on a fertile agricultural plain where a number of hamlets and villages are situated. The area was more secure than rural areas located beyond the surrounding hills which were occupied by U.S. Marines.

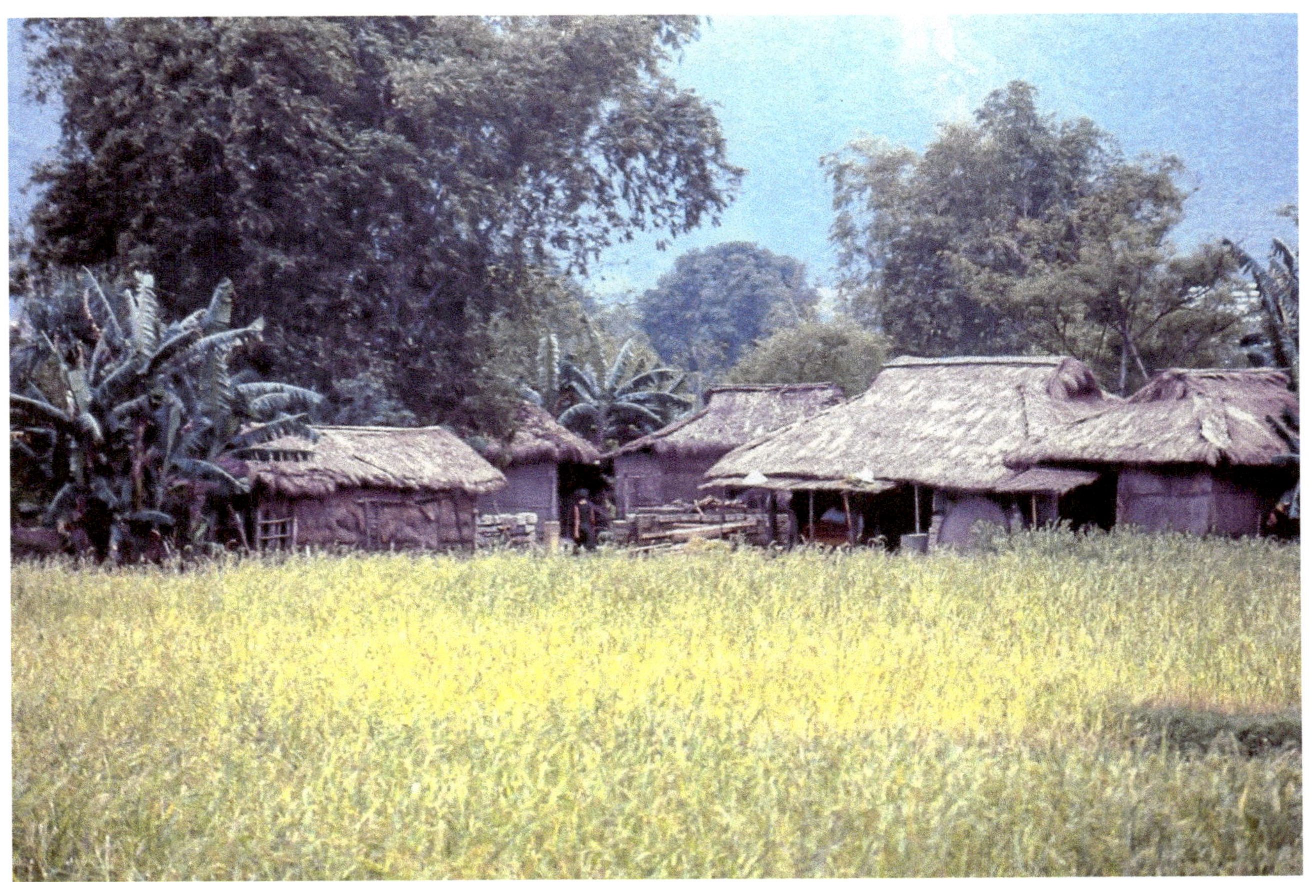

Thatched homes of Phuoc Ly Hamlet surrounded by paddies with mature rice stalks ready for harvest. 1966

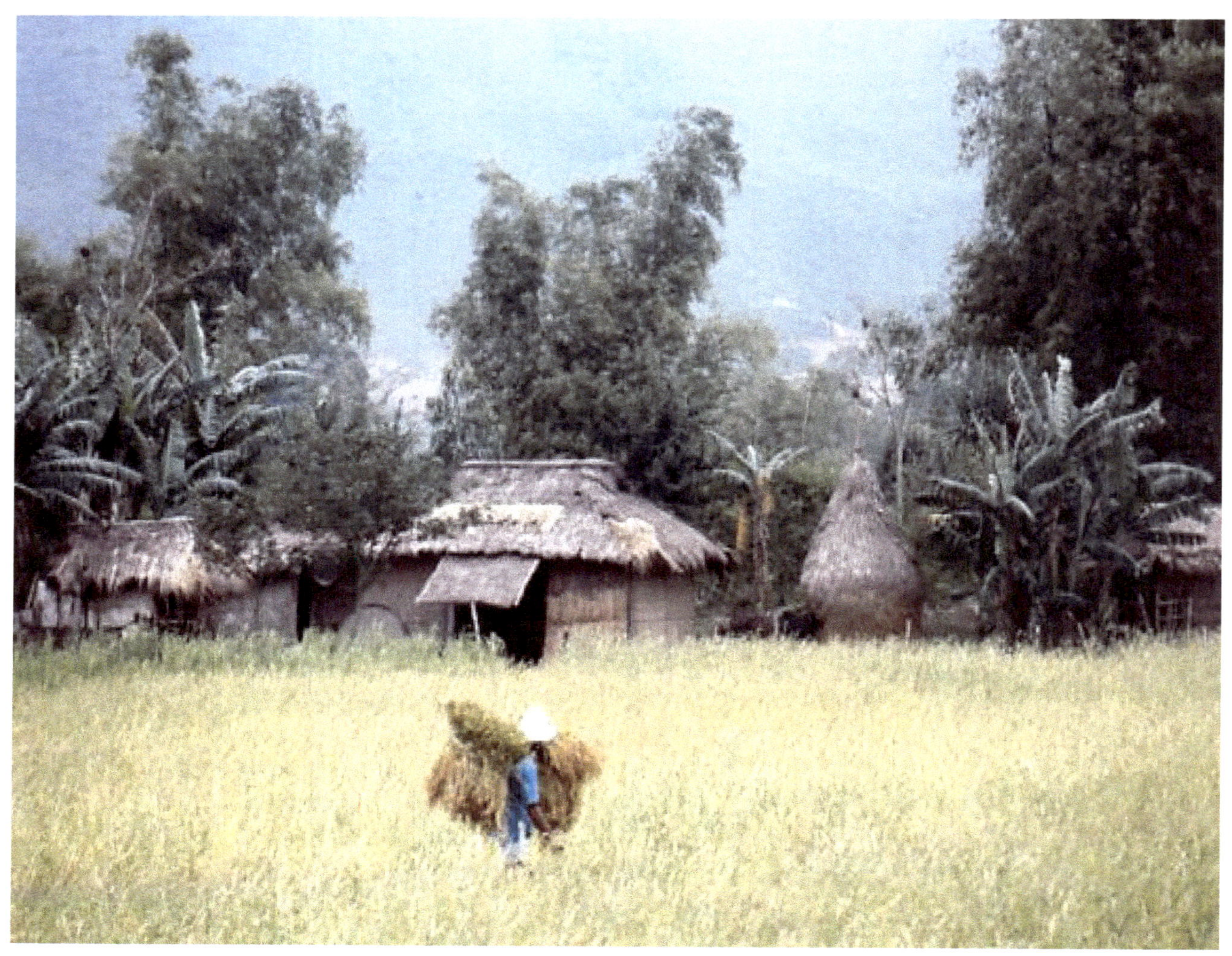

A hamlet resident carries freshly harvested rice to his home, where he will hand-thresh and dry the rice kernels.

Phuoc Ly Hamlet, 1966

Excerpt of a letter sent home, July, 1967,

Da Nang, Quang Nam Province

"Today we journeyed to an orphanage which is located about 8 miles out in the bush. The area is mountainous and lush with vegetation...really beautiful. We took medical supplies for the dispensary which is staffed by a Vietnamese Nun. We also took a large supply of hygiene sets which include soap, towels, washcloths, toothpaste, toothbrushes, and combs for the children to use. Before the kits were distributed, the children were required to listen while the dentist elaborated on the proper mechanics of tooth-brushing.

The dentist examined everyone's teeth, pulled several, and then we retired to a quiet lunch of rice and greens with the children who numbered about 30. We reluctantly departed about 1:30 p.m. so that we could keep a schedule which required us to be in Phuoc Ly Hamlet by 2 :00 p.m.

Across the paddies which border the hospital here, lies the Hamlet of Phuoc Ly. I have known the people of Phuoc Ly for as long as I have been in Viet Nam. Well over two years ago I participated in my first Medcap (Medical Civic Action Program) in that hamlet. If there is one reason for my decision to stay in Viet Nam this long, that reason was precipitated by my communion with those people at that time.

Quite frequently, the people of Phuoc Ly will solicit our assistance in problems which arise. We have always helped them to the best of our abilities, and in so doing, have maintained an excellent friendship.

Today we were invited to attend a Buddhist ceremony, which in essence, is a pre-Tet celebration signifying that everyone has repaired the ancestral graves. It is traditional to repair and otherwise beautify their ancestor's graves prior to the arrival of the Lunar New. The Vietnamese practice ancestor veneration, for their entire life cycle is based on the Lunar Calendar which consists of a 12-year cycle (Which repeats itself at the conclusion of the 12-year cycle). For instance, the Lunar New Year of 1969 is the year of the chicken. Twelve years from now the year of the chicken will return.

Deceased family members are worshipped because they are linked with the yet unborn generations. It is felt that the living is a link between that part of the family which has gone on (deceased) and that which is yet to come. The family is paramount. No individual's need is more important than the ongoing well fare of the family. There is a very strong desire to continue the family, to plan marriages, for the children, and to encourage large families.

Thusly, it is important that graves be maintained and kept clean, especially at Tet, since they are the resting place of the deceased. Only the graves of those who have no offspring are neglected.

The people of Phuoc Ly invited Lt. Steiner and I to this annual ceremony which is a time of great happiness. There is much food, rice, pig, vegetables and beer… rice beer. The elders dress in the traditional garb of their respective ruling status within the hamlet and assume a jovial disposition, as happiness is the word of the day.

Three large tables are placed with on the hamlet meeting house, upon which are placed heaping bowls of food which has been specially prepared for the occasion (the pig is ceremoniously slaughtered). The small children are seated at one table, the ladies at another. The middle table is reserved for the hamlet chief and elders, or quite simply...the men folk. The food is as palatable as it is plentiful. Between mouthfuls of pig, rice, and vegetables, there is incessant laughter; genuine guffaws which penetrate the soul and serve to demonstrate that these people have a singular communion with life despite the war. I will remember the generosity of these people because they not only shared their food with me, but their happiness as well."

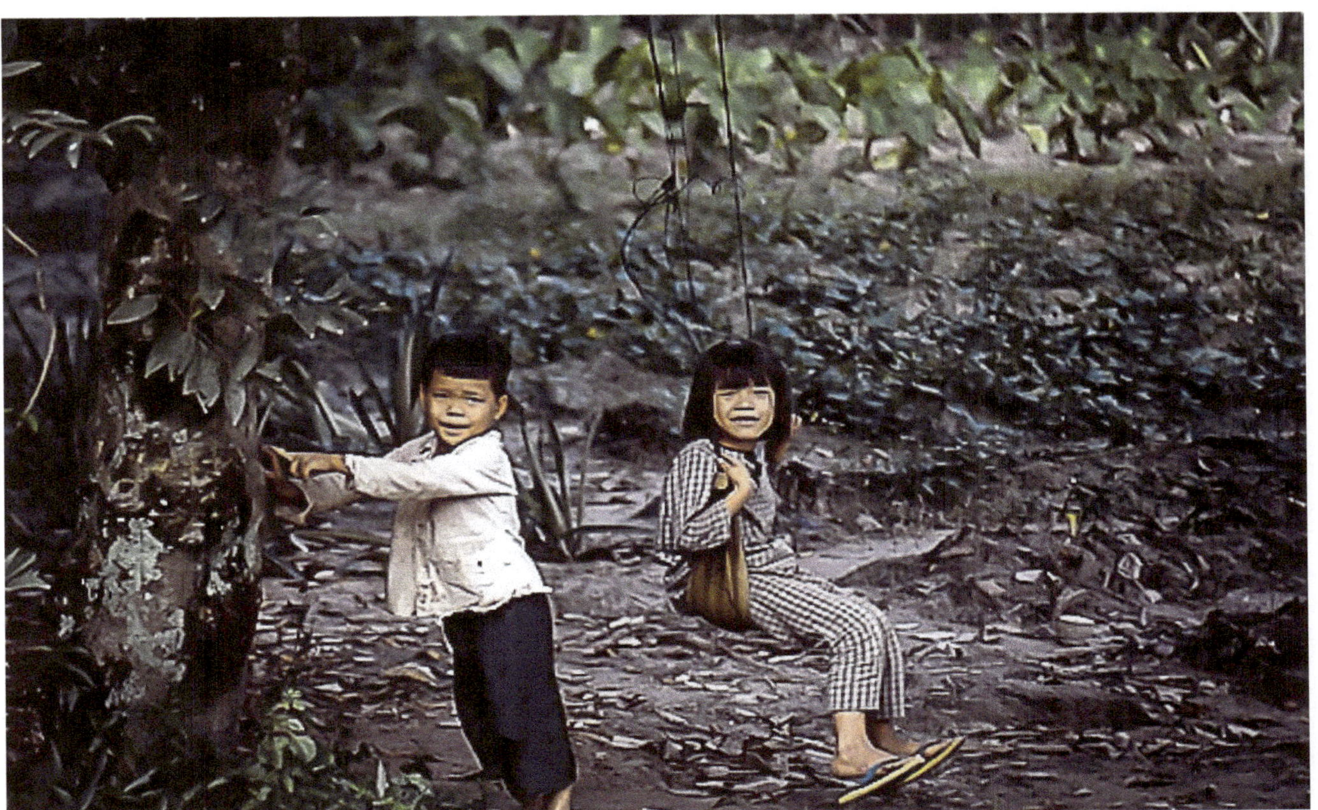

Brother and sister swing-playing adjacent to the family garden plot. Peasant families grew all of their food for consumption, some of which may have been sold or traded in the village marketplace.

Phuoc Ly, 1967

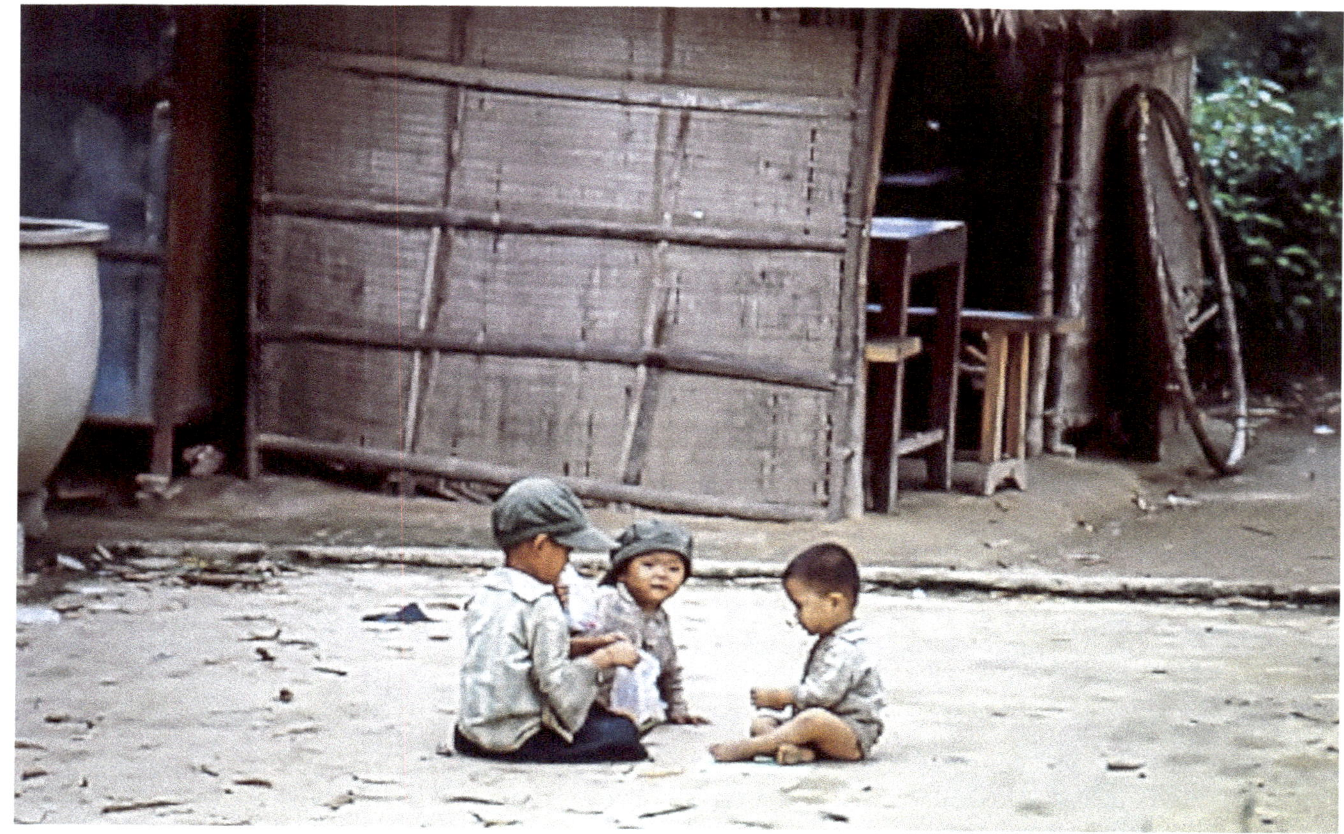

Phuoc Ly

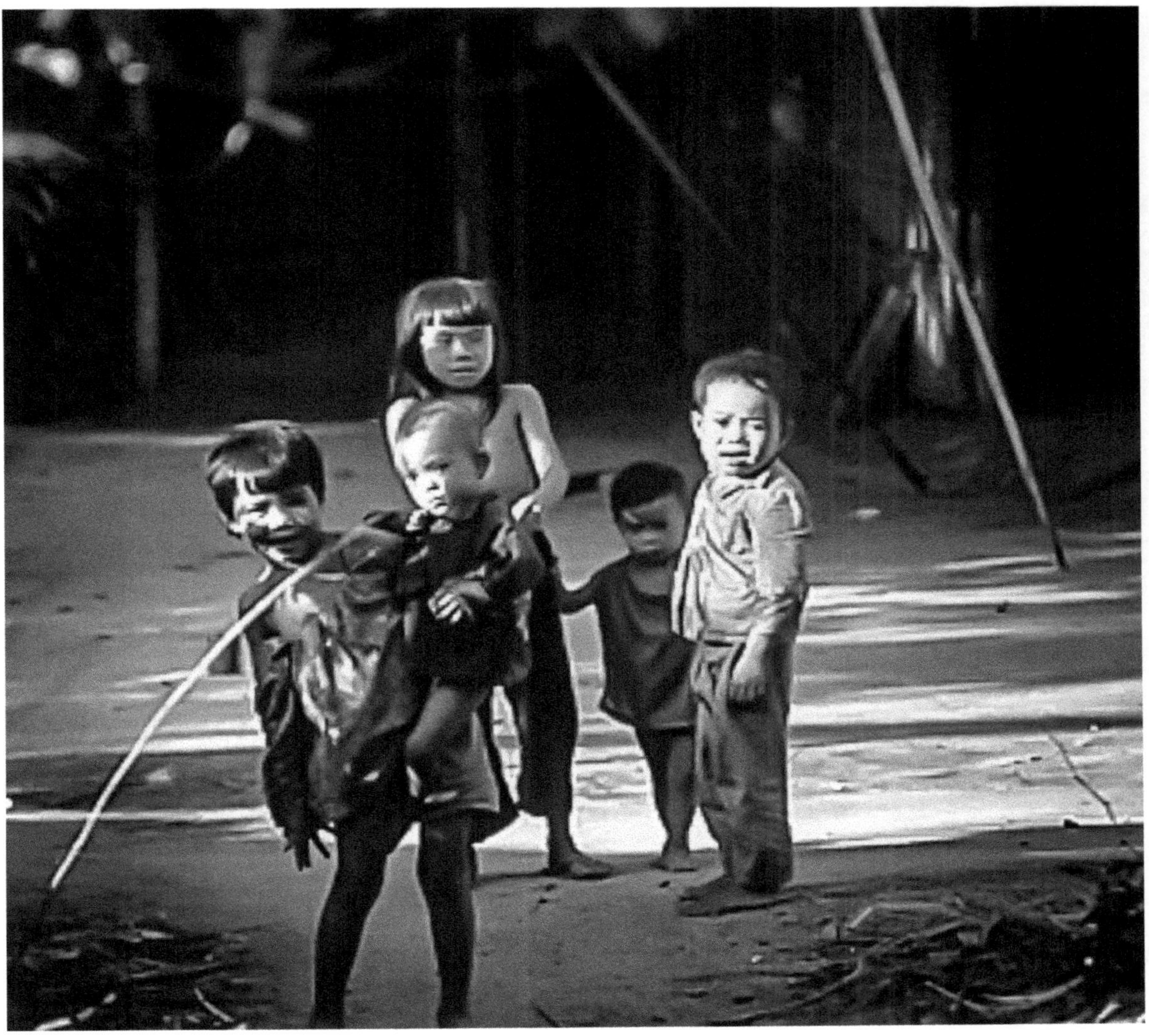

A Family of Children

In rural Viet Nam there was a need to have many children. The agrarian existence was labor intensive requiring large families and cooperative community support. Young children cared for siblings and livestock as their parents worked in the rice paddies and fields. Disease, malnutrition, and the lack of clean water contributed to a high infant and child mortality rate. Decades of war had consumed and continued to consume lives of young men as well as females.

Phuoc Ly Hamlet, 1968

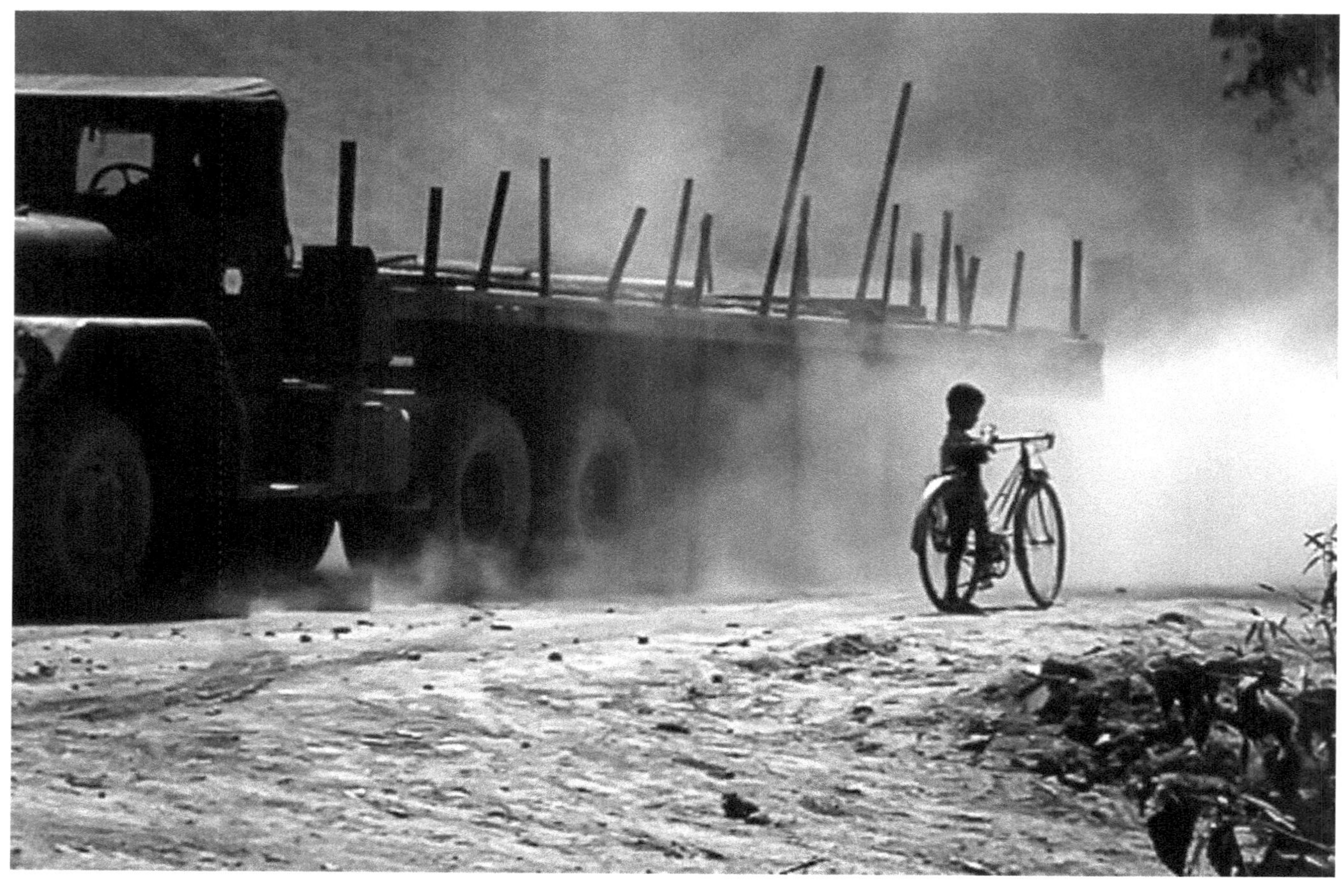

A Lesser-Known Hazard

The road to Da Nang, passed through Phouc Ly and became a major thoroughfare for military vehicles from outlying posts as the war progressed.

Phuoc Ly Hamlet, 1966

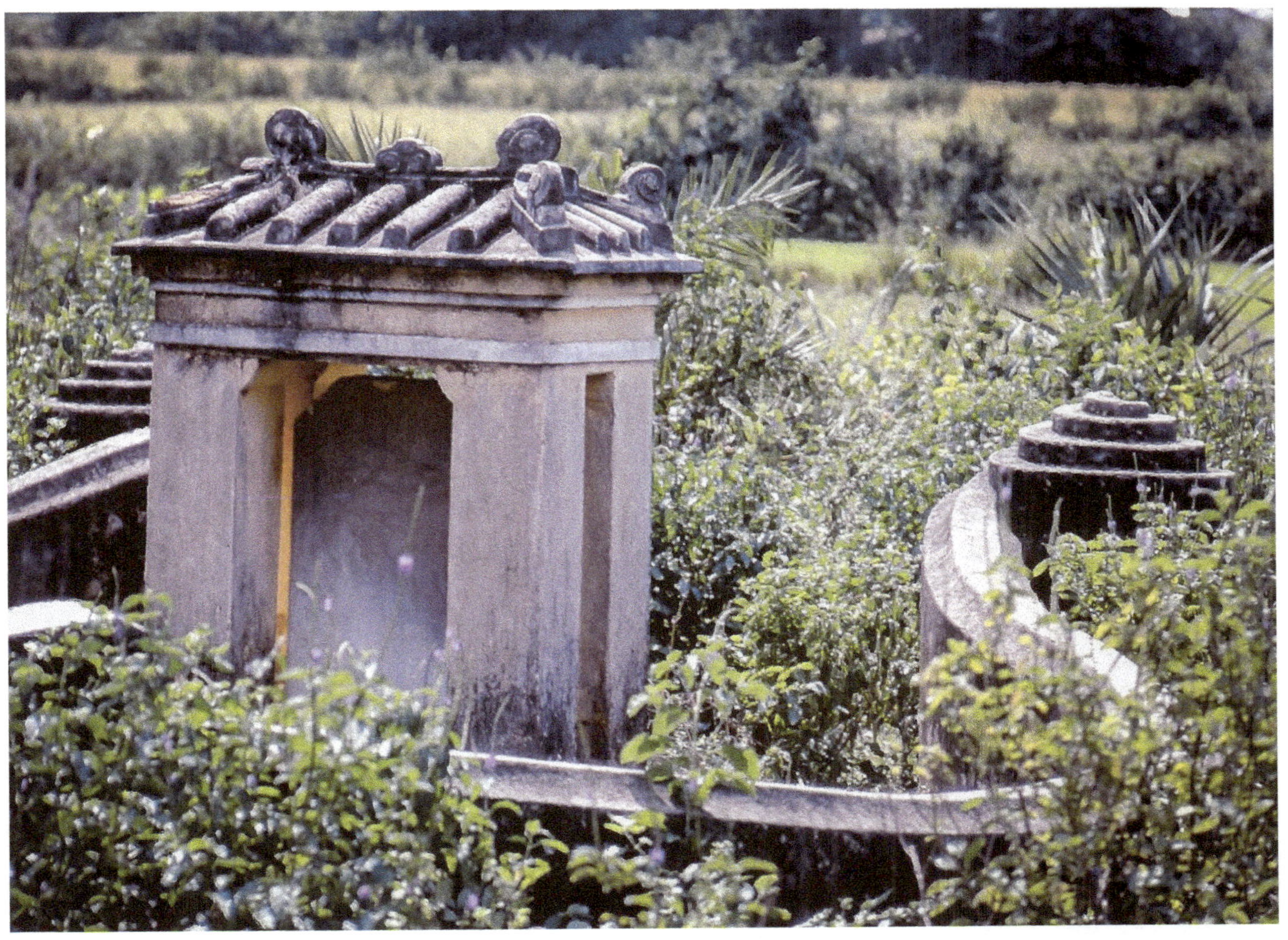

Ornate Vietnamese grave

This grave was placed by a wealthier family. Peasant graves in the countryside were constructed of circular mounds of dirt.

Phuoc Ly, 1968

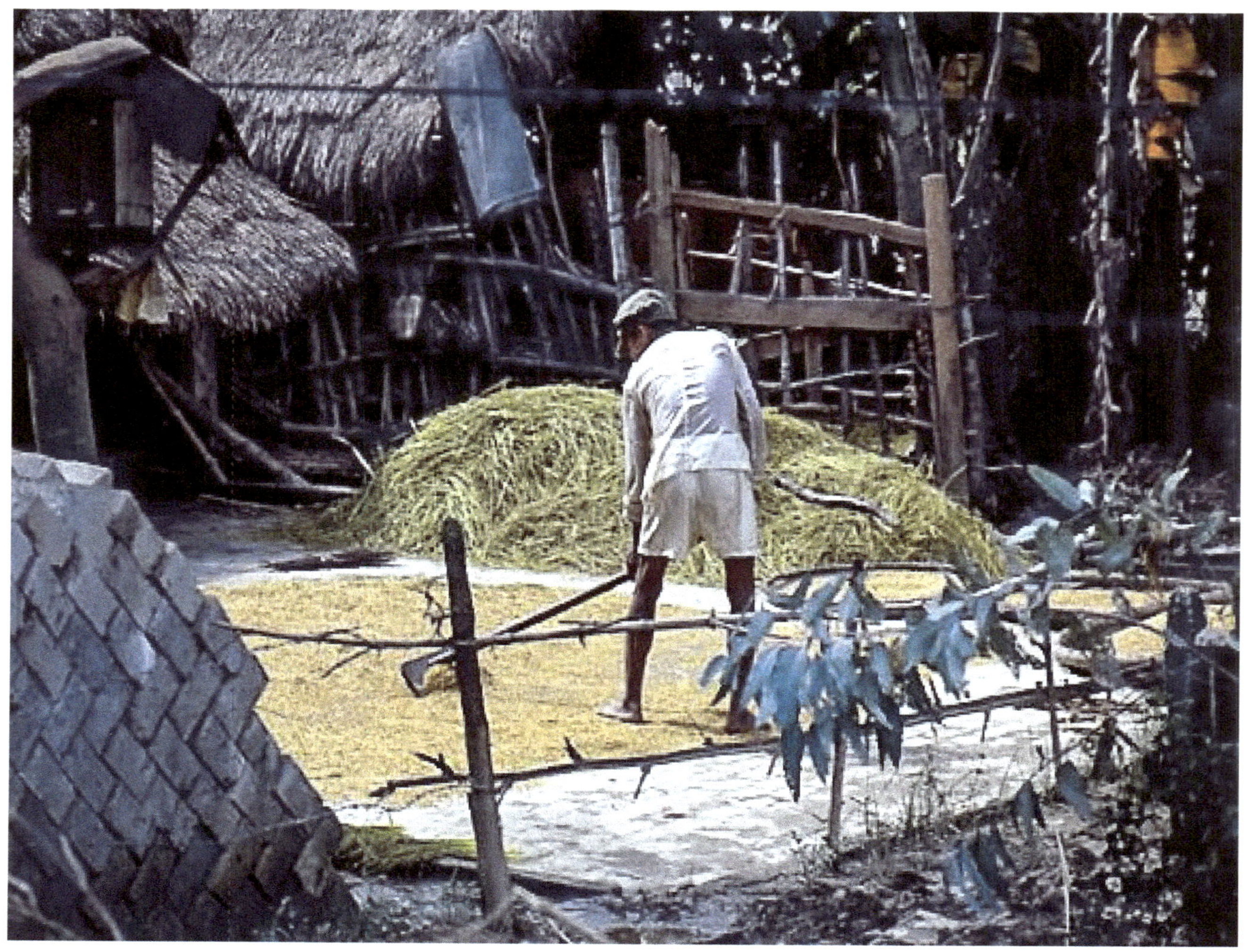

An Elder spreads rice to dry on his home patio. Phuoc Ly

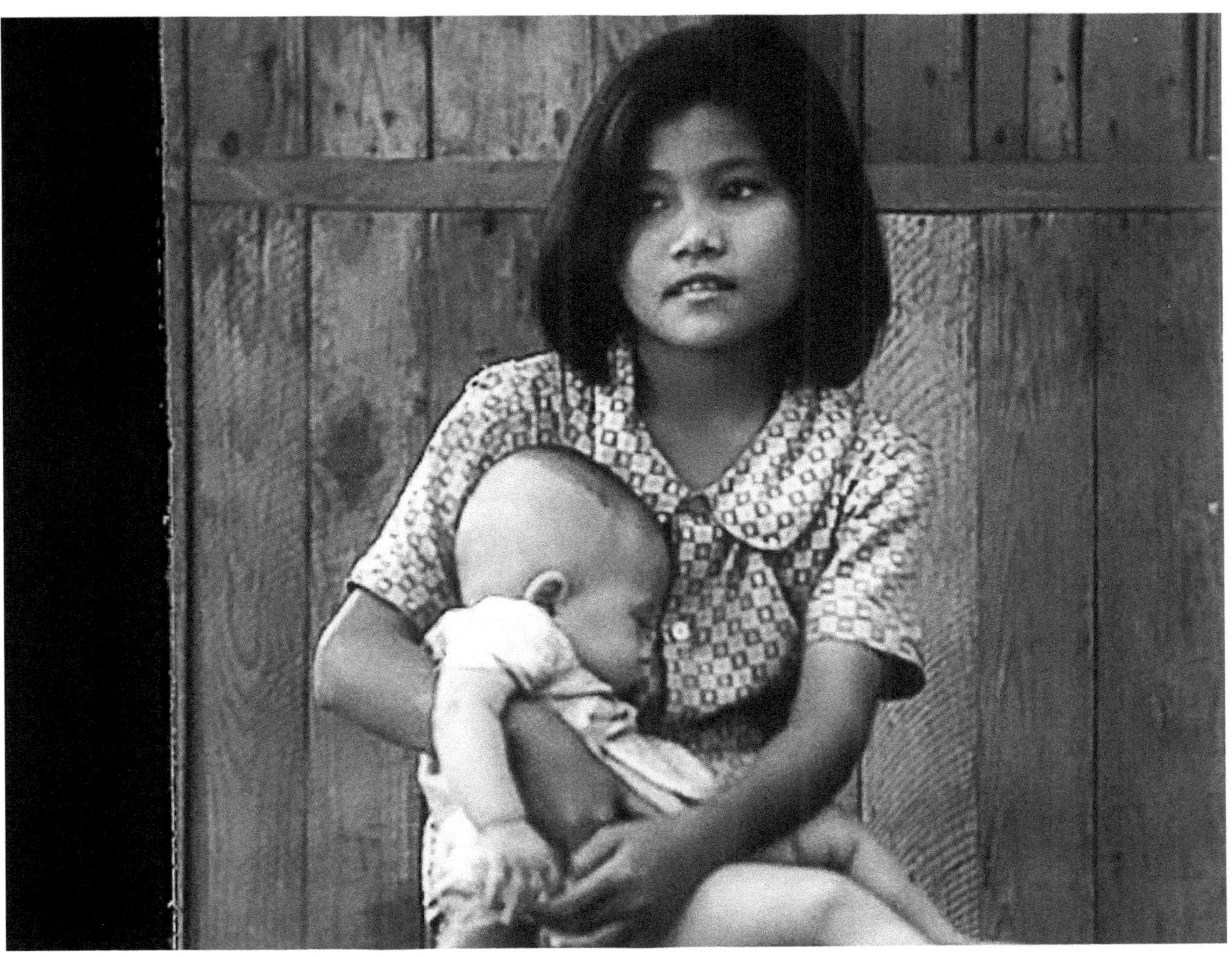

Girls of rural families are tasked with responsibilities that prepare them for the culturally essential role in their future as wives and mothers.

Phuoc Ly, 1967.

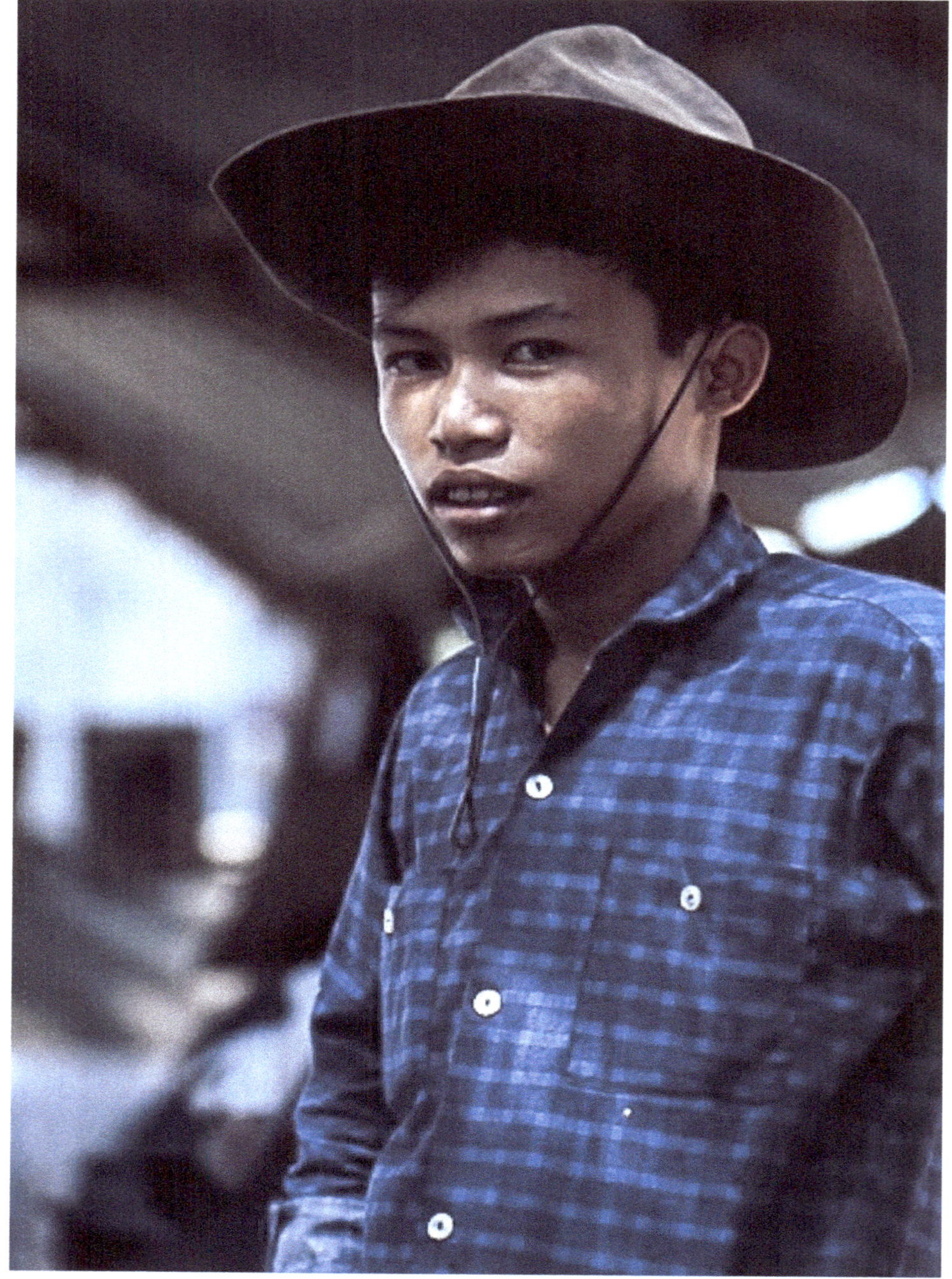

Vietnamese teenager wearing a shirt not commonly seen in more rural areas. Phuoc Ly, 1967

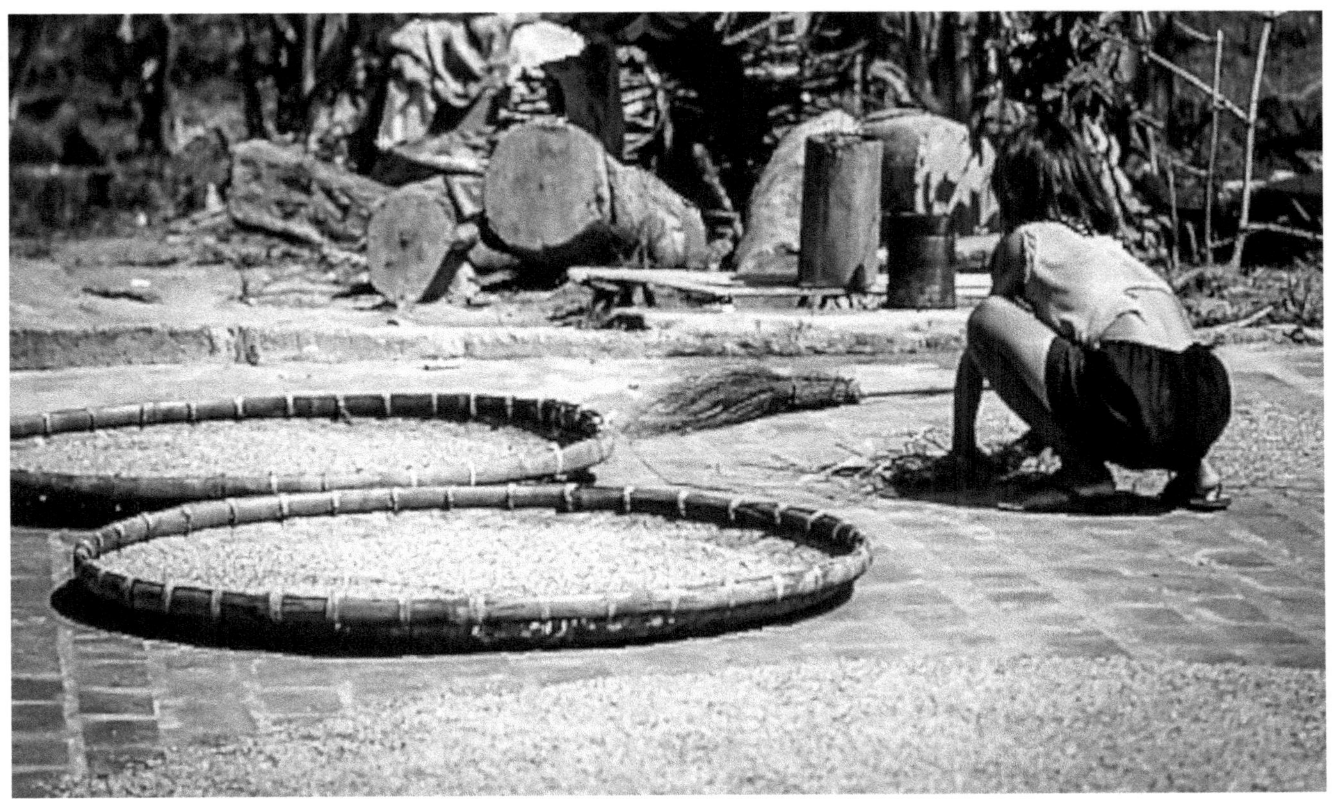

Rice is Life

A young girl removes rice kernels from stalks as she prepares them for drying on woven mats. Rice is a pivot of life for the Vietnamese people. It is a symbol and part of ceremonies and offerings. The family...adults and children are essential to a successful harvest. Without rice, famine will follow. The Viet Cong exacted a severe rice tax on the peasantry in areas that it controlled. Phuoc Ly, 1967

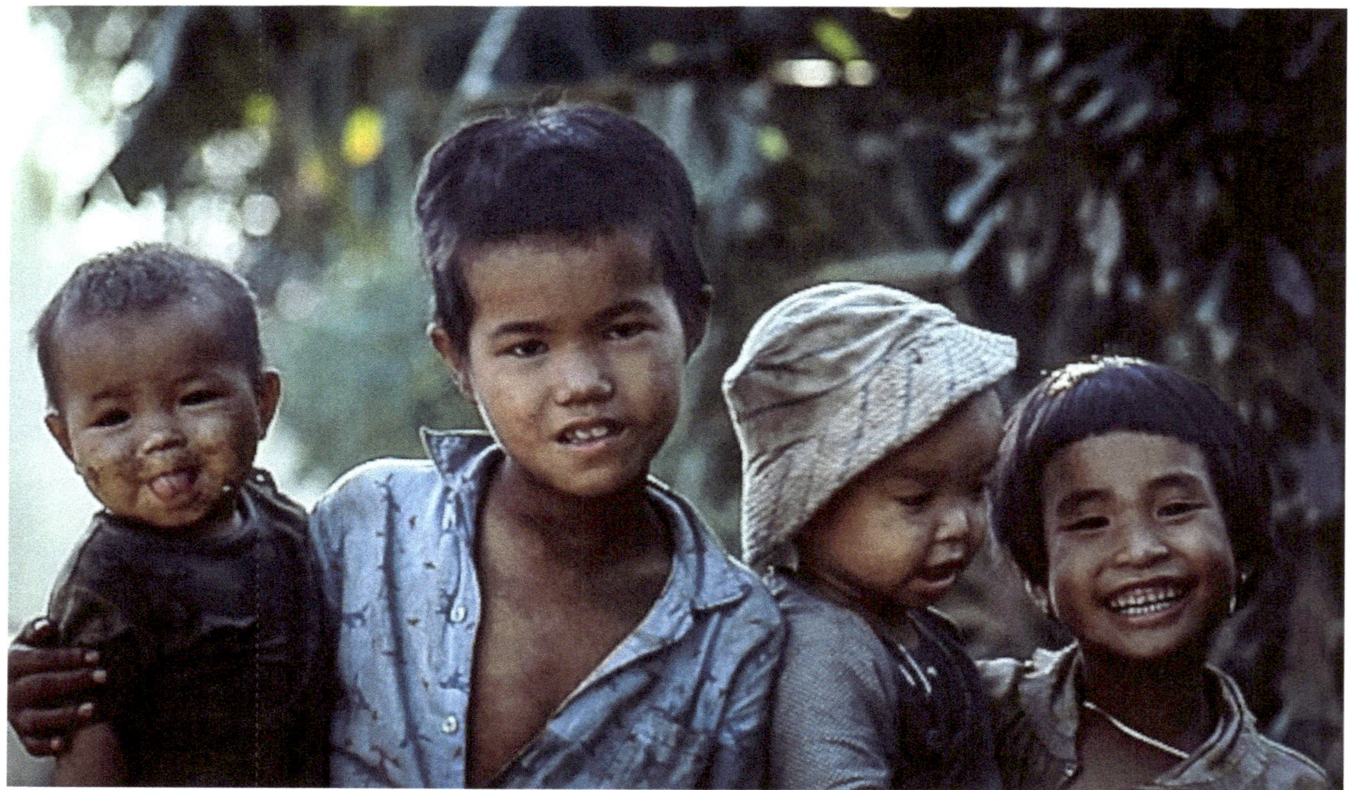

The love and care that siblings share for each other is evident in this image. I found this to be a cultural norm that I witnessed in the rural areas. A stark exception to this occurred when the Viet Cong recruited family members, including children, to terrorize other family members.

Phuoc Ly, 1967

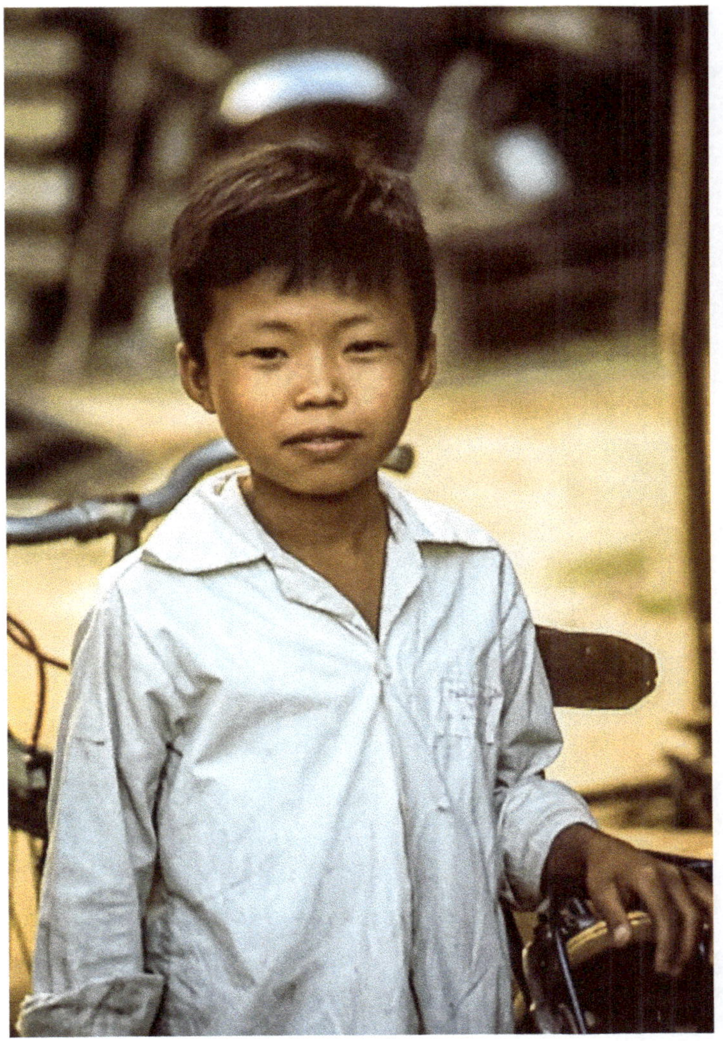

Young boy standing next to his bicycle, the only means of transportation for many Vietnamese.

Phuoc Ly, 1968.

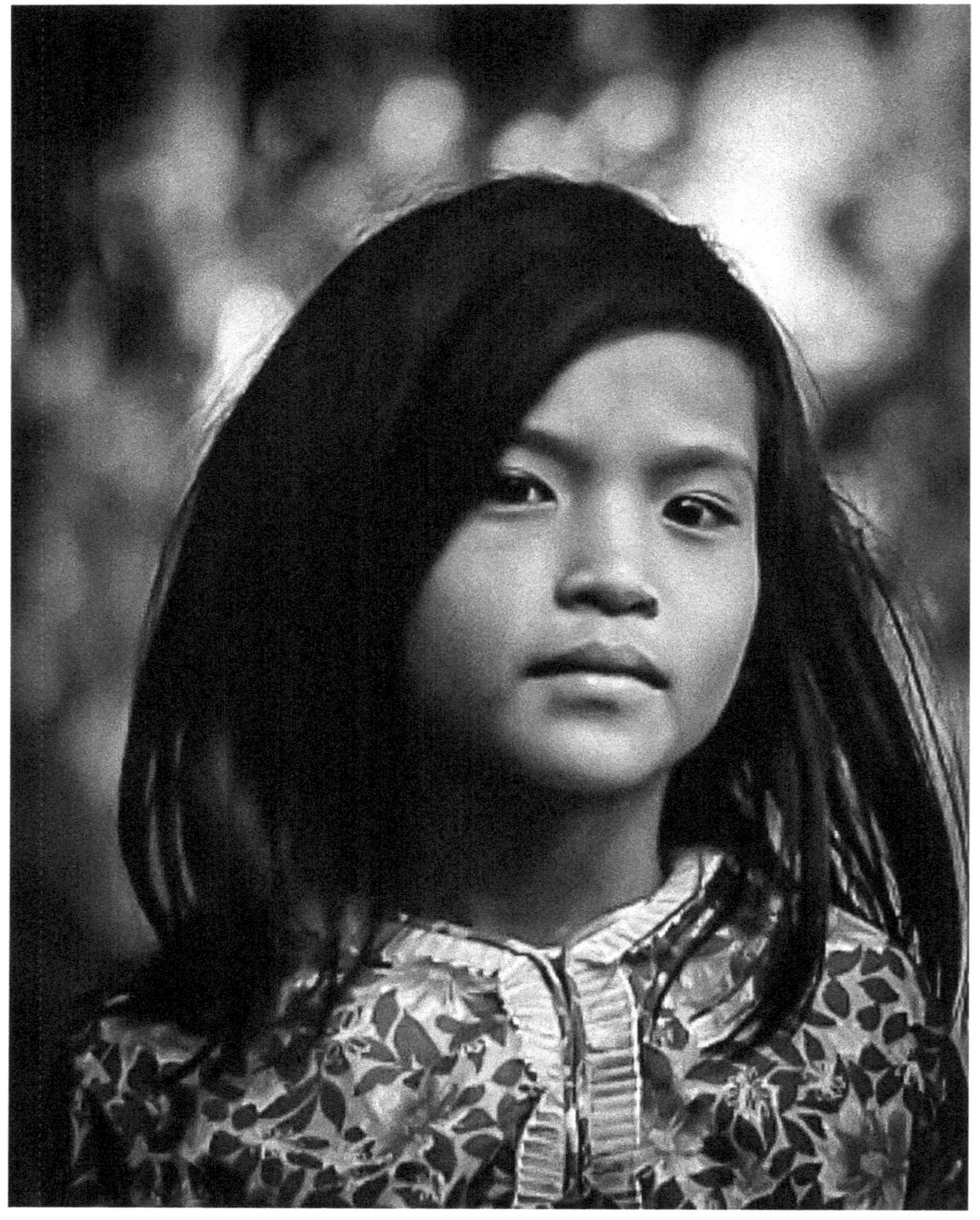

The children of Phuoc Ly wore much finer clothing than children in the more remote hamlets and villages where extreme poverty was common. 1967

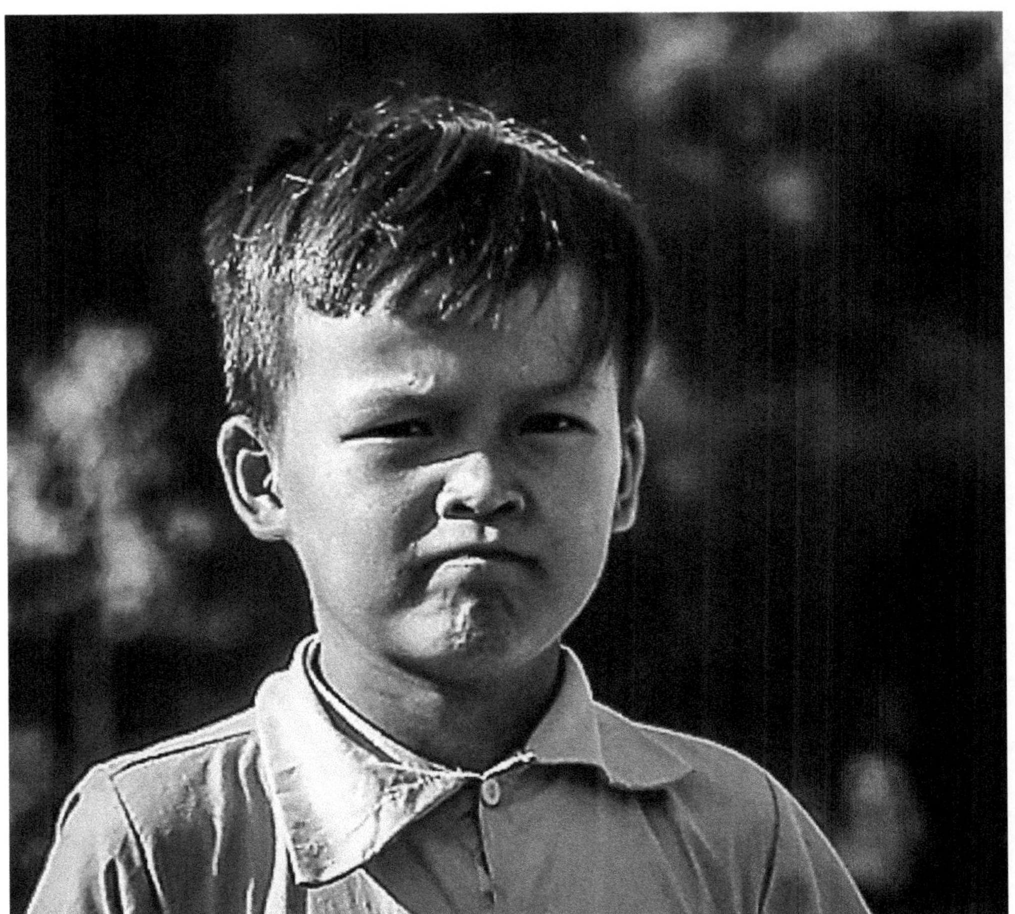

Phuoc Ly Hamlet

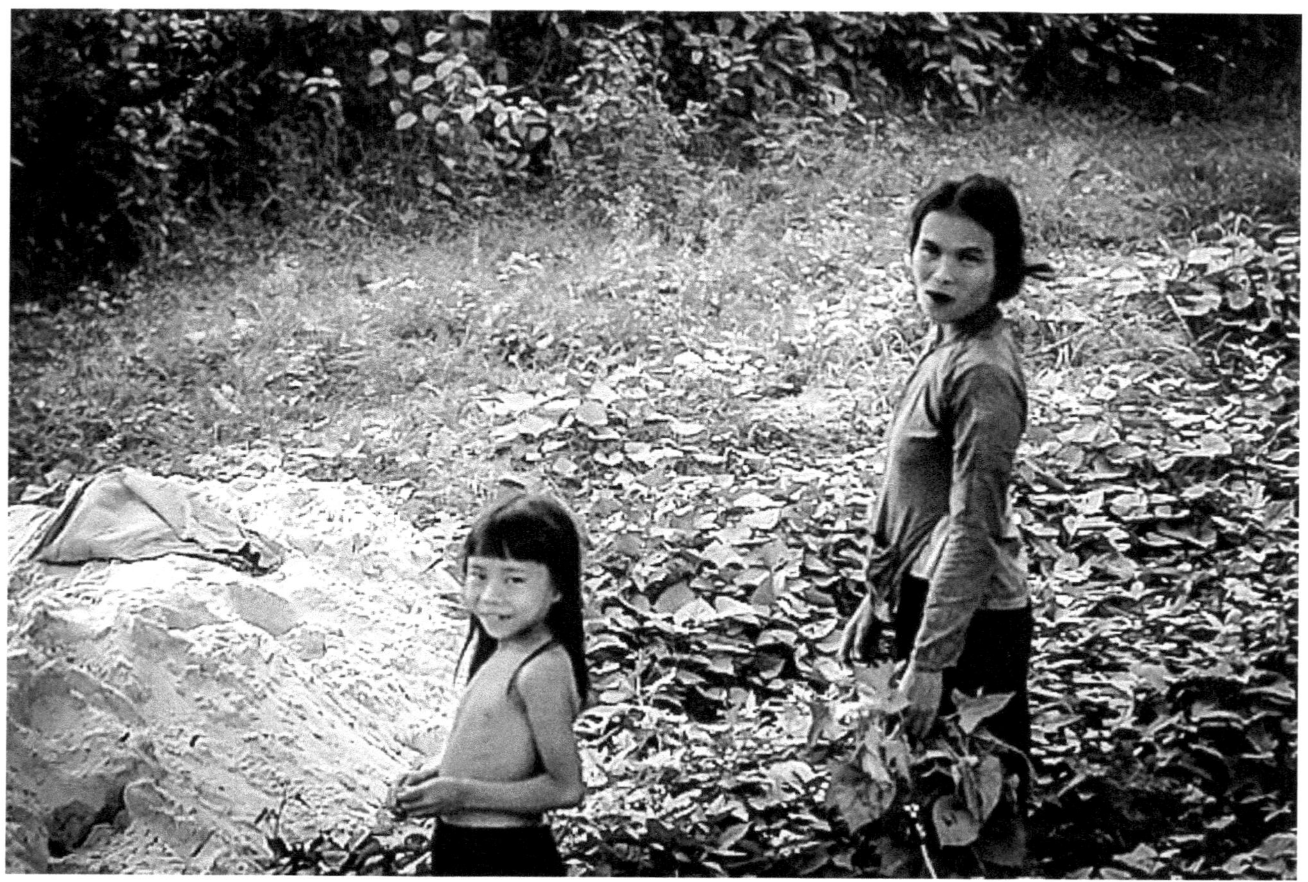

Mother and daughter harvesting the family garden in preparation for the family meal. Rural families obtained all of their food from the land. Each family member, adults and children who were old enough, participated in the cultivation and harvesting process. Phuoc Ly Hamlet, 1966

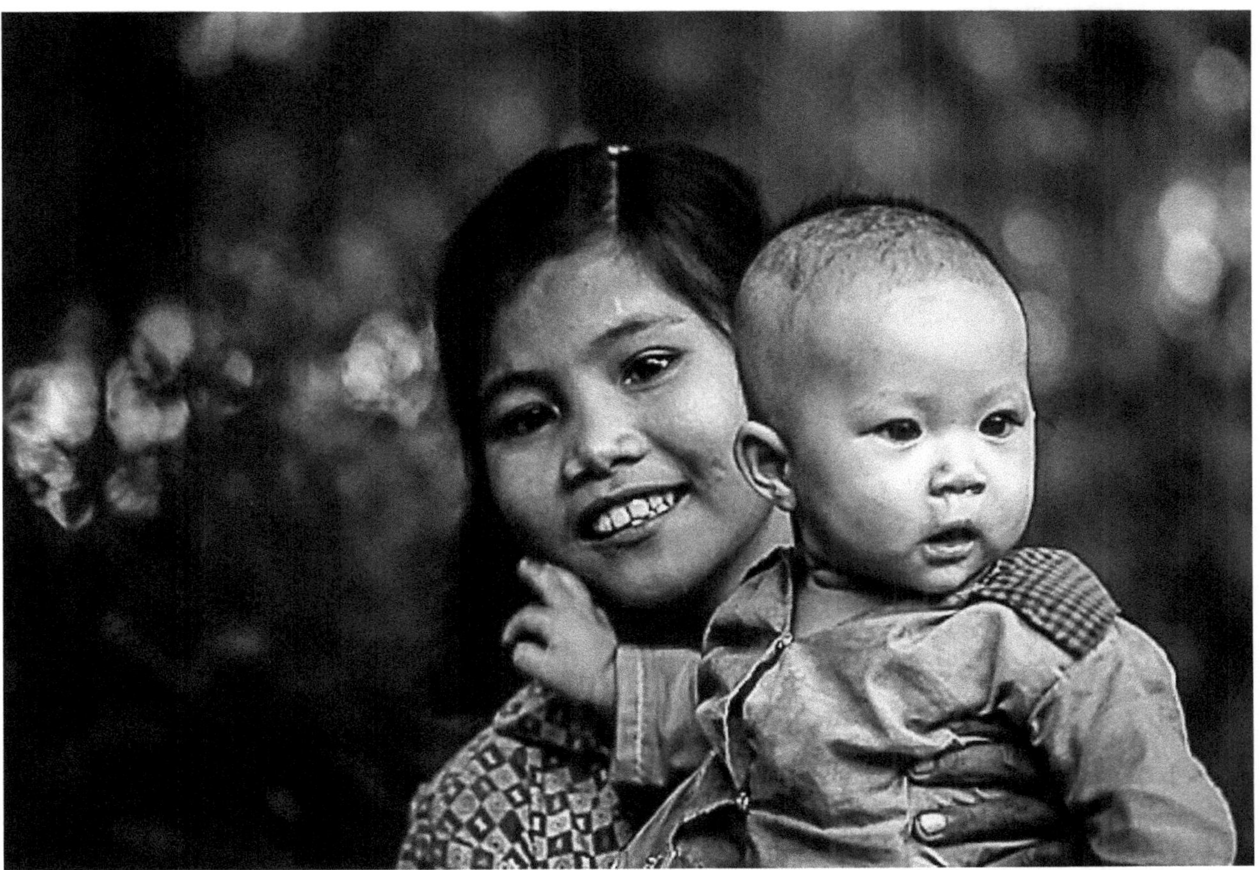

The children of Phuoc Ly, were relatively safe from the daily threat of the war compared to children in more remote areas. However, close proximity to the Da Nang Airbase and military installations, put them at greater risk of being victims of rocket and mortar attacks intended to hit those installations.

Big sister and little brother, Phuoc Ly Hamlet.

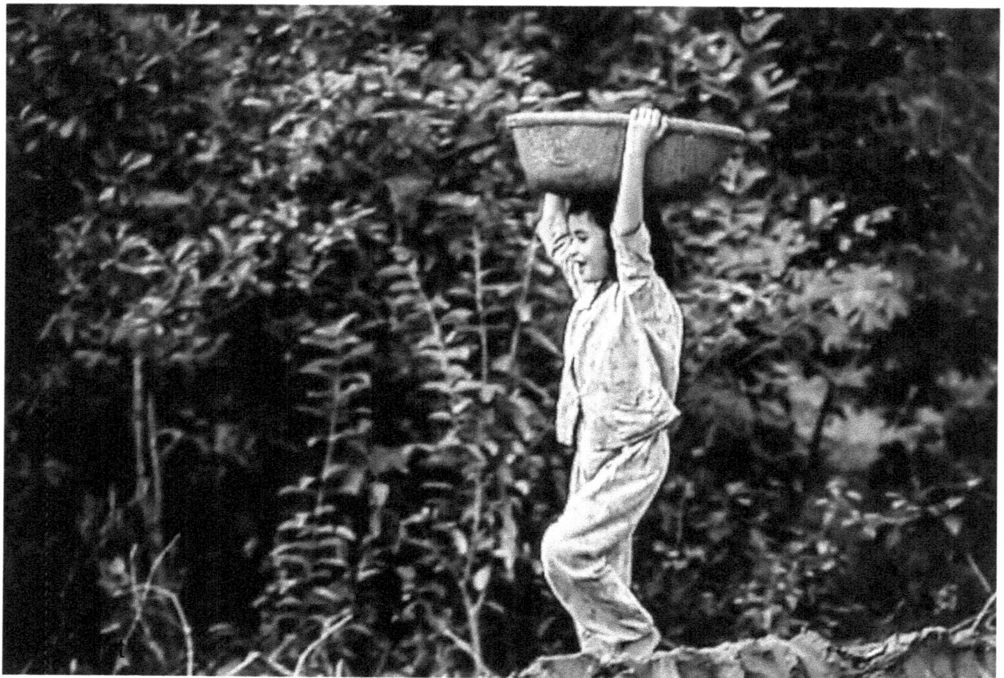

Young hamlet girl carrying freshly harvested vegetables to the Village Market

Phuoc Ly 1967

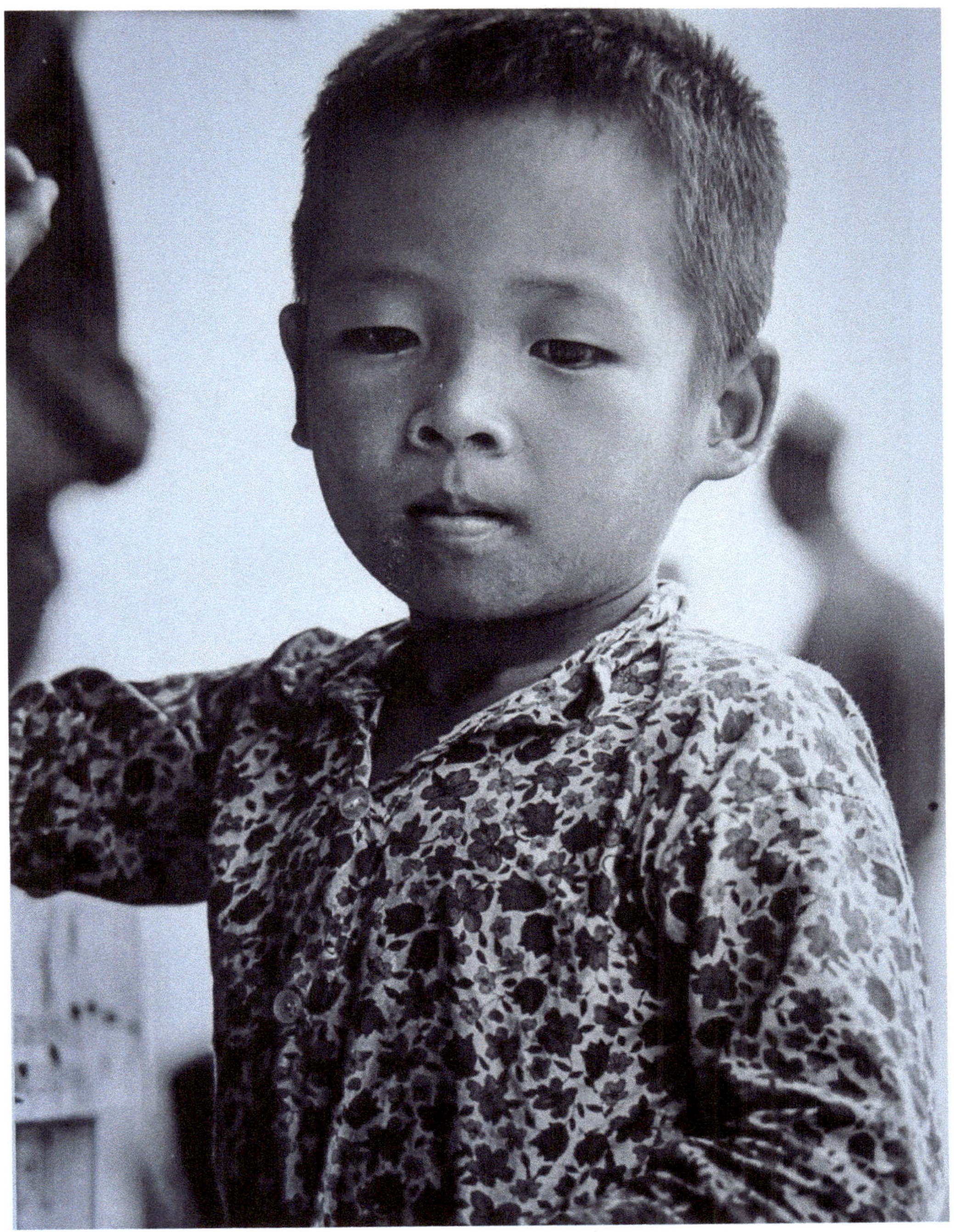

The expression hints at the perplexity of thought and memories of a war that many Vietnamese children carried with them daily. Phuoc Ly 1967

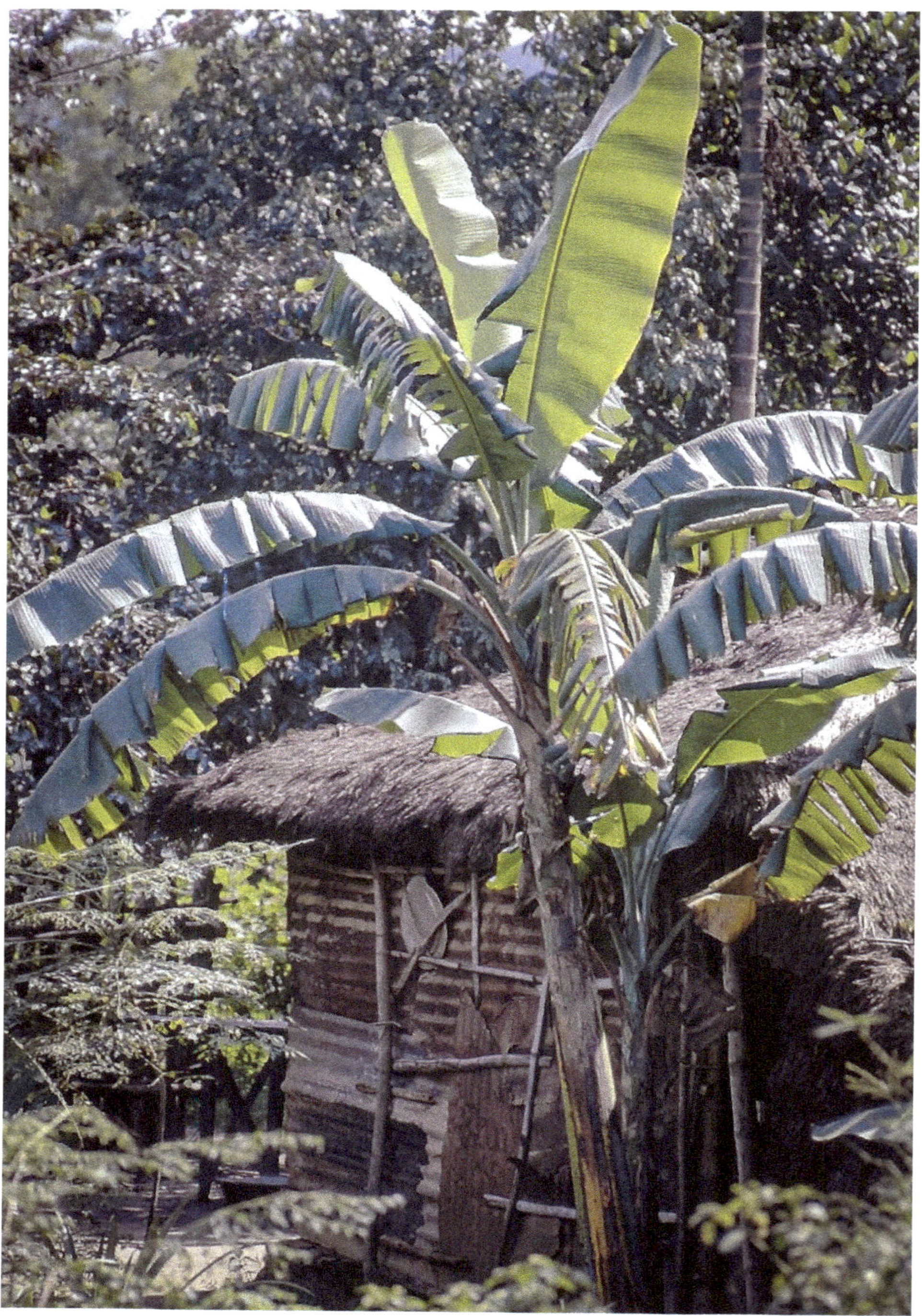

Typical Phuoc Ly Home, the side of the hut is covered with discarded metal roof sheeting and braced with bamboo.1967

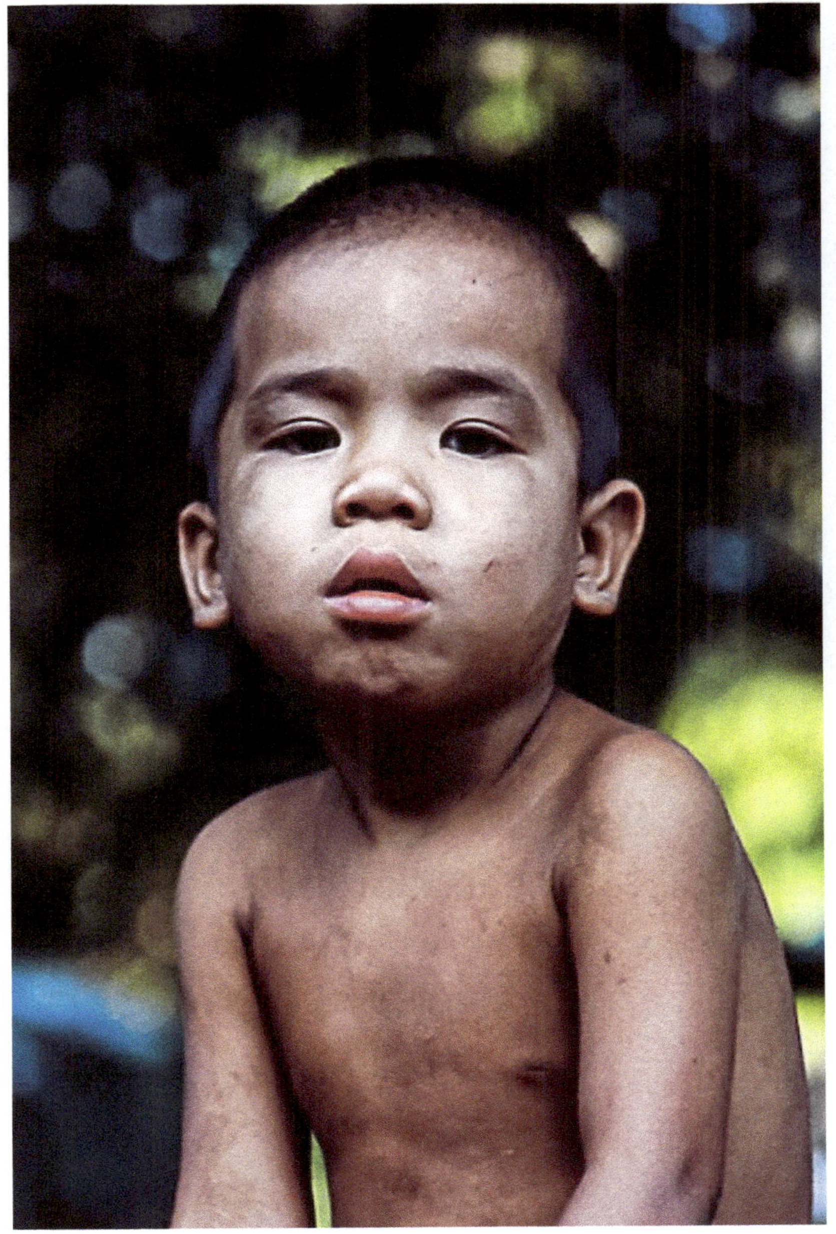

Evidence of an early near total body skin infection were evident on this boy's skin. A lack of soap contributed to a high prevalence infectious skin infections among children. Lack of a clean water source in most rural areas also contributed to widespread intestinal parasitic infestation in children.

Phuoc Ly 1967.

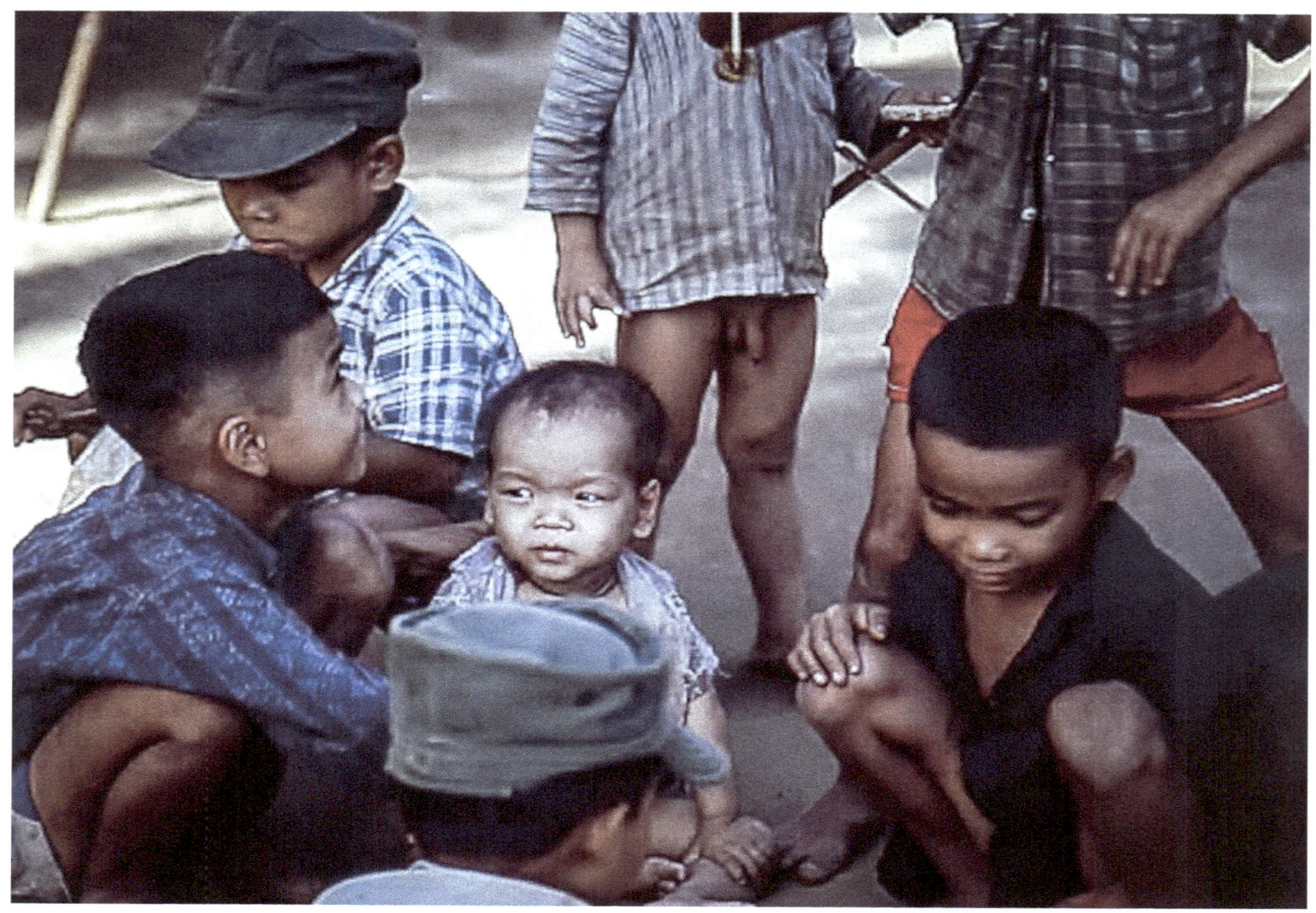

Boys of varying ages coming together in Phuoc Ly Hamlet. 1967

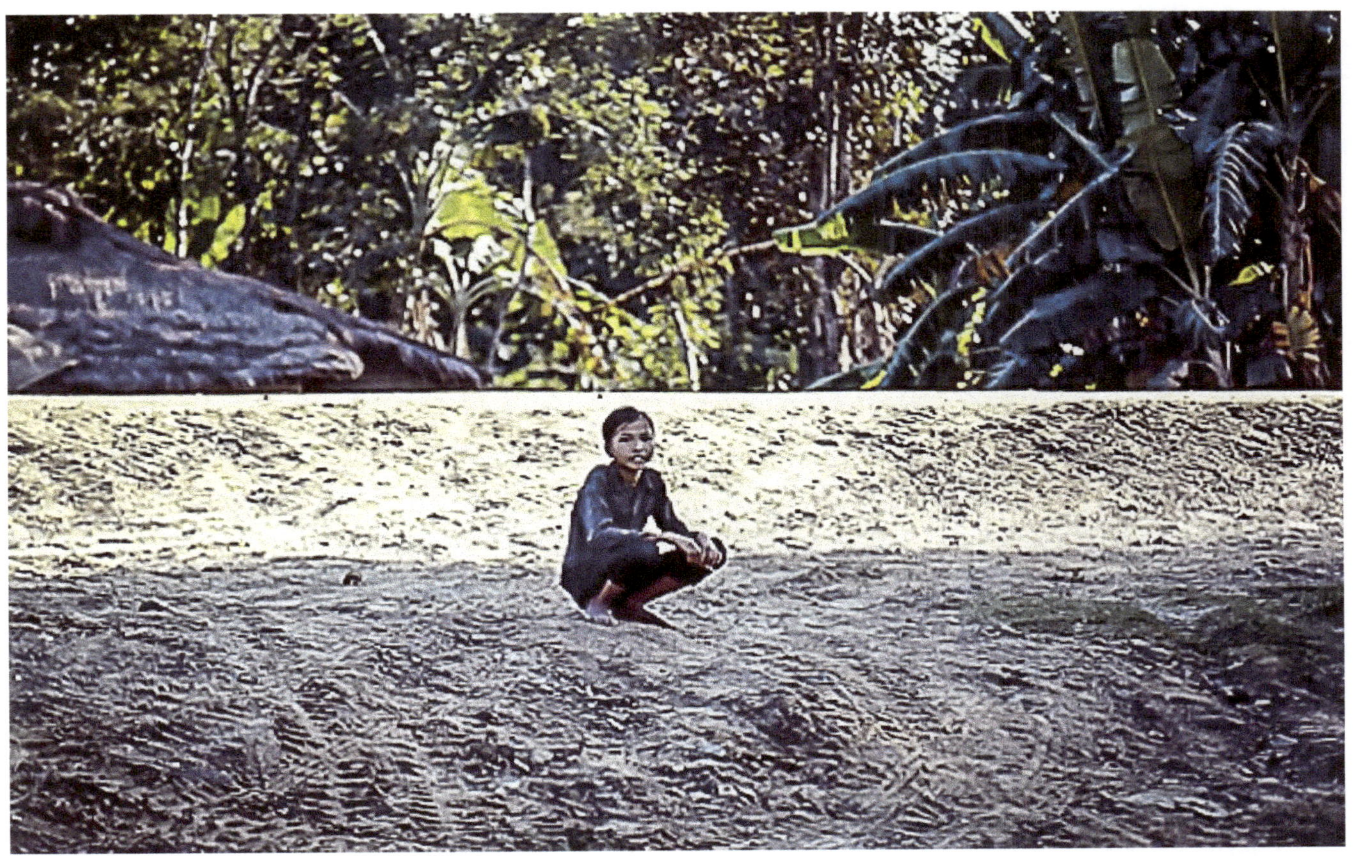

This girl assumes the normal position of sitting for Vietnamese in the countryside when no chairs are available. Phuoc Ly 1967.

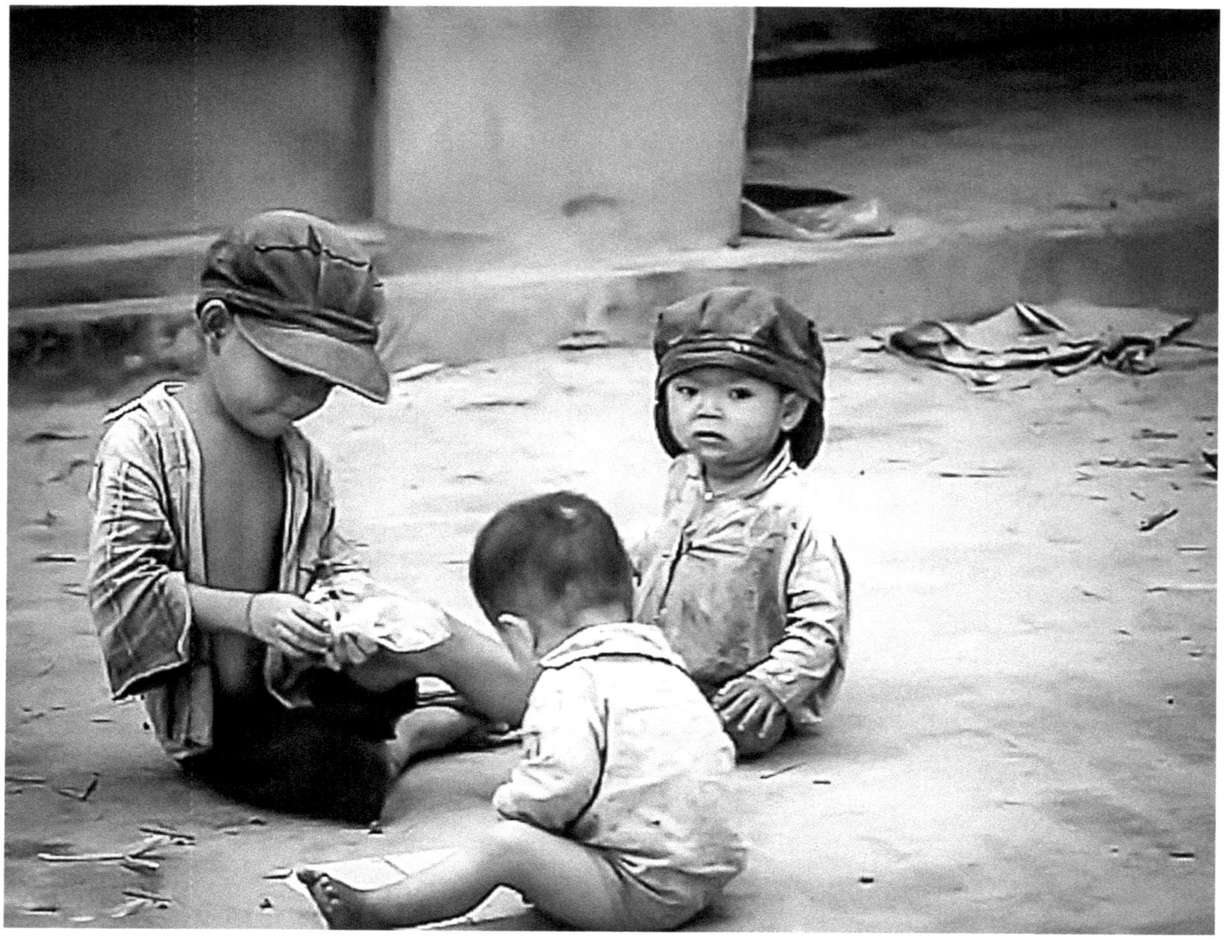

Innovative play among three brothers outside the family home. The two older boys wear hats given to them by Marines. Phuoc Ly 1967.

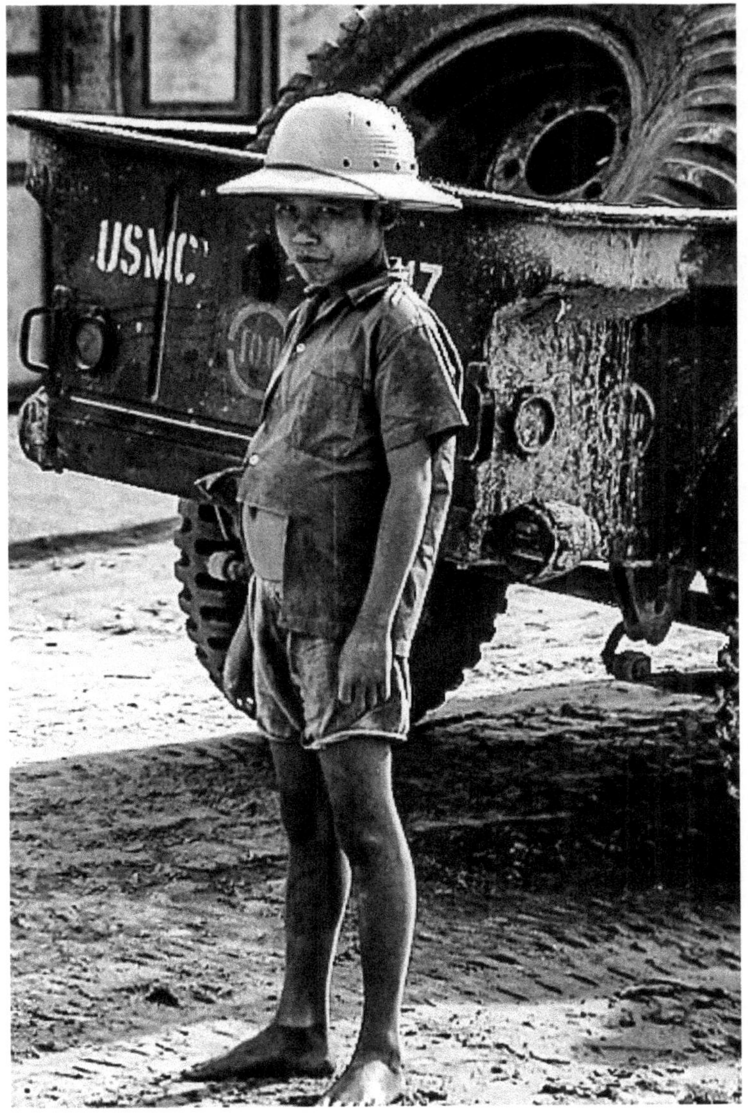

The stern expression of this boy puzzled me because the children of Phuoc Ly were generally friendly, outgoing, and happy. 1967

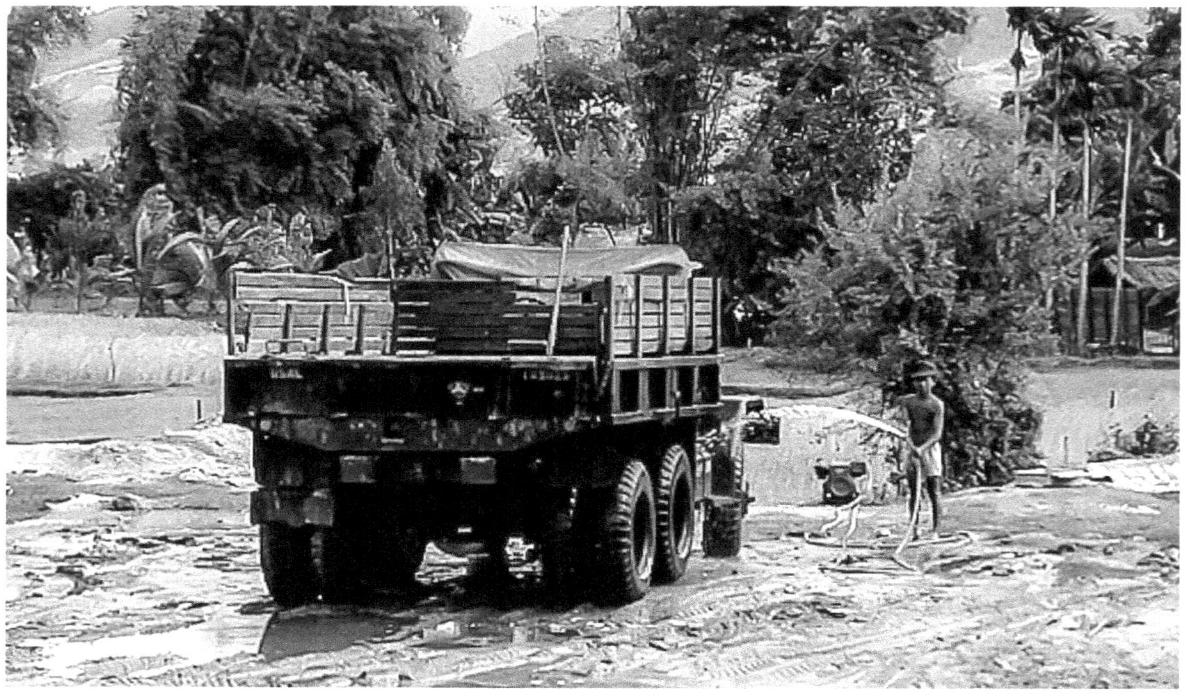

Young boy washes a U.S. Marine truck for a fee.

Phuoc Ly 1966.

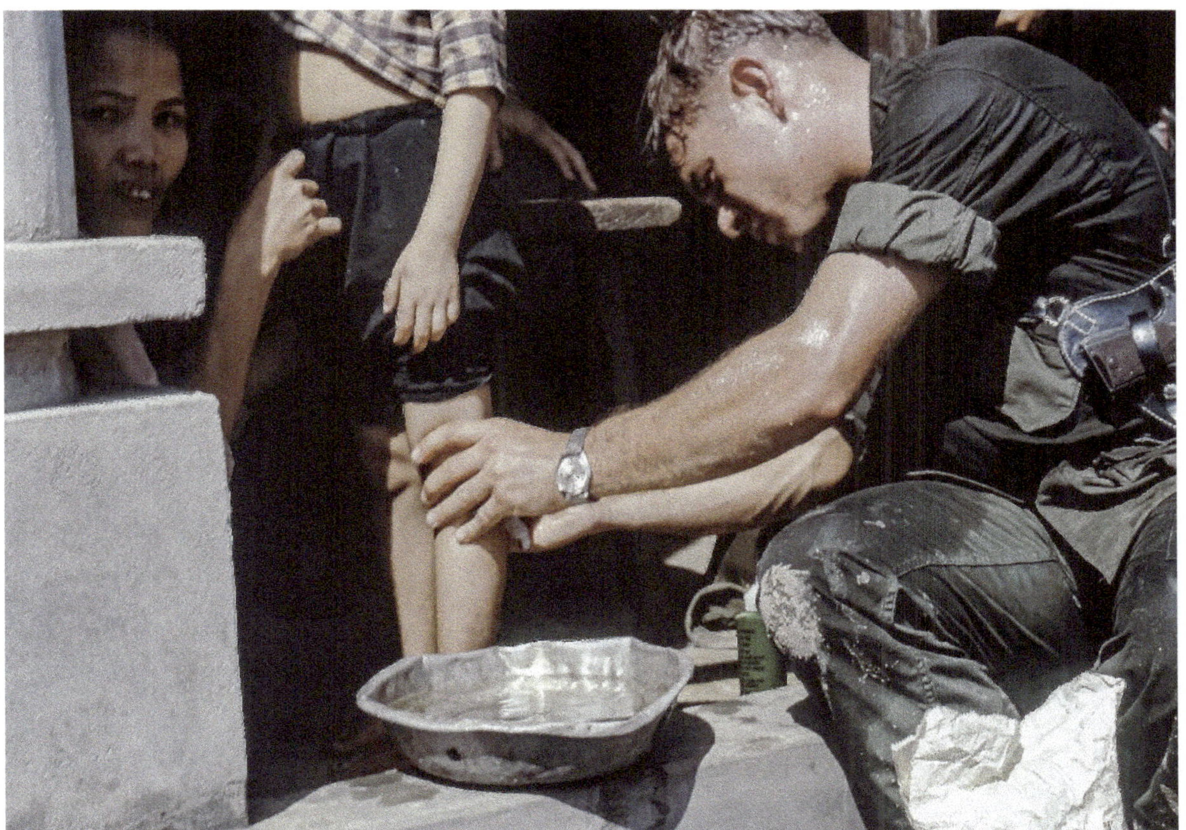

The author treating a Vietnamese girl with a leg infection.

Phuoc Ly 1967.

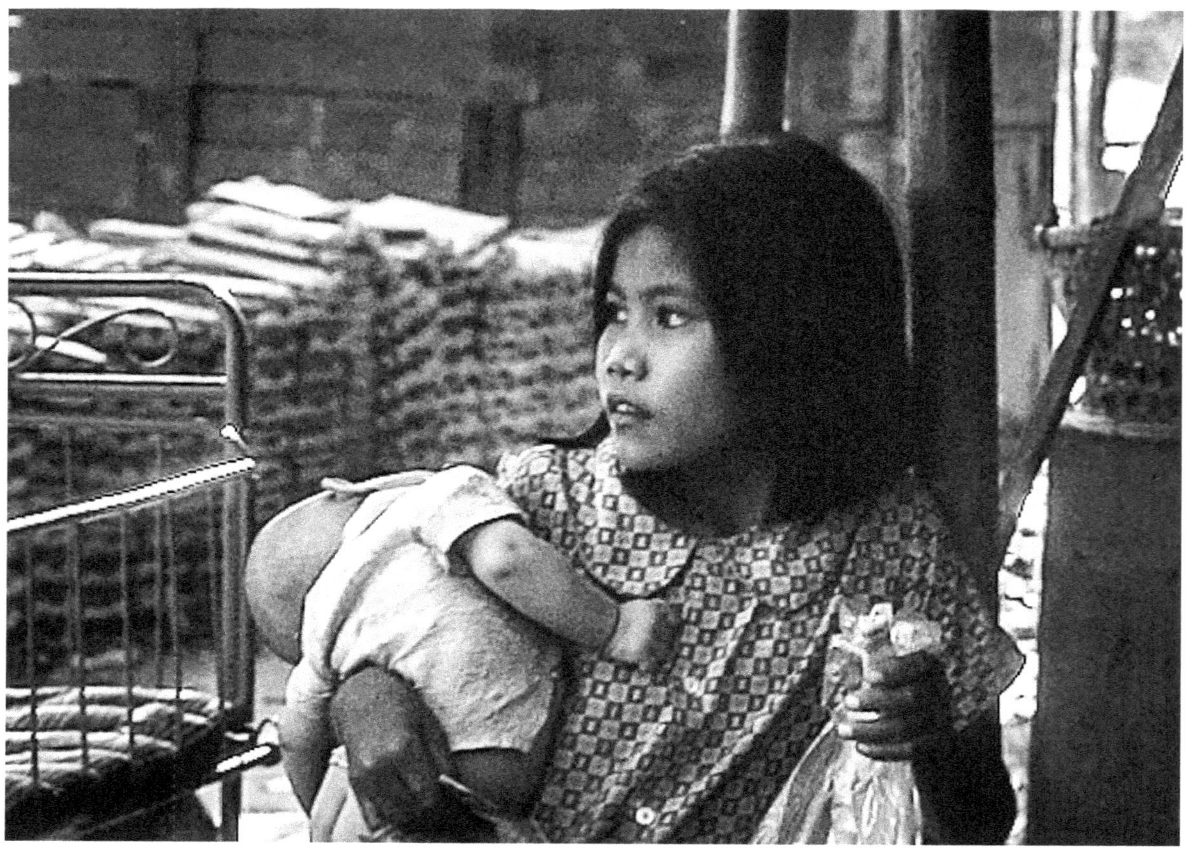

A Young girl Cares for her infant sister as her parents work in the field and rice paddies.

Phuoc Ly Hamlet 1967.

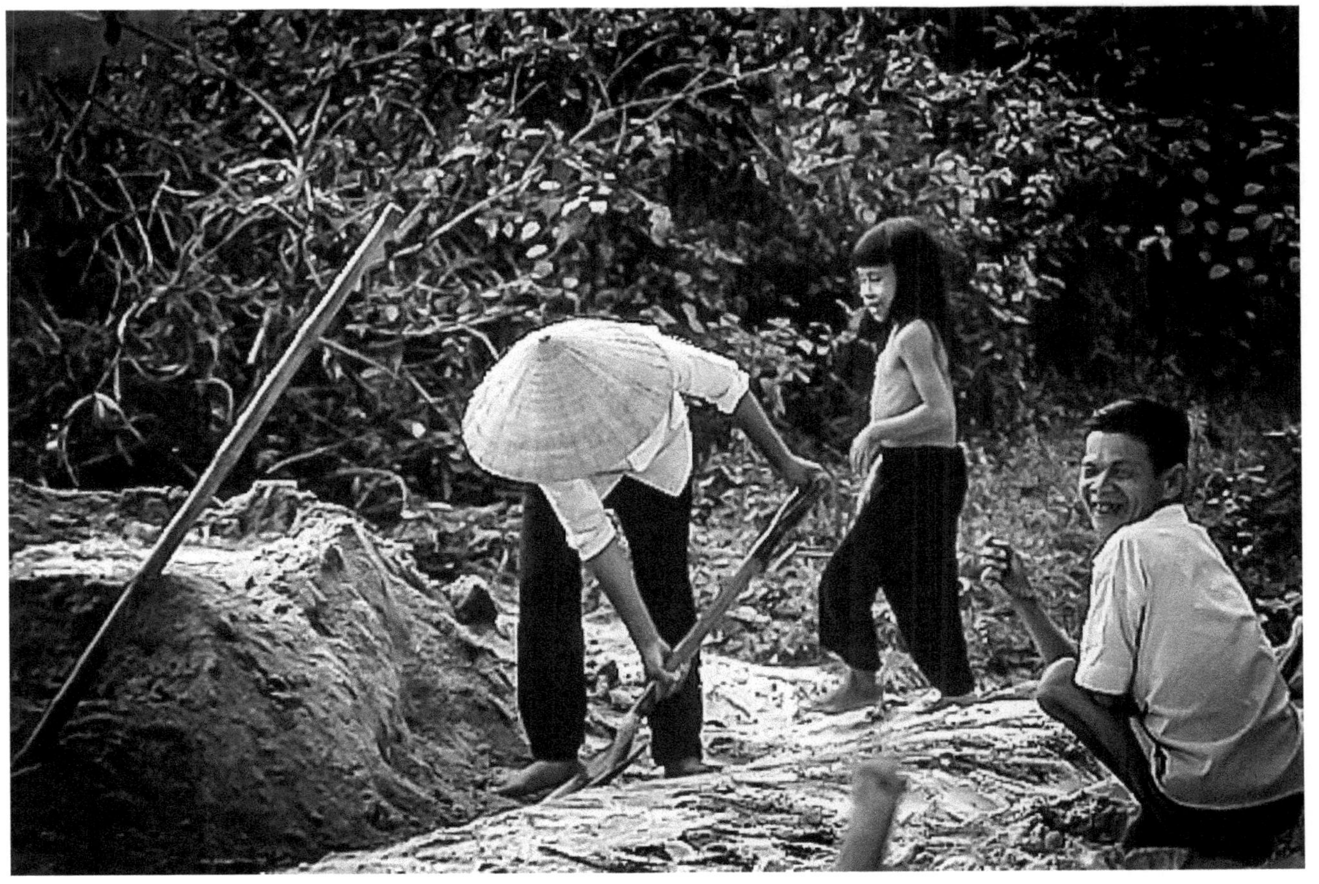

The Family

Mother, father, and daughter prepare mortar for repair of their stucco home. Home constructed of stucco in the rural countryside was a rarity. Most homes in rural areas were constructed of thatch.

Phuoc Ly 1966.

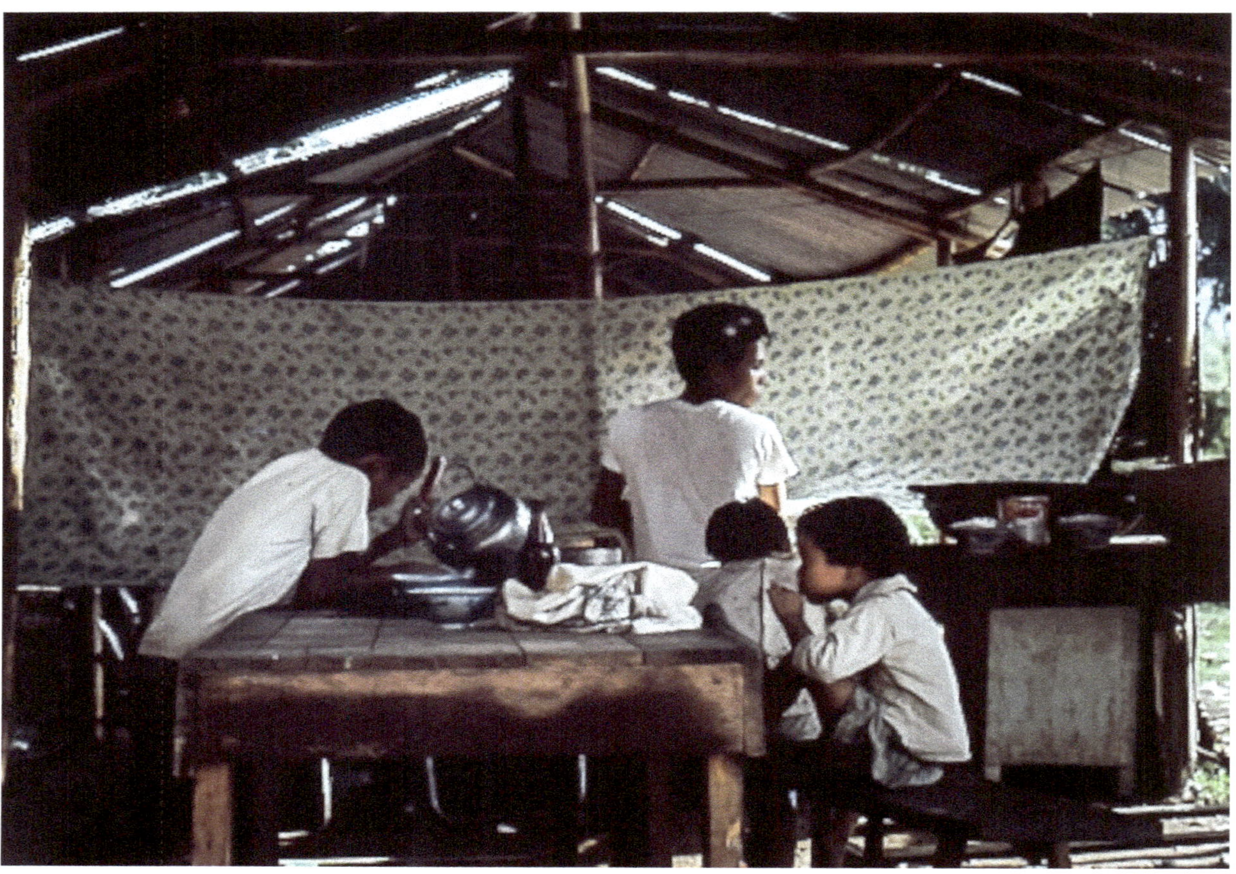

A Vietnamese father and his children eat a mid-day meal in the Phuoc Ly market. The floors were packed dirt and the market stalls were constructed of bamboo frame with tin and thatched roofs.

Phuoc Ly 1967.

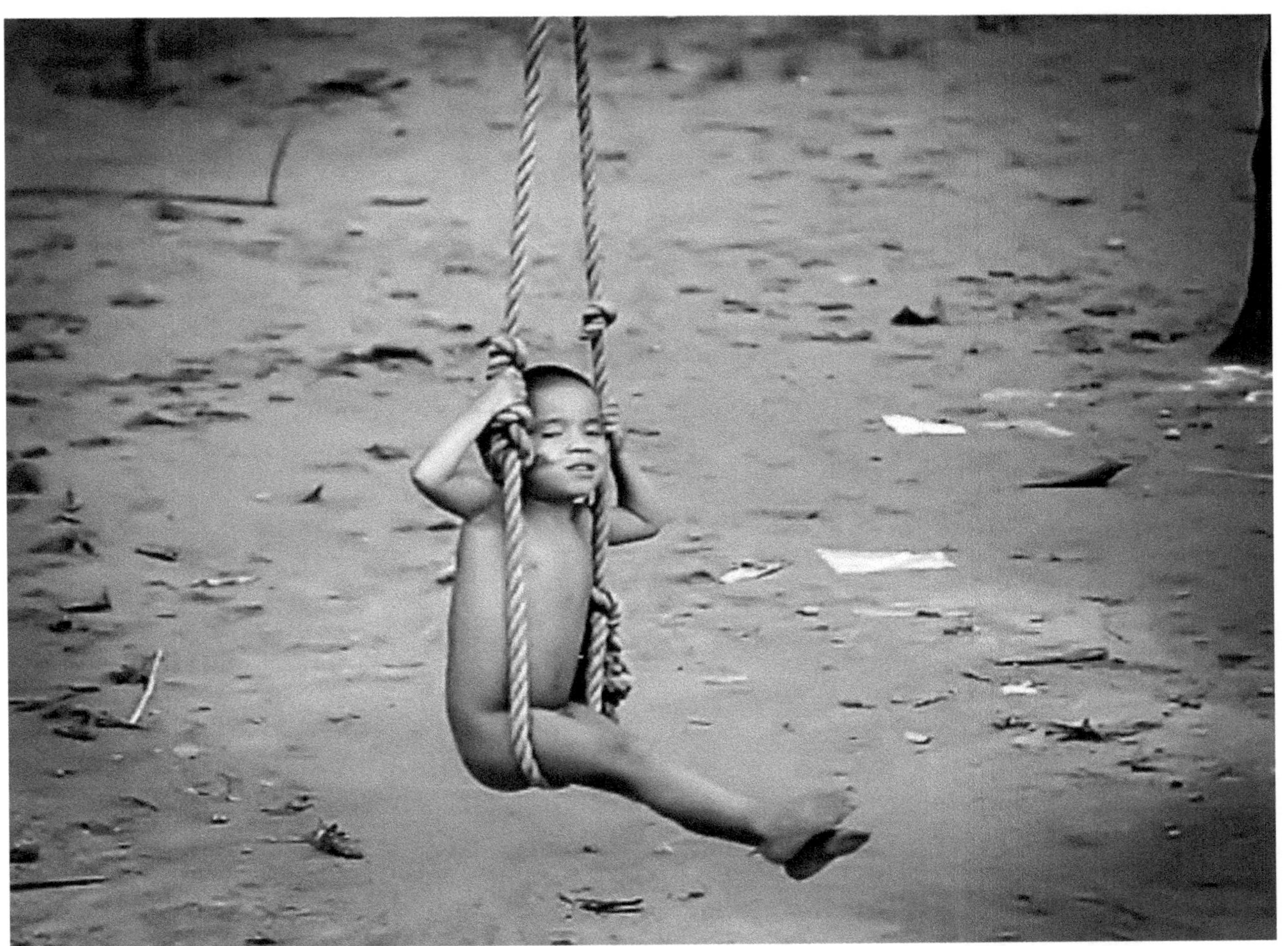

Diapers were unavailable in the rural countryside, and so young infants and toddlers did not wear clothing on the lower half of the body, or simply no clothing during the hot dry season.

Phuoc Ly 1966.

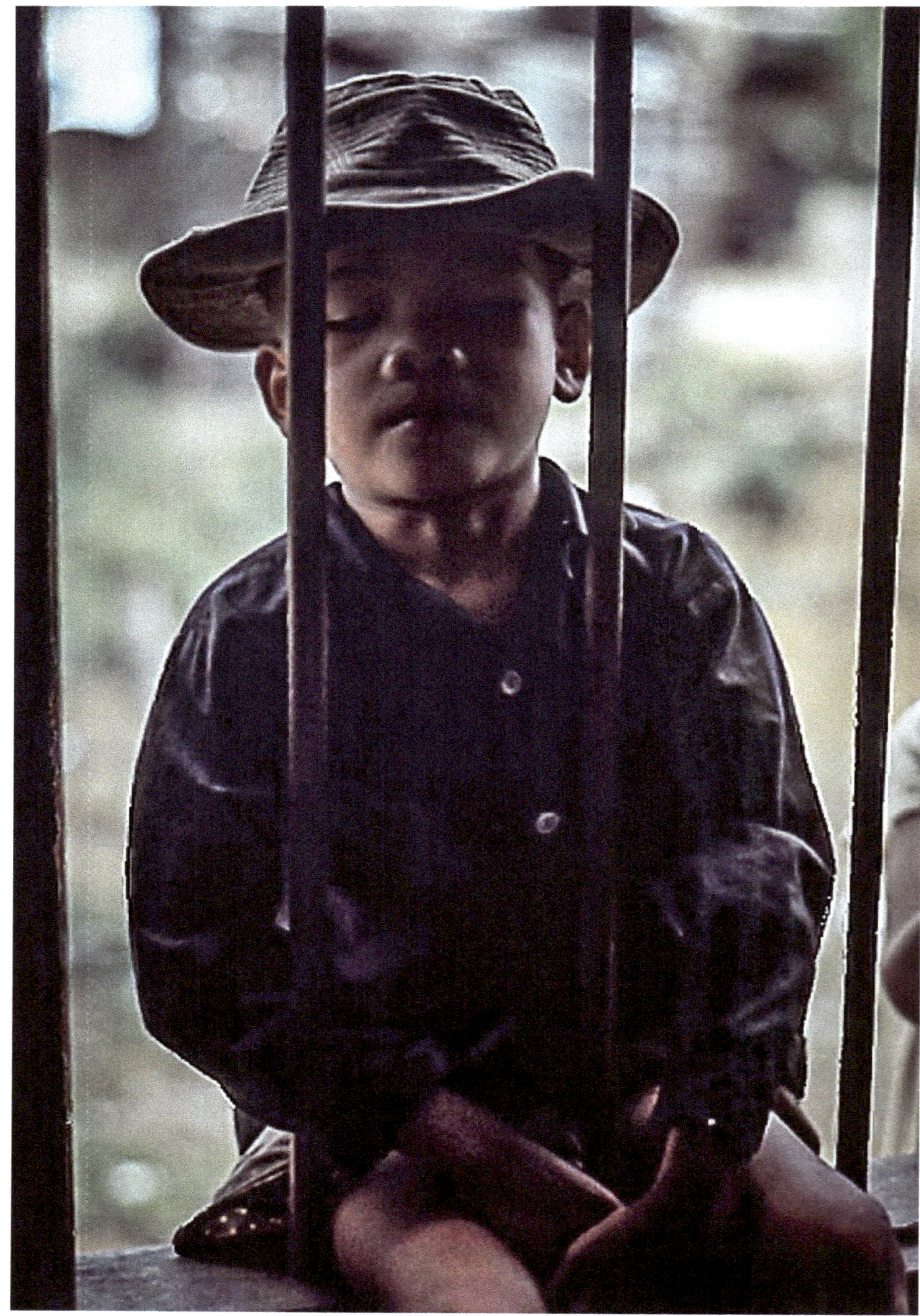

A young boy observes hamlet residents as they seek medical care within family home that we used as a temporary clinic. Phuoc Ly 1967.

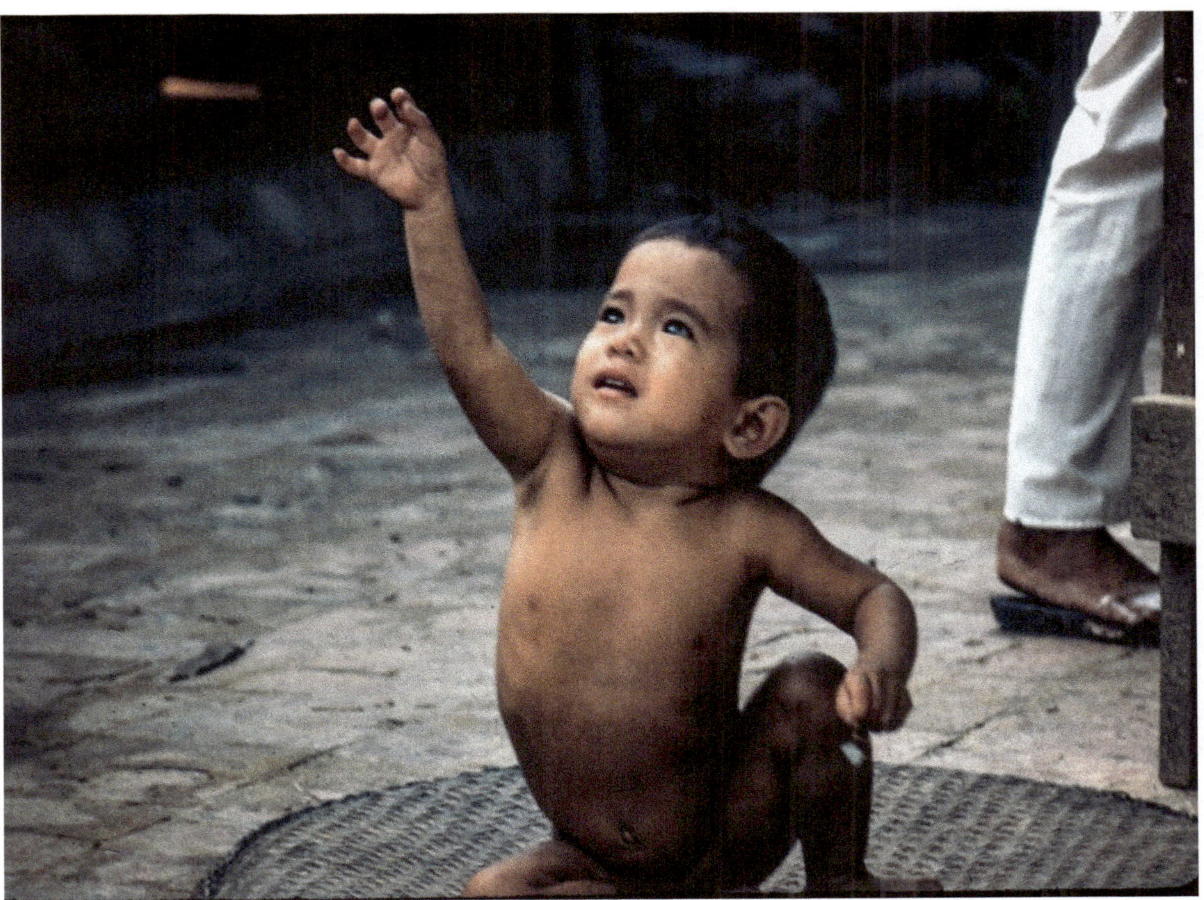

Phuoc Ly

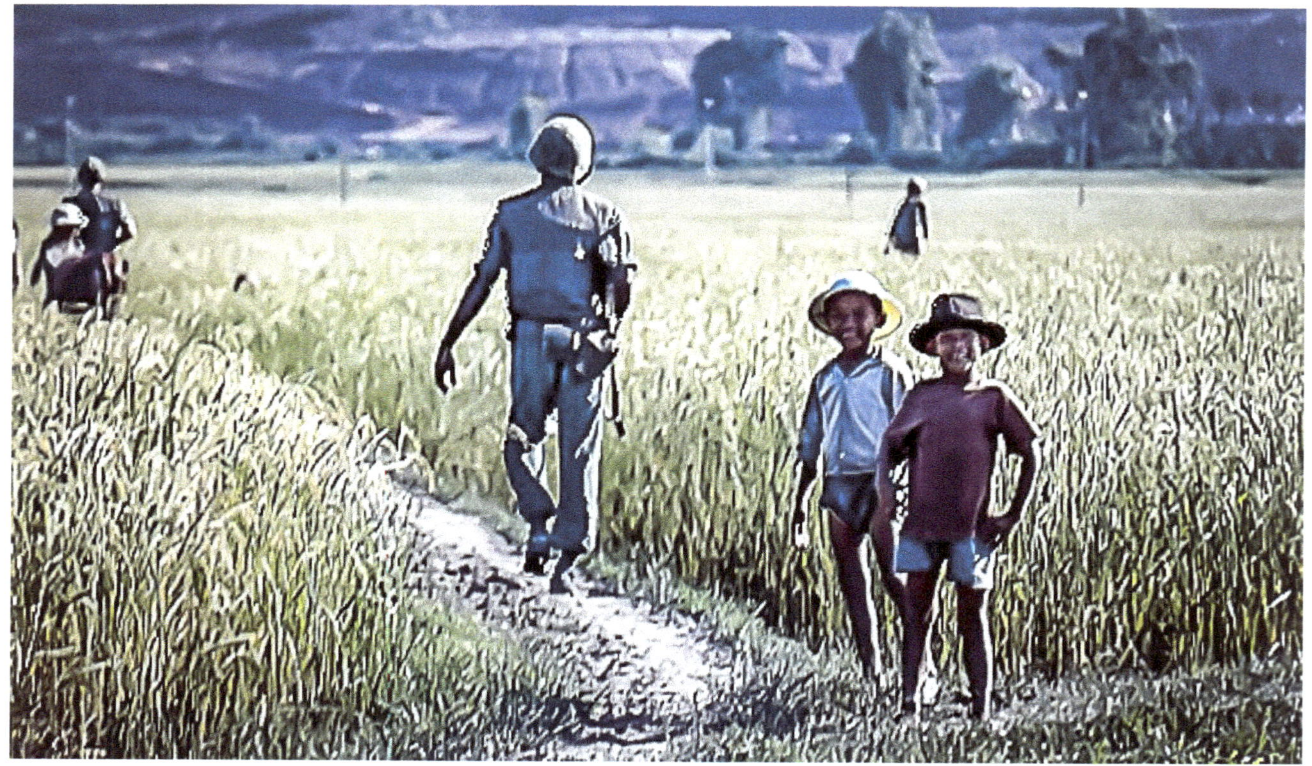

The presence of children on the trail always made our day. When not present...our concern for the presence of booby traps or an ambush was heightened.

Phuoc Ly 1967.

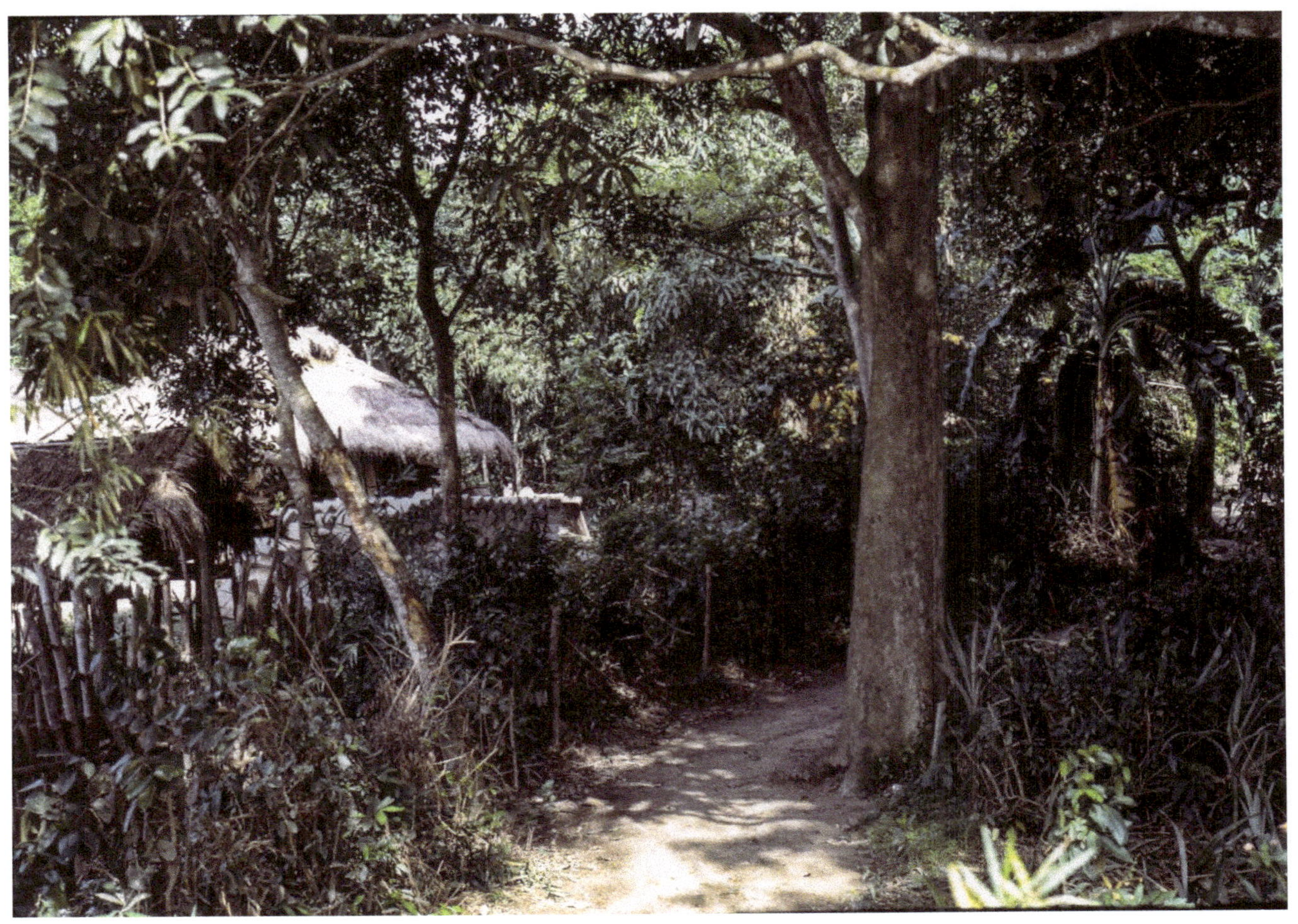

One trail through Phuoc Ly. As in all rural hamlets and villages, there was no electricity, Water for domestic use was drawn from a shallow well, fallow rice paddies served for the deposition of raw sewage, and medical care was non-existent. 1967.

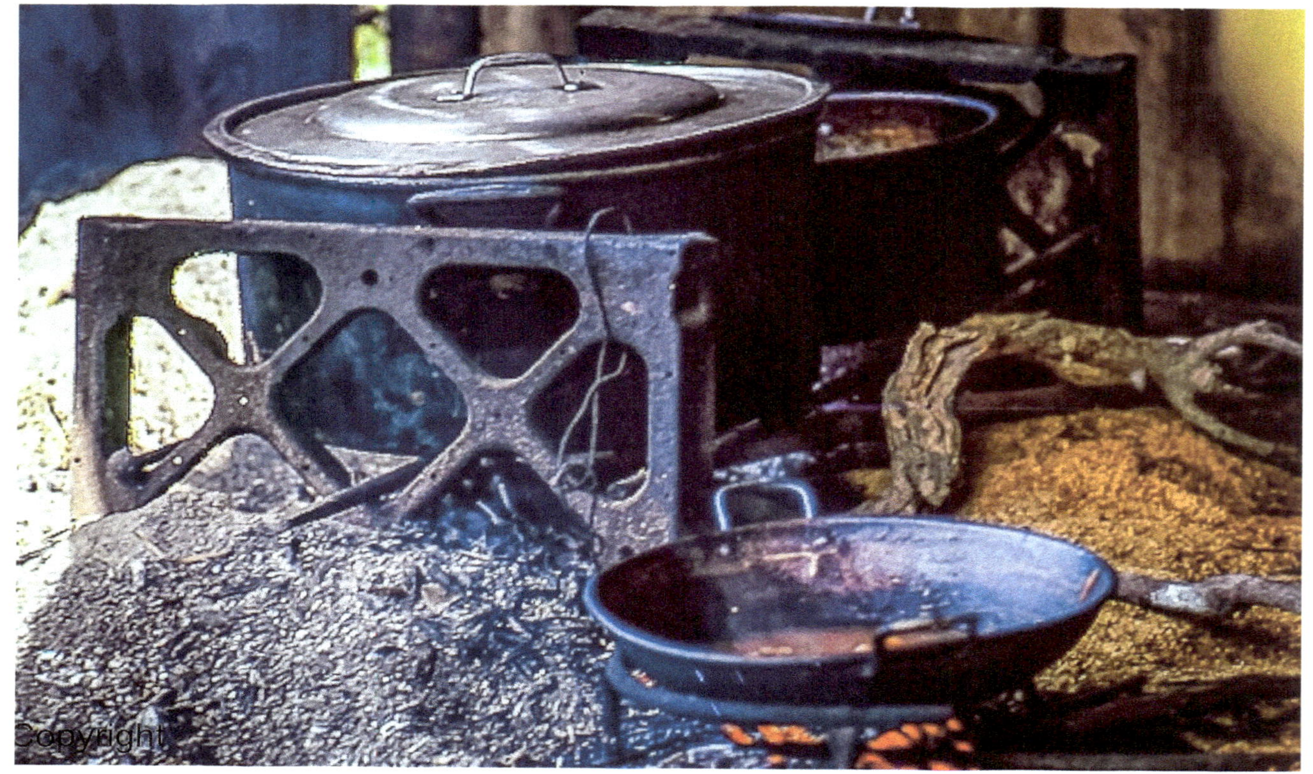

Typical peasant home cooking area.

Phuoc Ly,

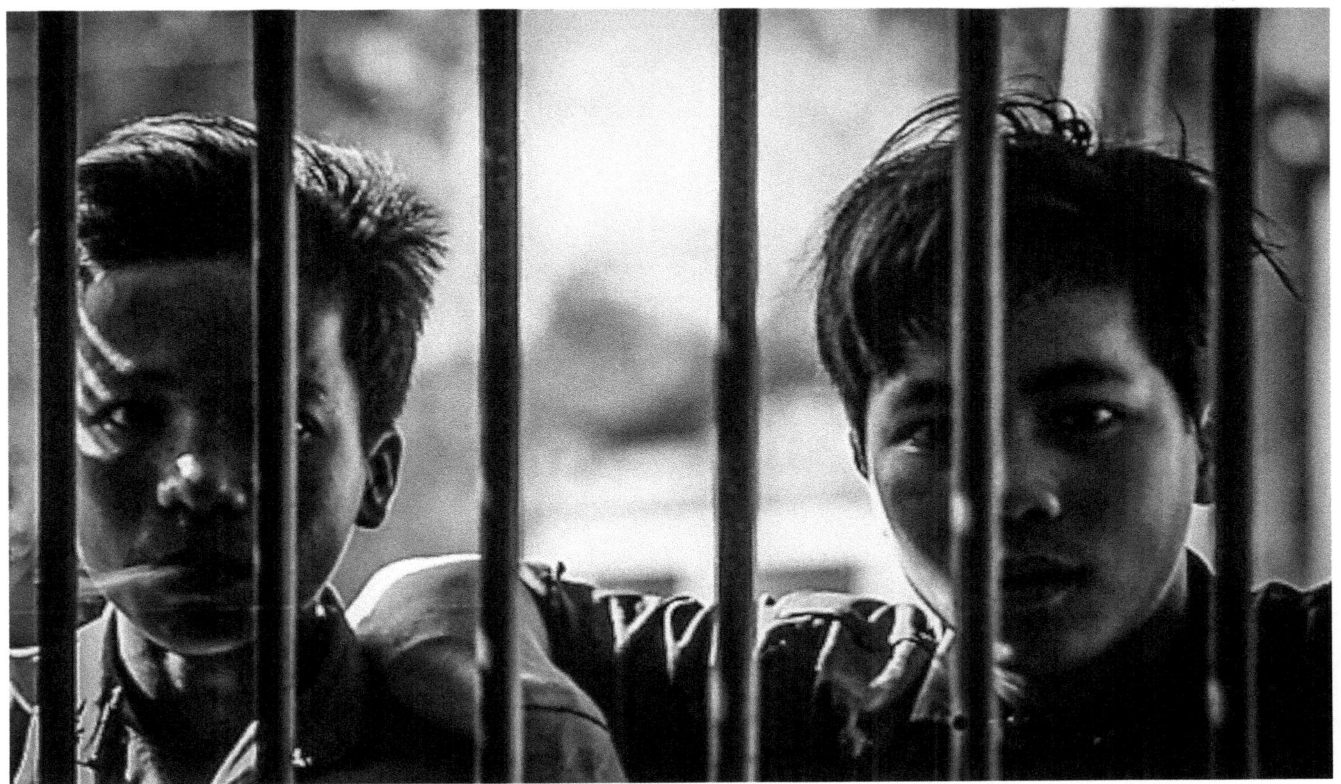

The Sudden Arrival… of the boys attracted my attention as I was treating villagers in Phuoc Ly. They did not ask for medical care. The hostile nature of their demeanor concerned me as I did not know whether or not they were Viet Cong. I finished caring for hamlet residents and had an uneventful walk back to our base camp.

Phuoc Ly, 1967.

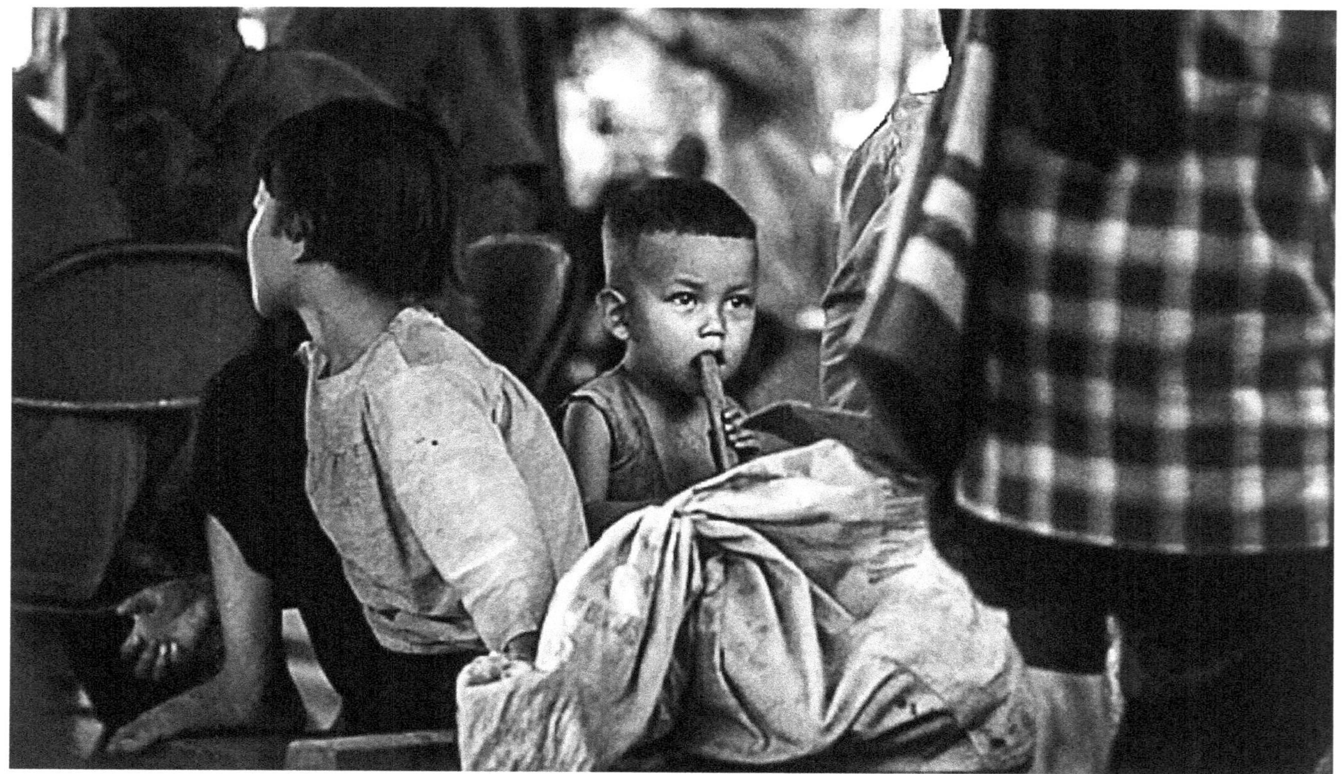

Vietnamese boy, seated next to his sister, eats his noon meal in the Phuoc Ly marketplace.

Phuoc Ly 1967.

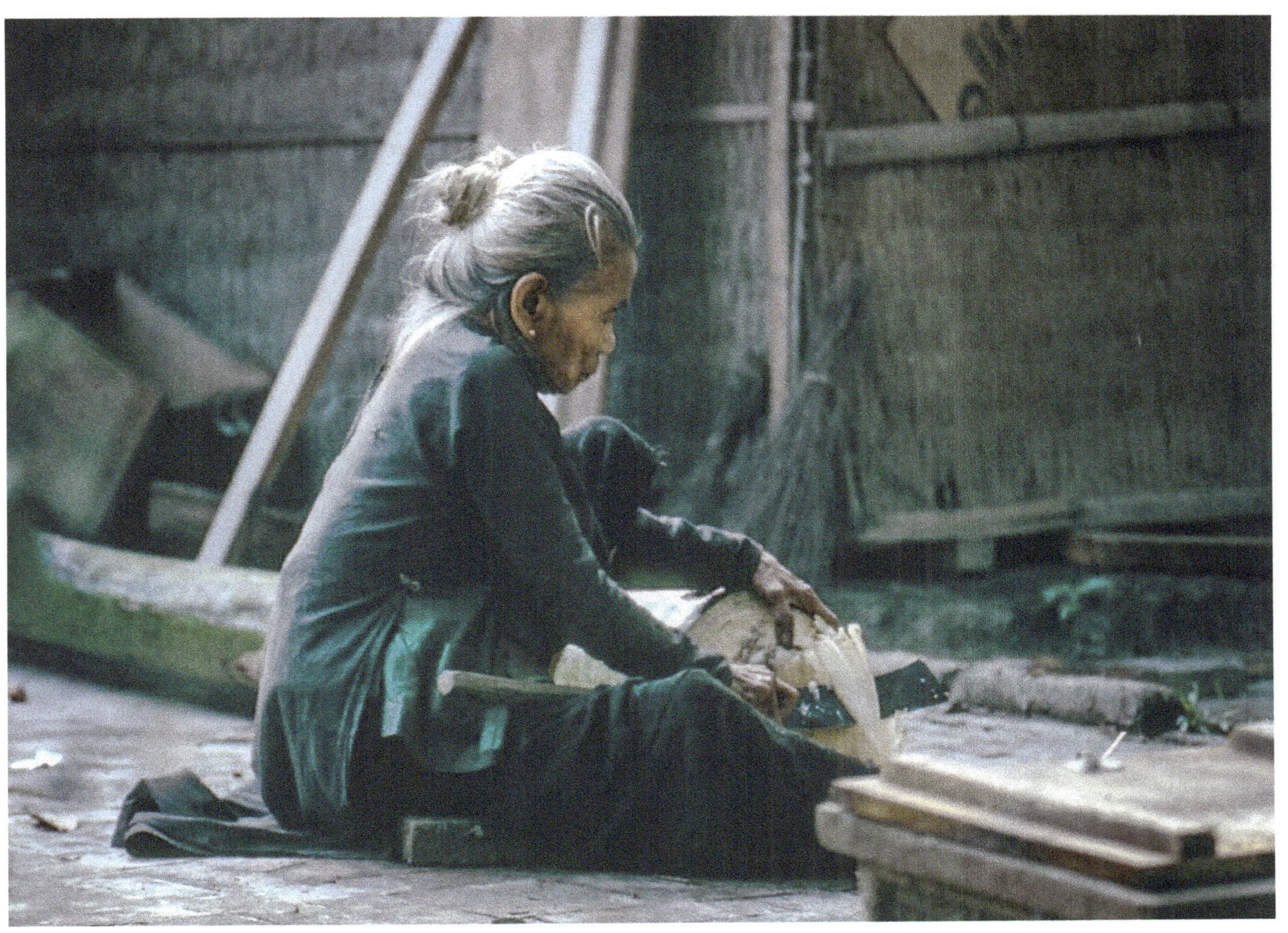

Vietnamese Elder slices the trunk of a banana tree for pig food.

Phuoc Ly 1967.

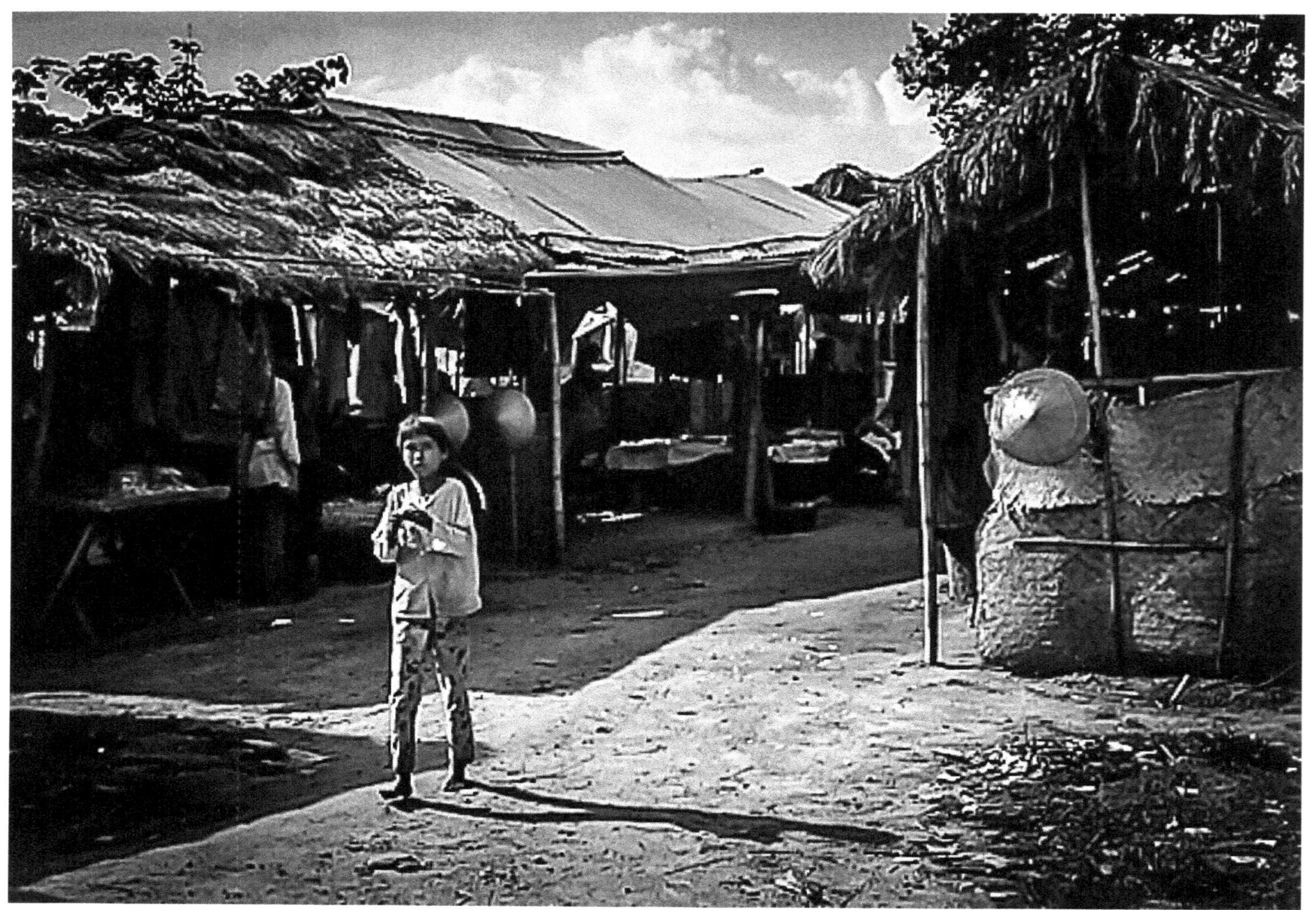

Villagers of Phuoc Ly and surrounding hamlets sold or bartered their crops and wares in this marketplace. 1967

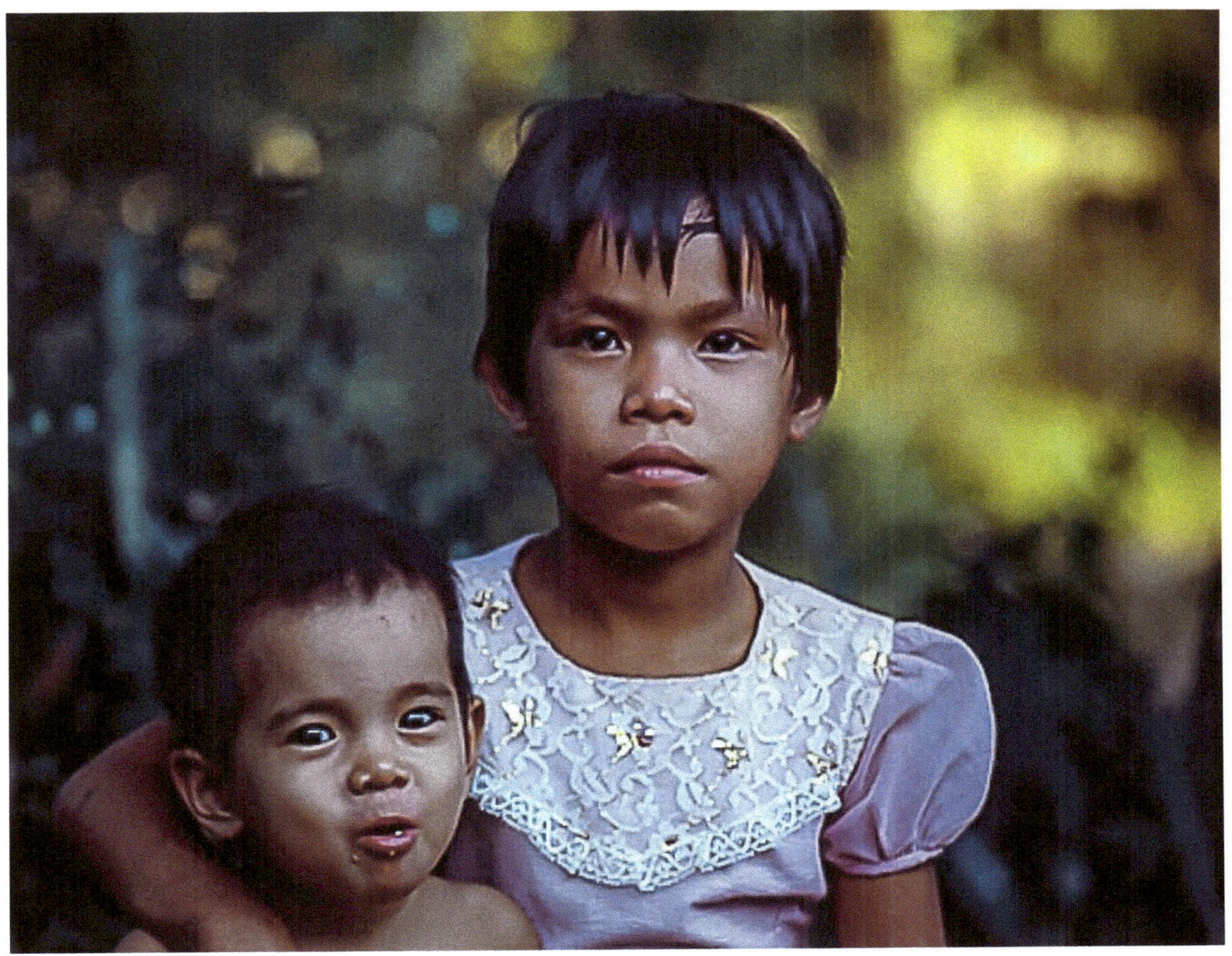

Big Sister... put her special dress on to be photographed with her little brother. A singular event for me, for her, and her brother. In the countryside, fancy clothing such as this was unobtainable because of poverty.

Phuoc Ly, 1966.

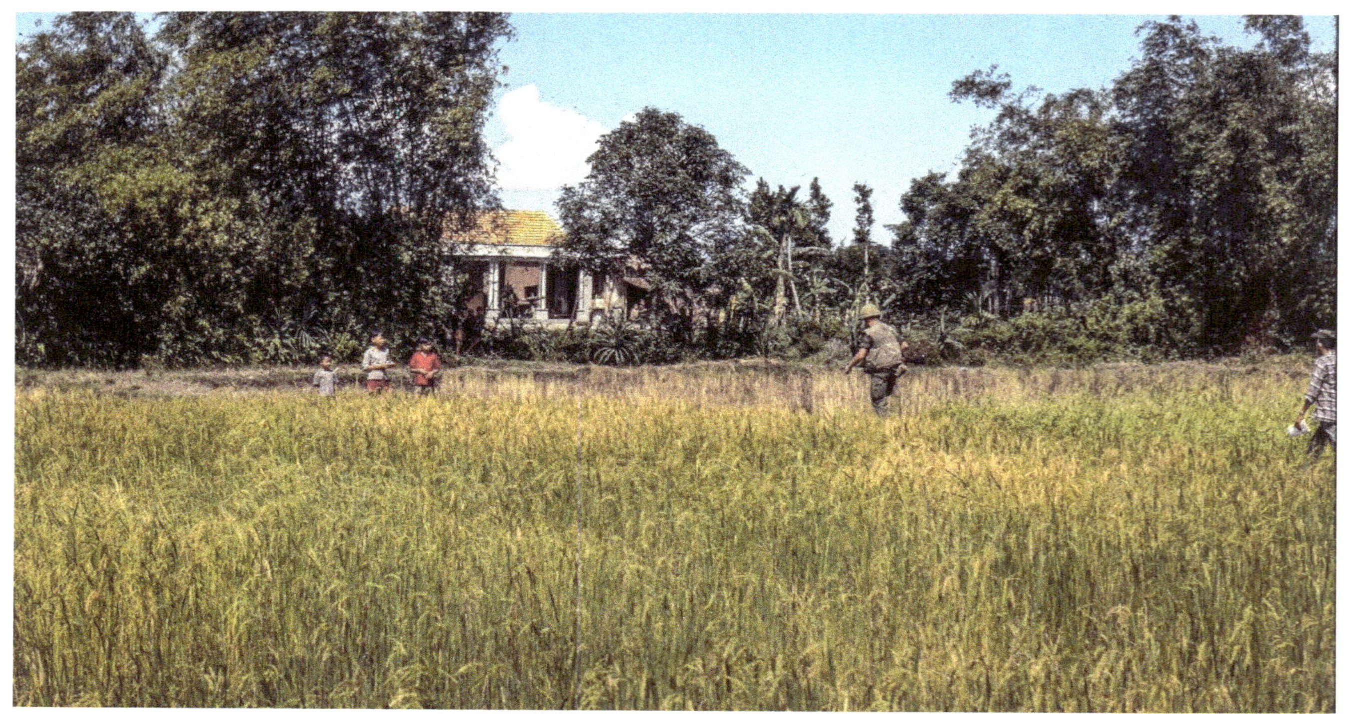

Young boys greet us as we approach Phuoc Ly on a rice paddy dike.

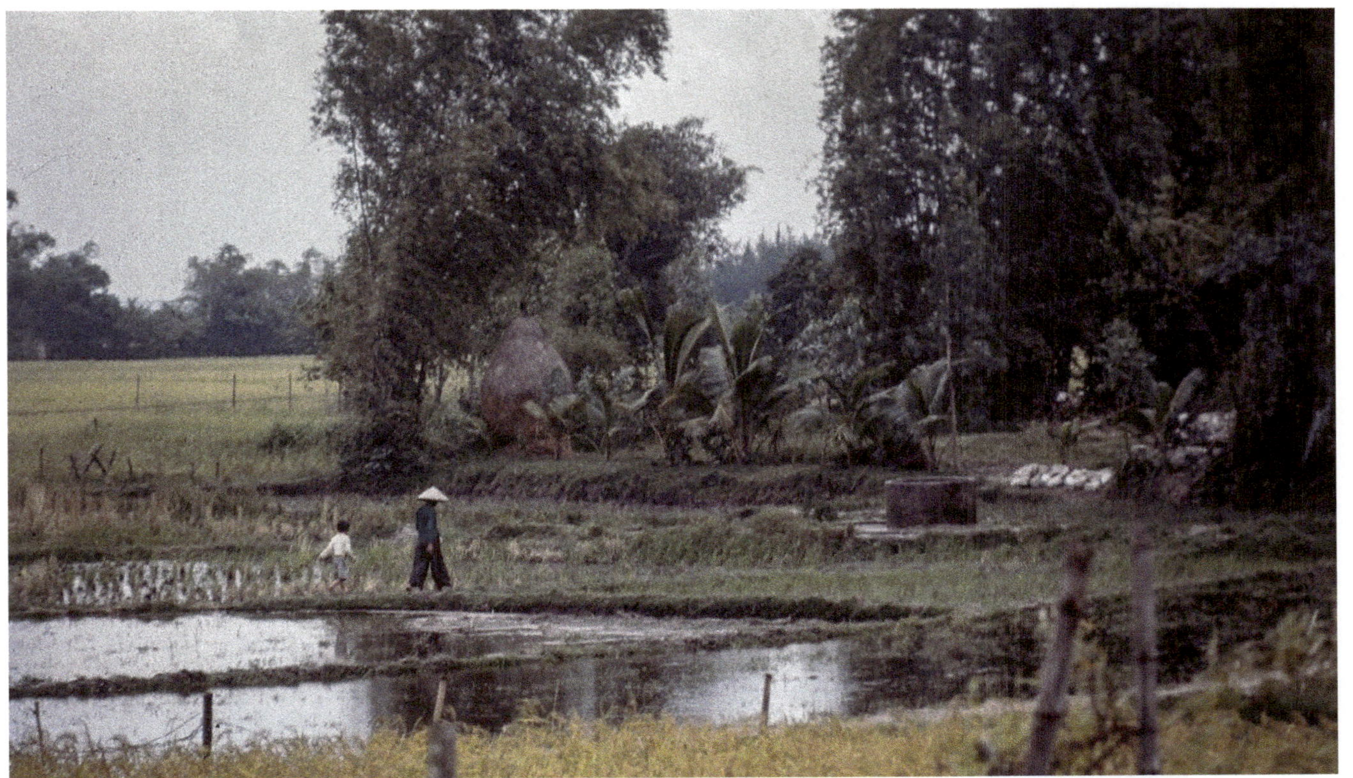

A Vietnamese mother walks with her child on a rice paddy dike. The flooded paddies lie adjacent to a hamlet well which increases the likelihood of contamination making it unsuitable for human use. It was however, used by families for cooking.

Phuoc Ly 1966.

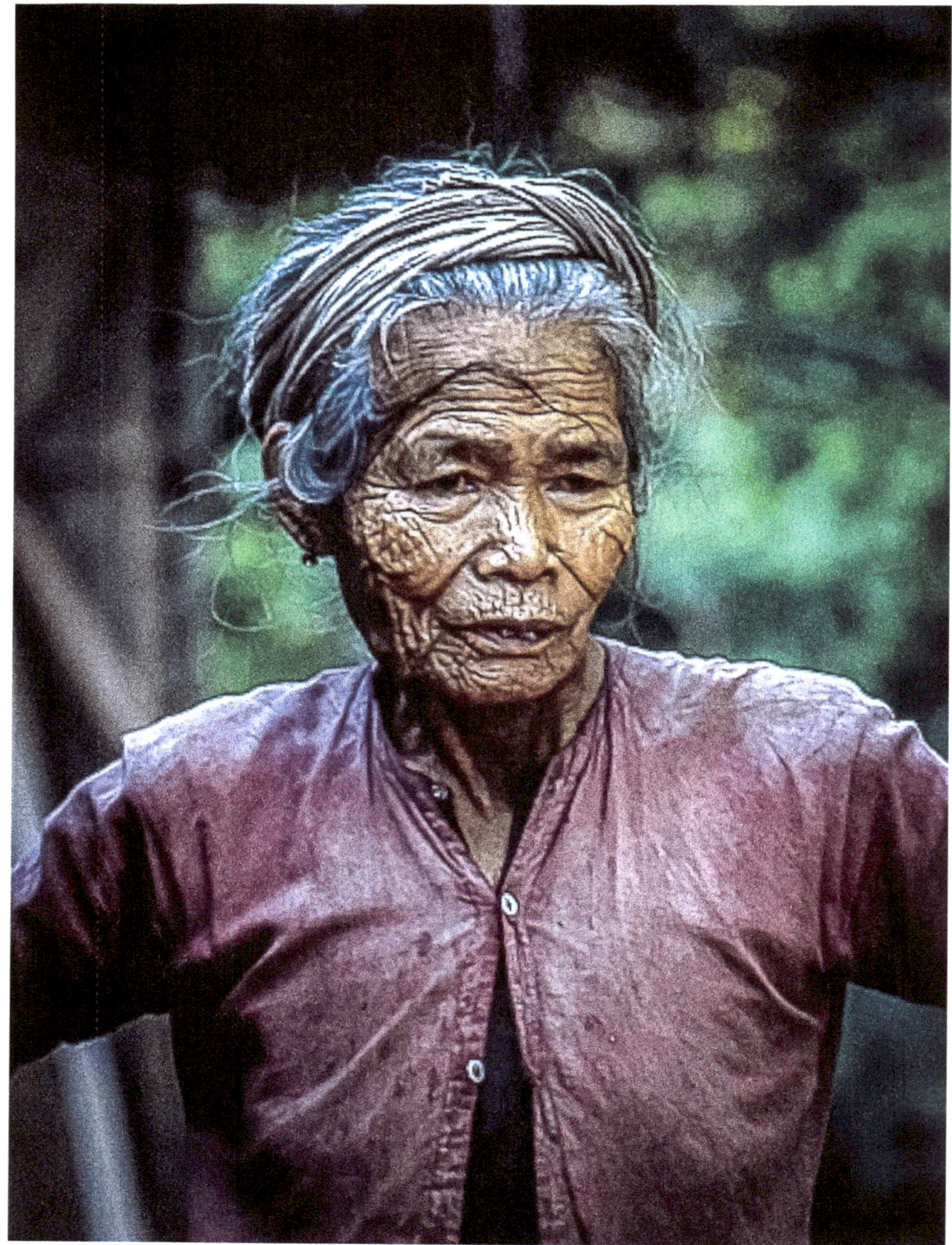

Phuoc Ly Elder

Phuoc Tuong Hamlet

Was situated just outside the western perimeter of the sprawling Da Nang airbase used jointly by the U.S. and Vietnamese air forces. The hamlet was a conglomeration of closely packed houses, huts, and lean-to structures constructed by local residents and war refugees and Vietnamese who were displaced by the war.

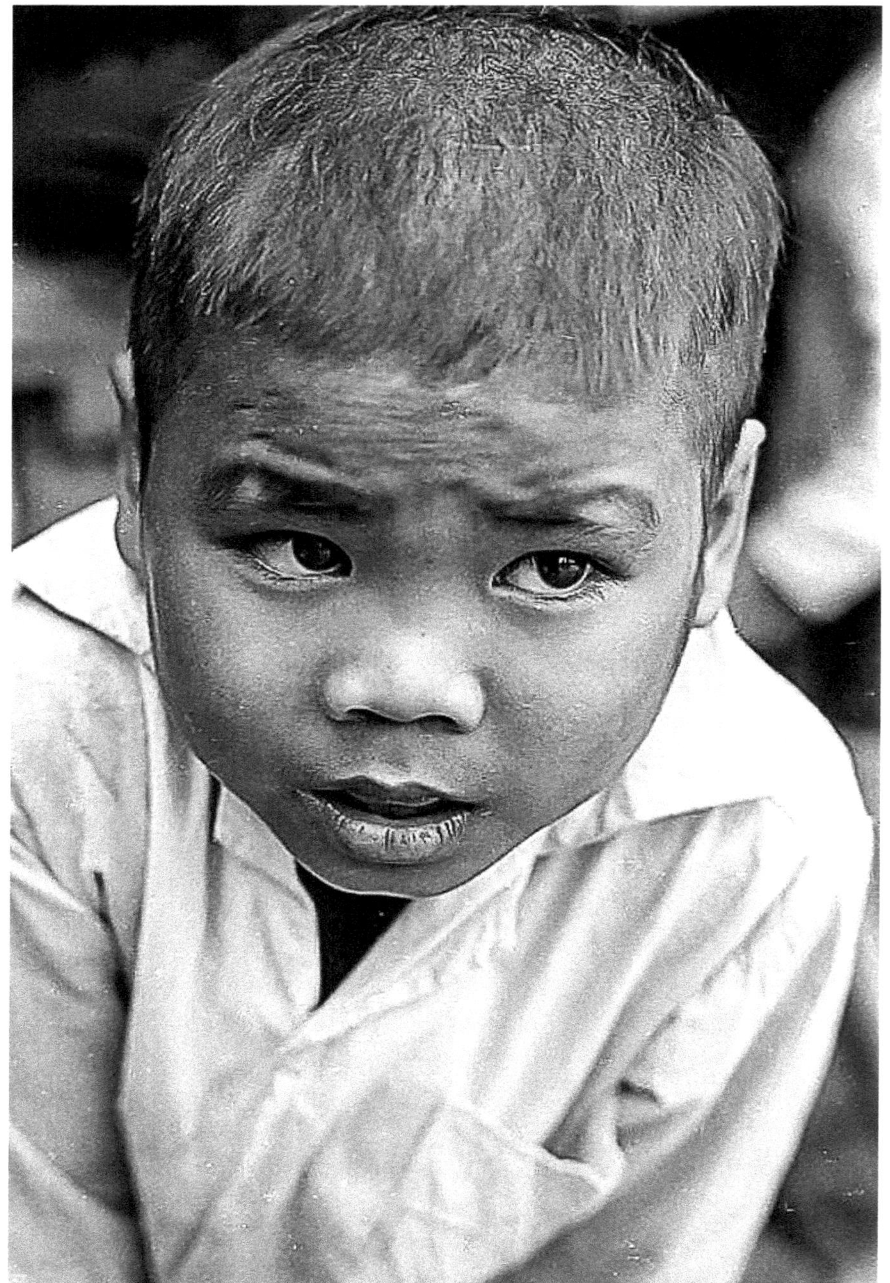

The Children of Phuoc Tuong Hamlet were always inquisitive and friendly, anxious to form a friendship. 1966

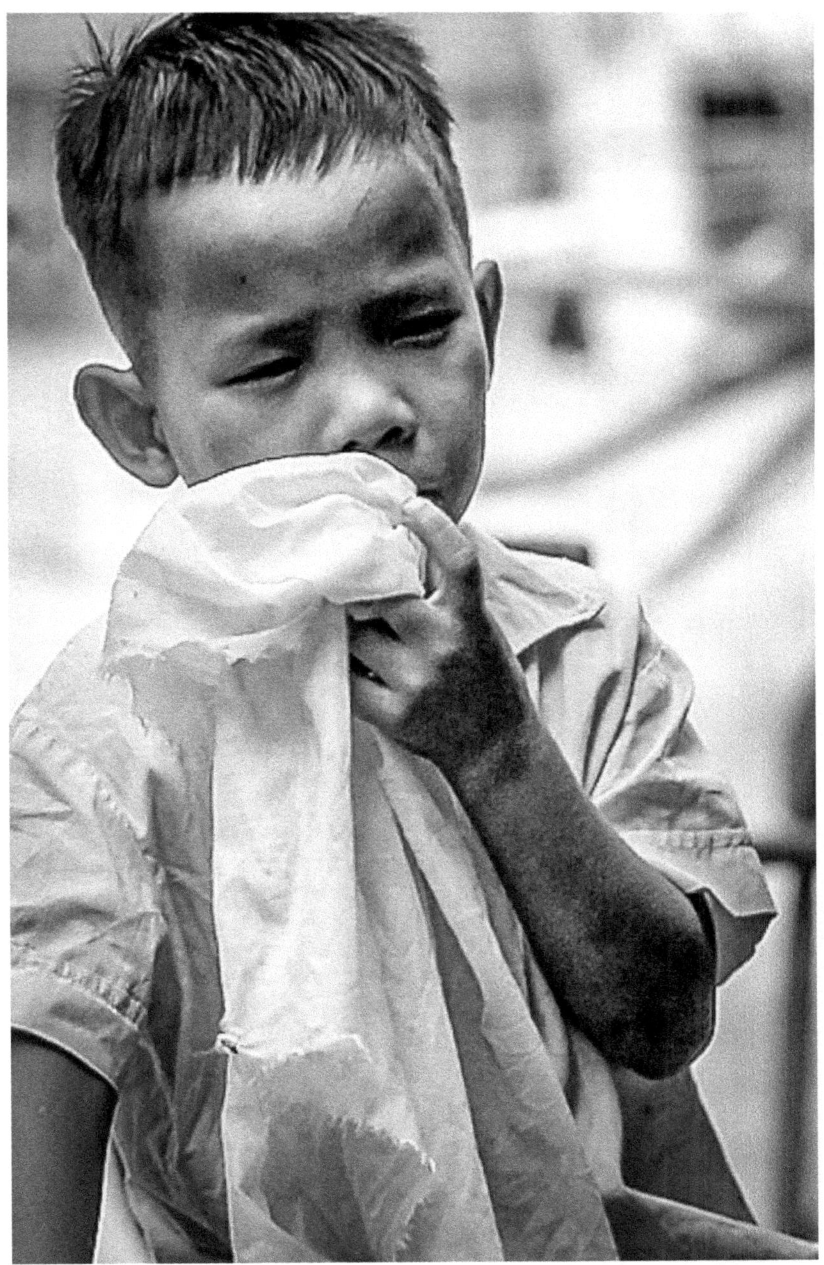

Waiting to be seen for medical care outside the Phuoc Tong Hamlet School. 1966

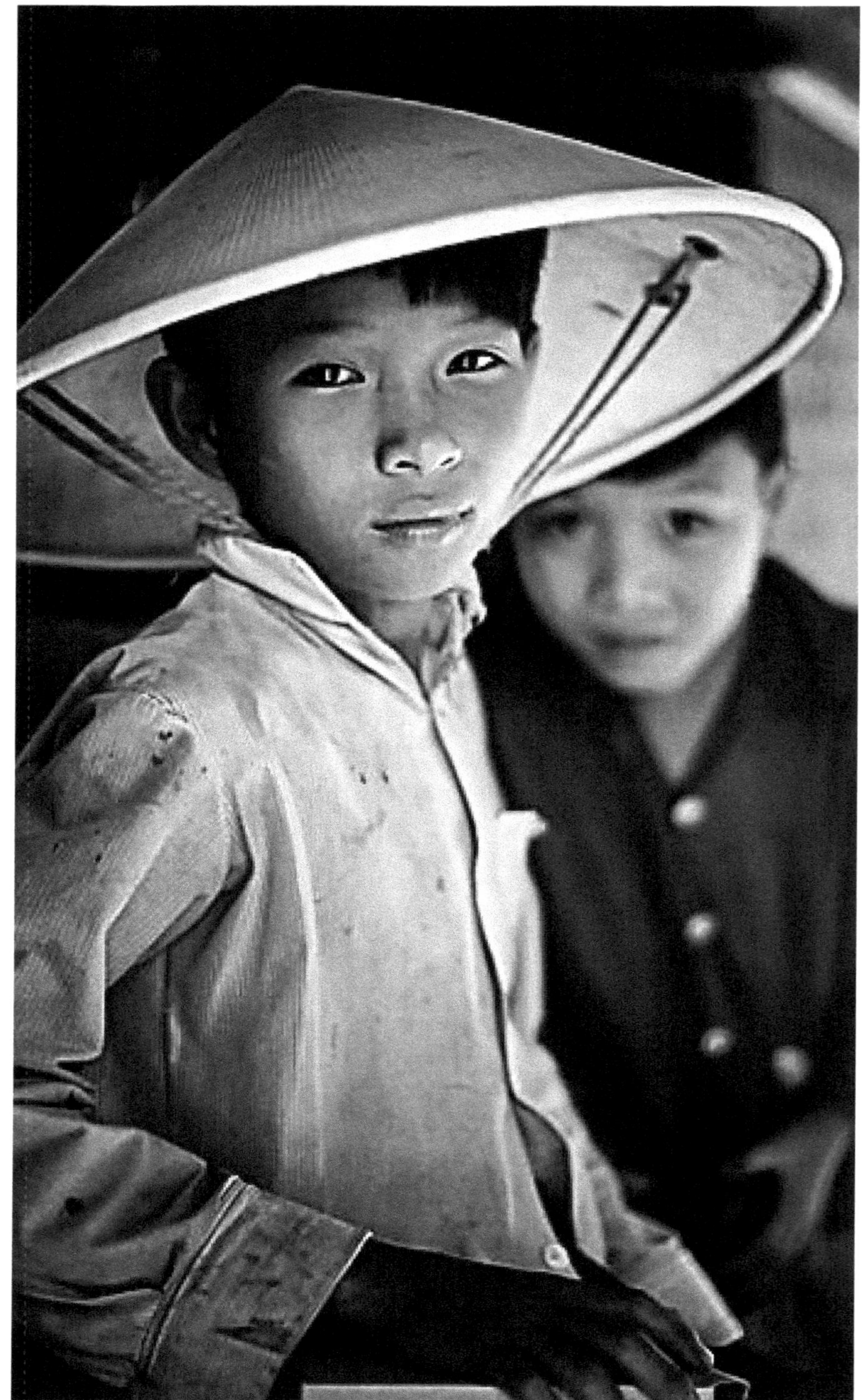

A Young Vietnamese boy wears the traditional and practical Vietnamese hat, the Non La. This model is made of a synthetic material, while most Non La hats are made of woven plant fiber. 1966

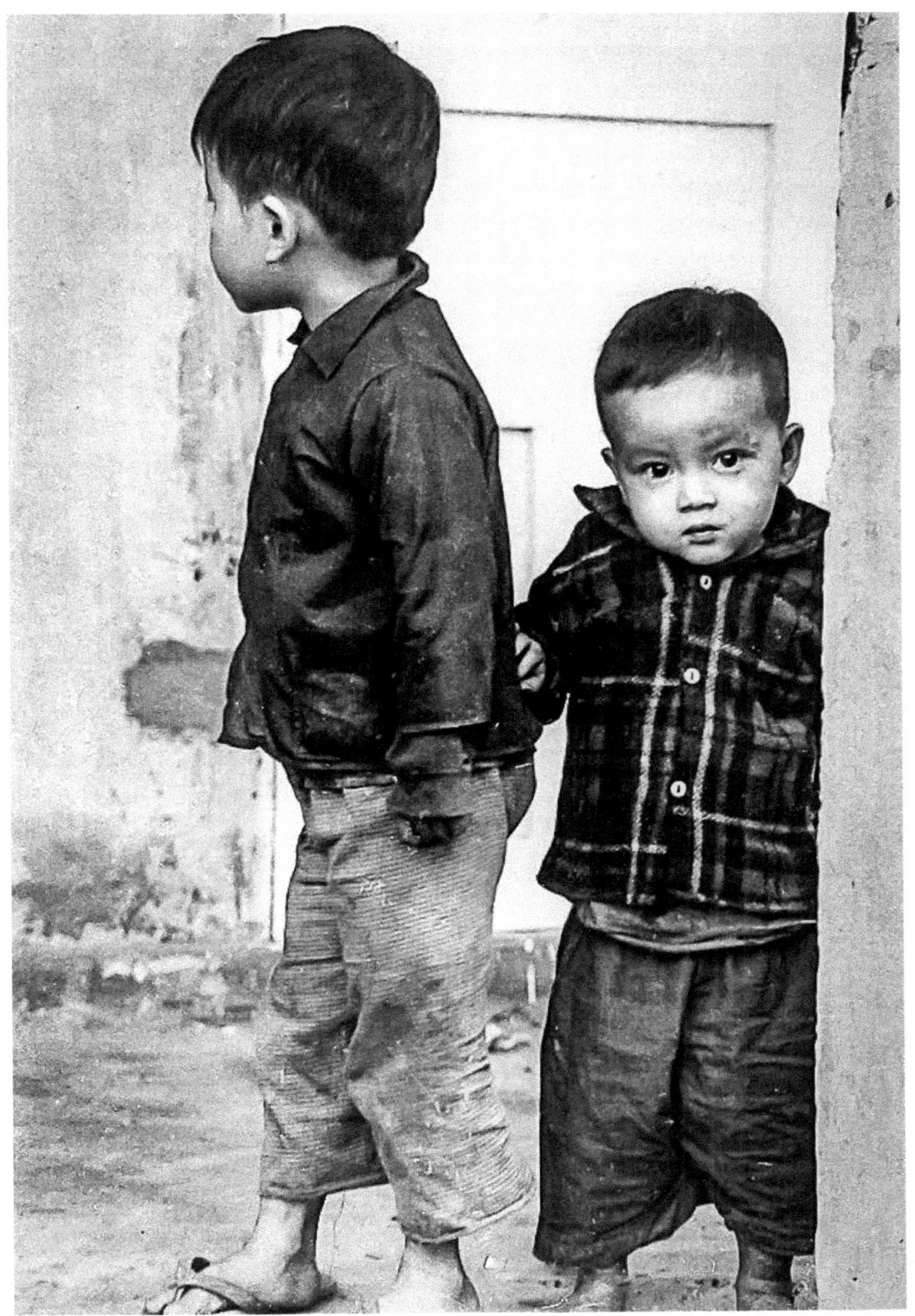

Brothers searching... they came with other children seeking medical care. Neither their mother nor father were with them. 1966

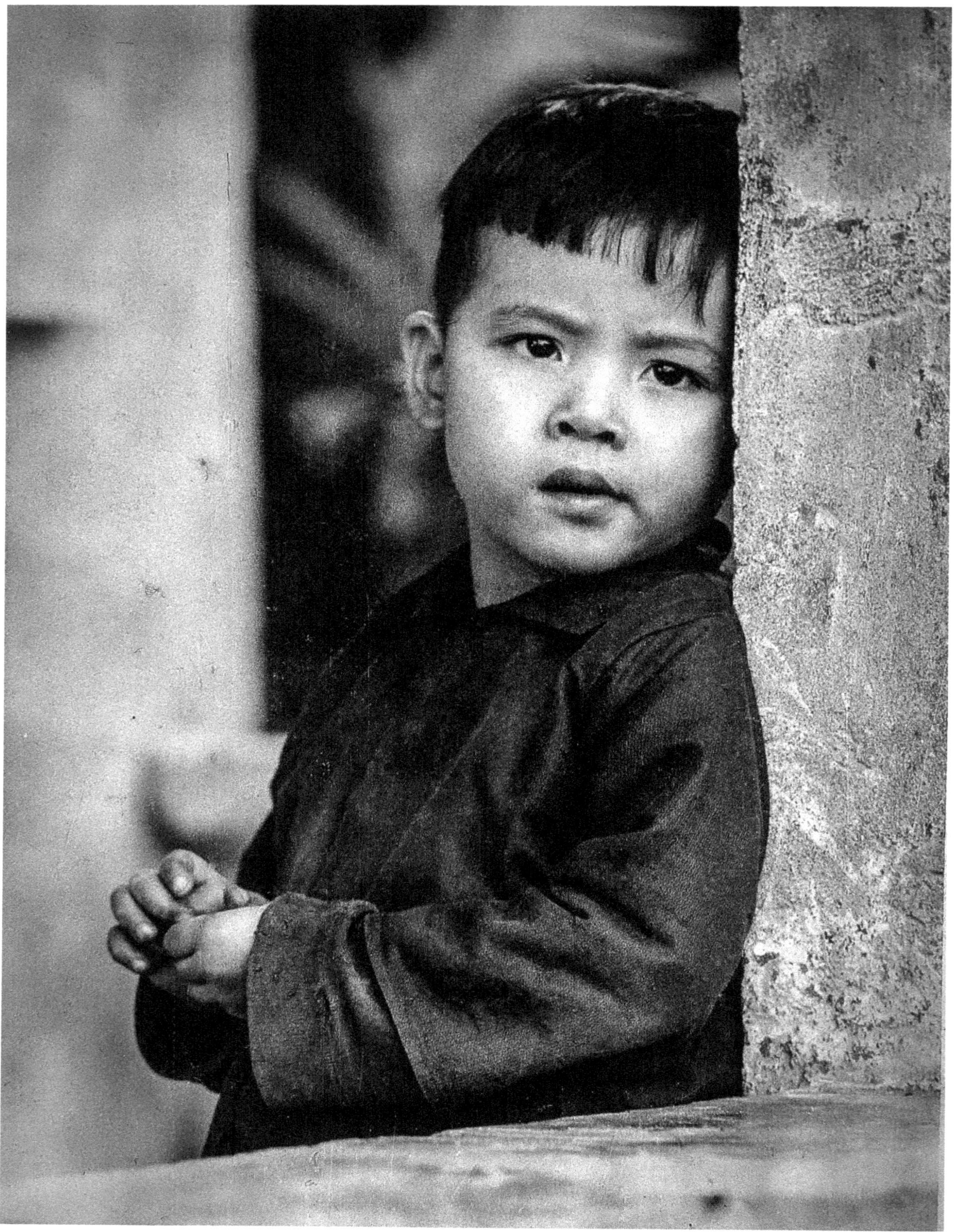

Phuoc Tuong 1966.

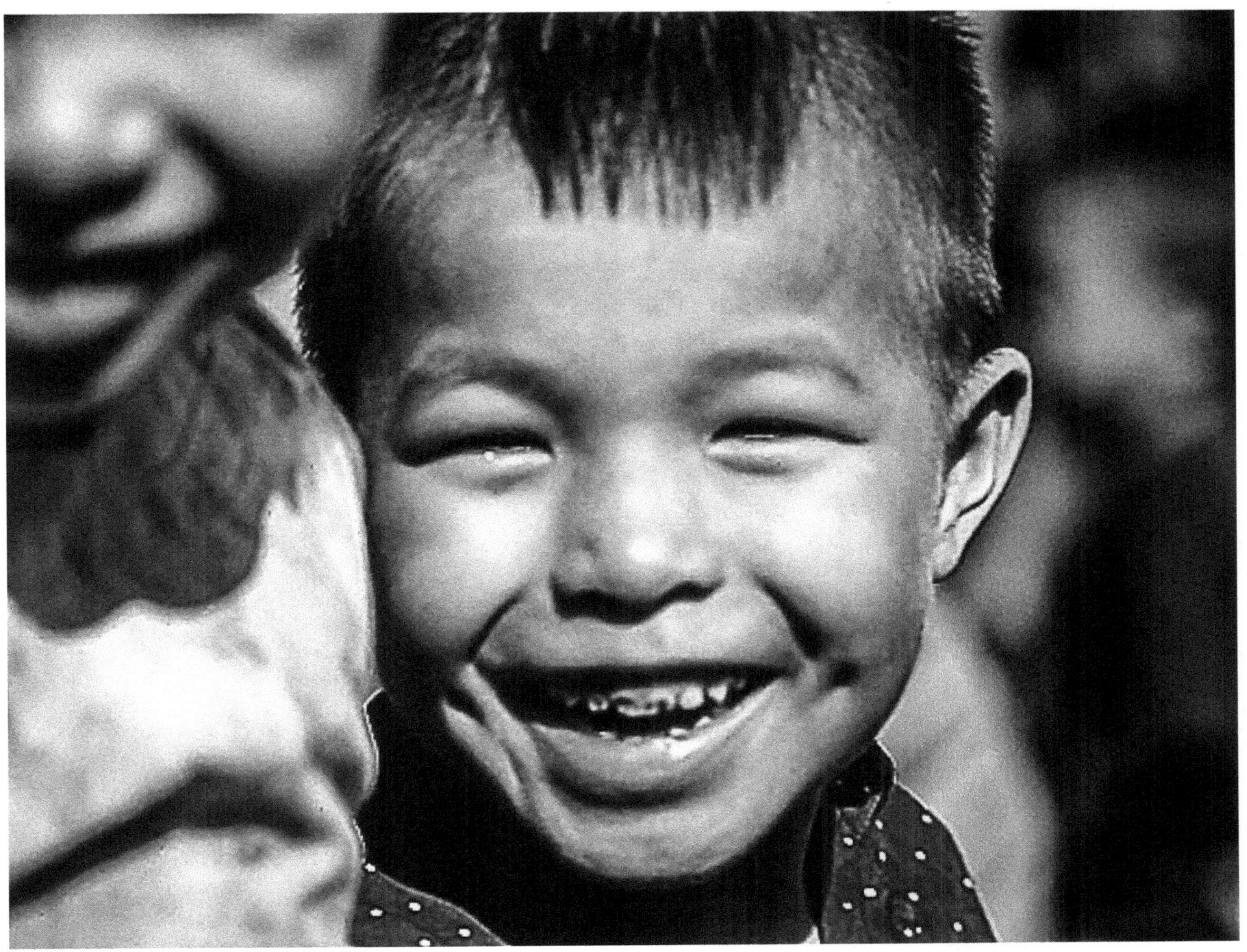

The lack of regular dental hygiene as evidenced in this boy's caries, was a major problem in the rural population. When possible, dentists accompanied us to remote hamlets to provide dental care.

Phuoc Tuong 1966.

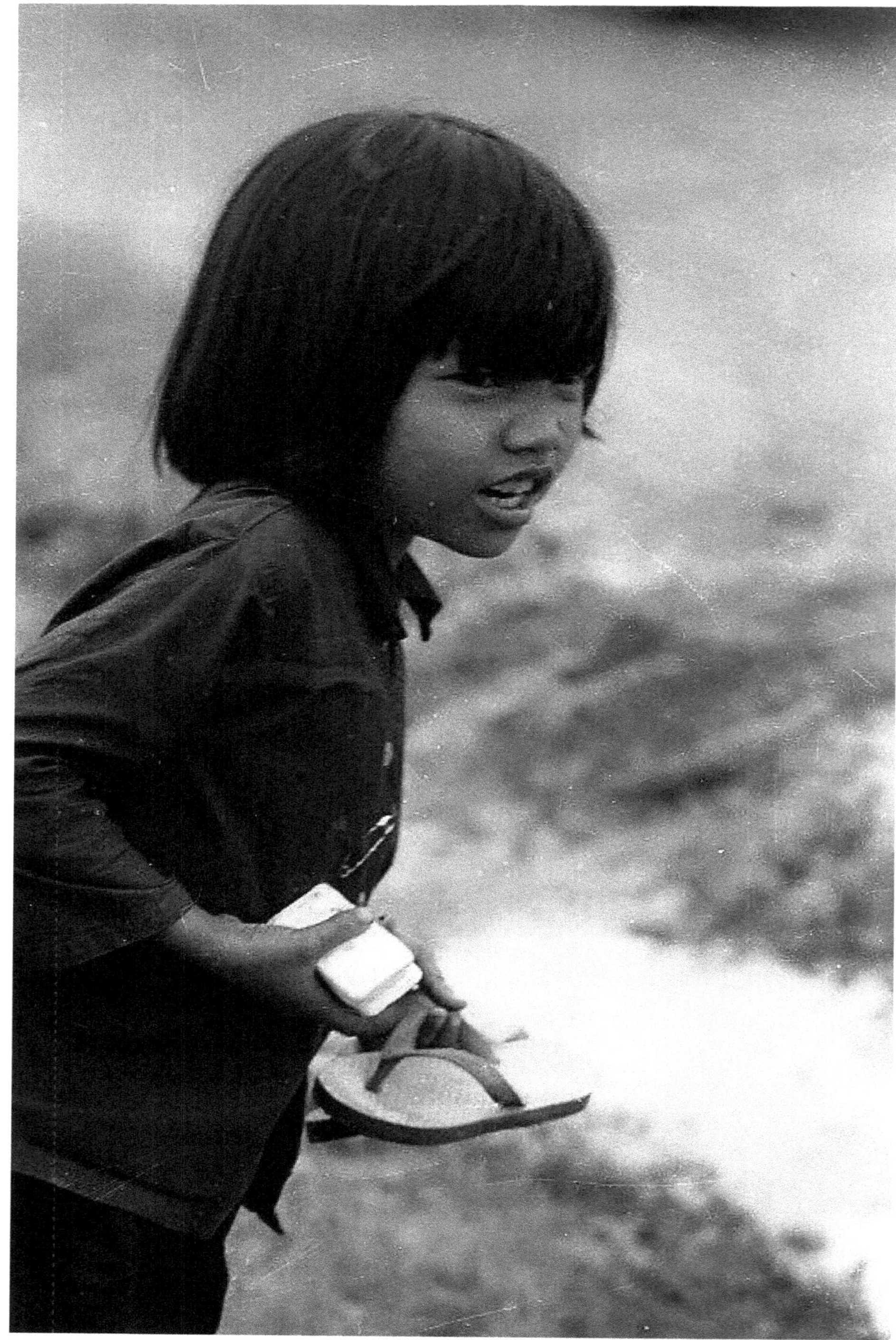

A young Vietnamese girl heads homeward with newly acquired soap which was very difficult for the average Vietnamese to obtain. In the rural countryside, many Vietnamese in very remote areas did not know what soap was or what it was intended for.

Phuoc Tuong 1966.

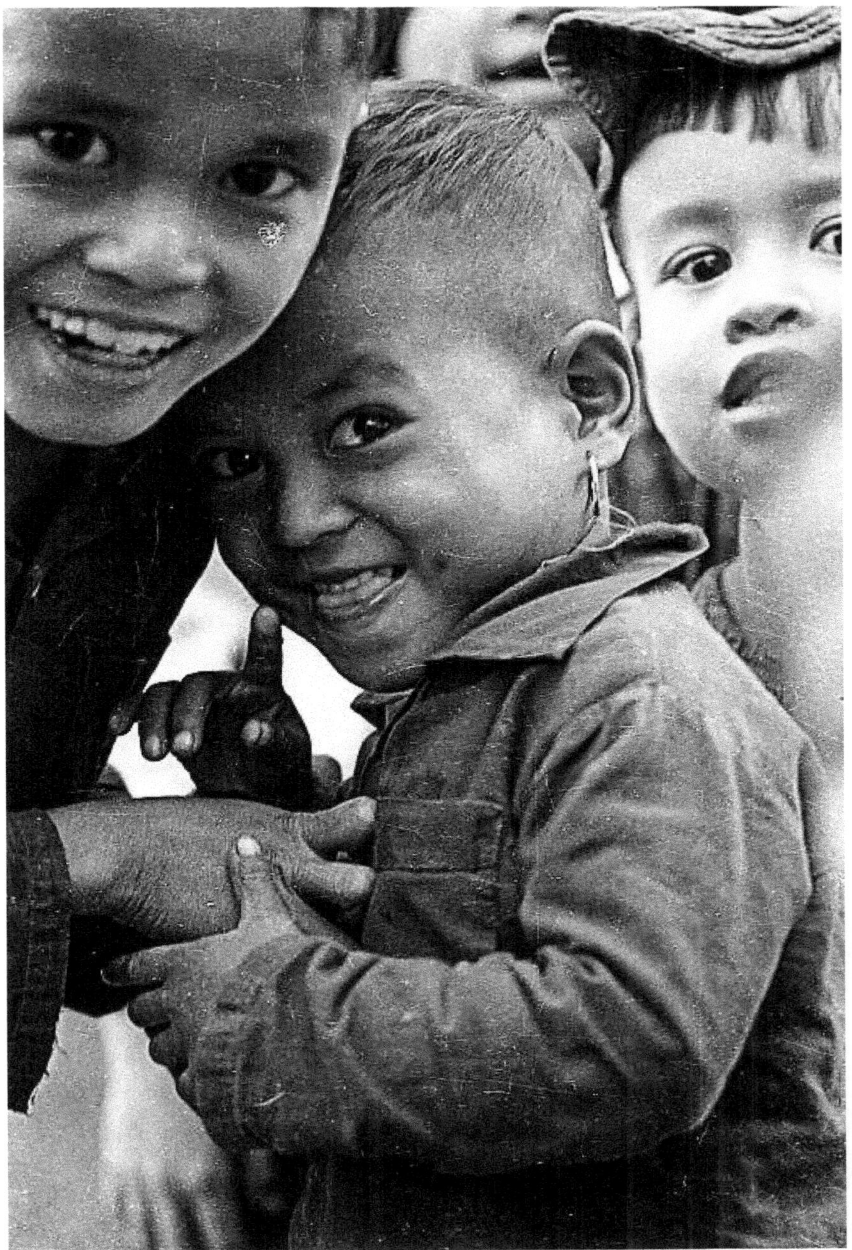

Young Vietnamese boy with a gold ear ring…

For Buddhists, gold is the universal symbol for happiness, purity, enlightenment, and freedom. Vietnamese who could afford gold adorned their children thusly. Adults would have a gold tooth placed or wear jewelry.

Phuoc Tuong 1966.

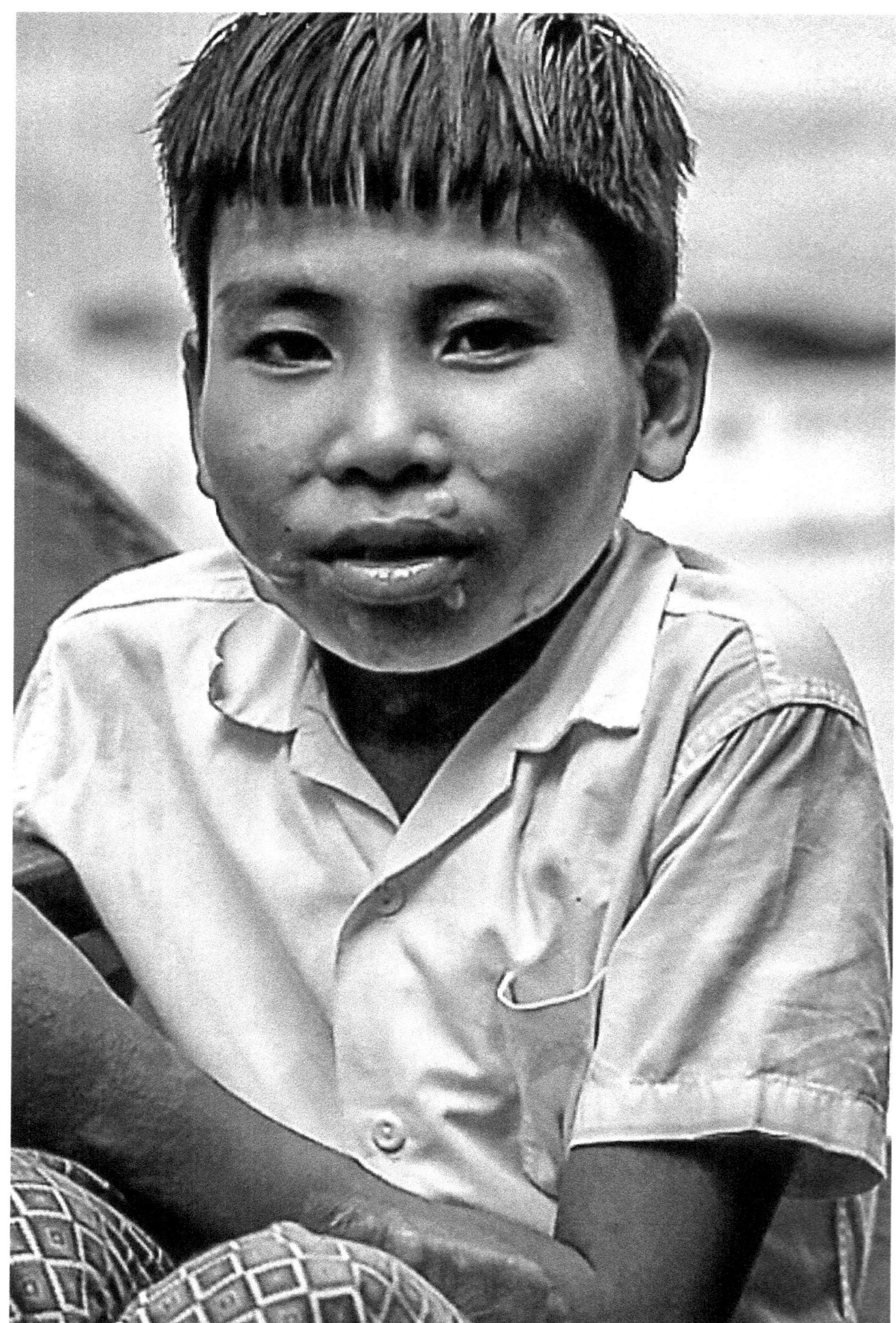

Facial scars from white phosphorus ordinance.

Phuoc Tuong, 1966.

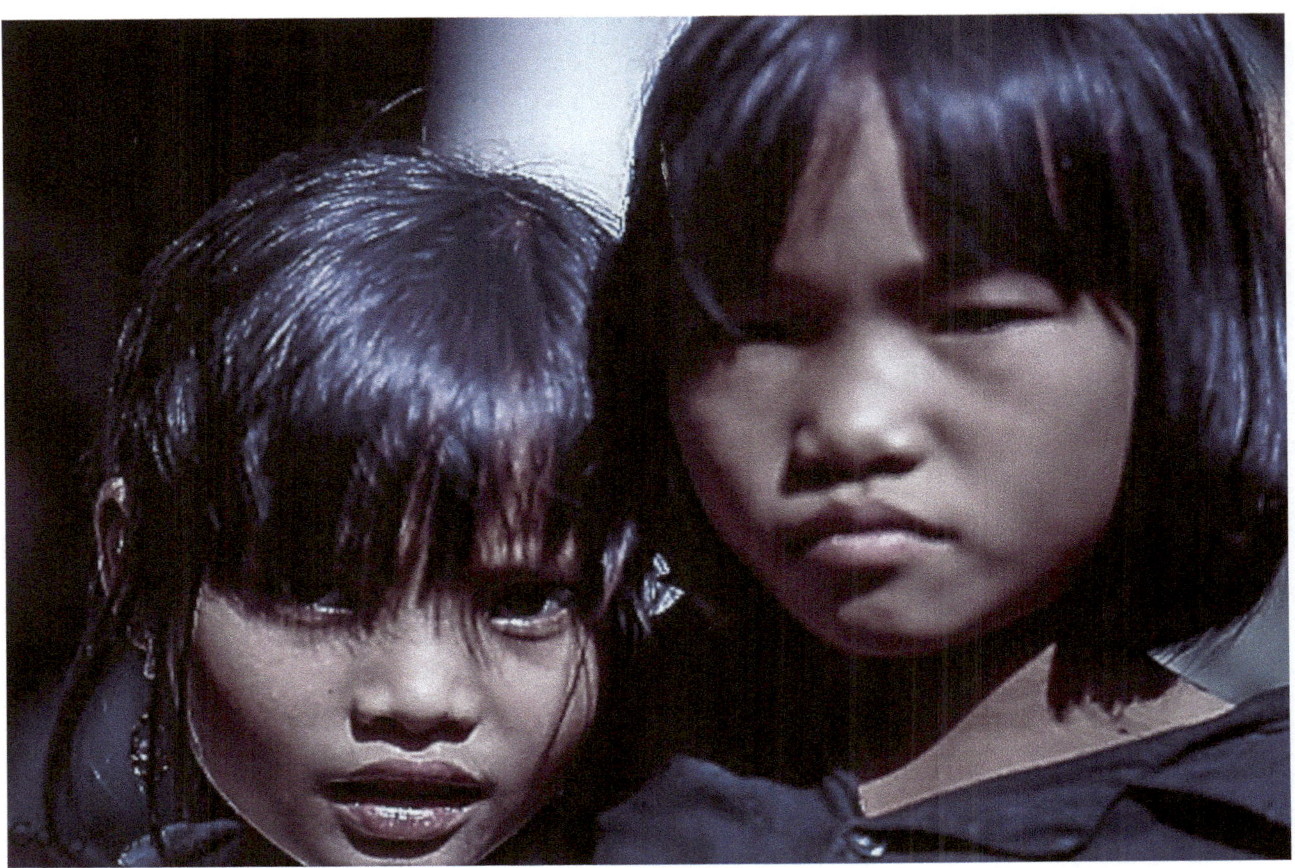

Phuoc Tuong 1966

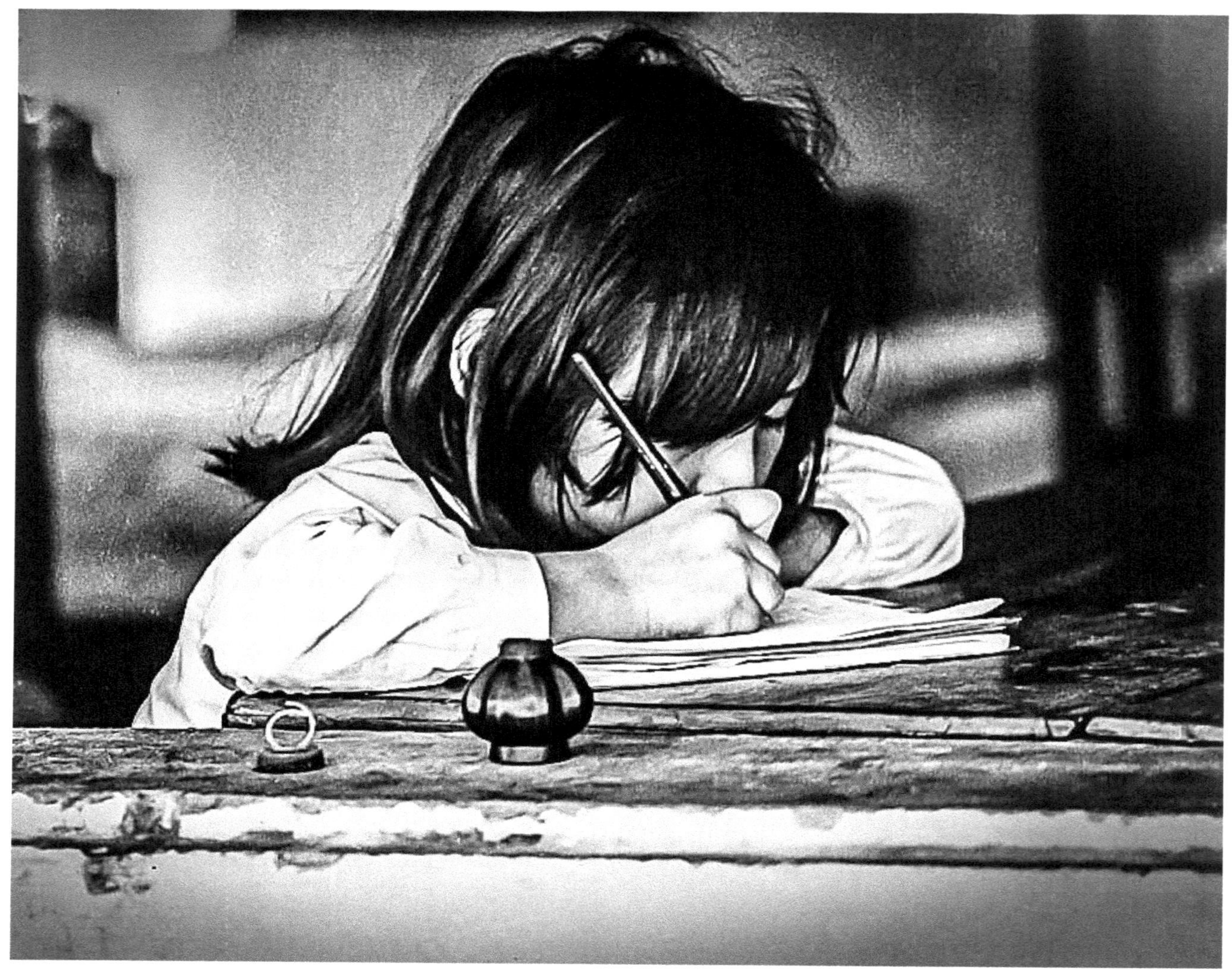

The Sacred Heart Orphanage

They were known as the Sisters of Saint. Paul de Chartes, with the congregation located in the City of Da Nang. The congregation existed since 1906 when the orphanage and school were founded. The orphanage and sisters endured Japanese occupation in WW11, escaped to Hue and returned in 1947 and re-established the school and orphanage. We provided medical and dental care to them when possible.

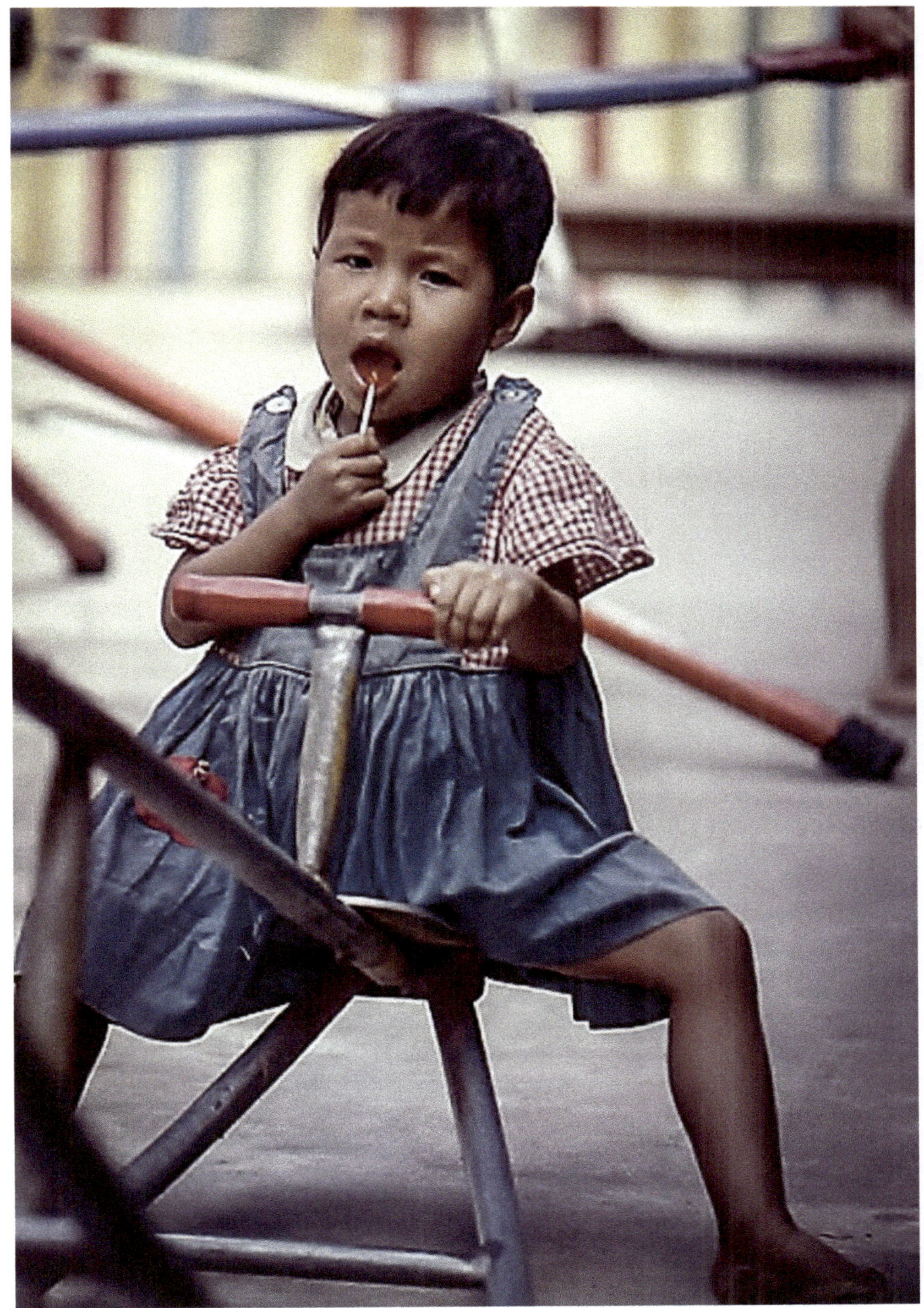

Children who lived in the orphanage were dressed in newer clothing, donated by charities.

Sacred Heart 1967.

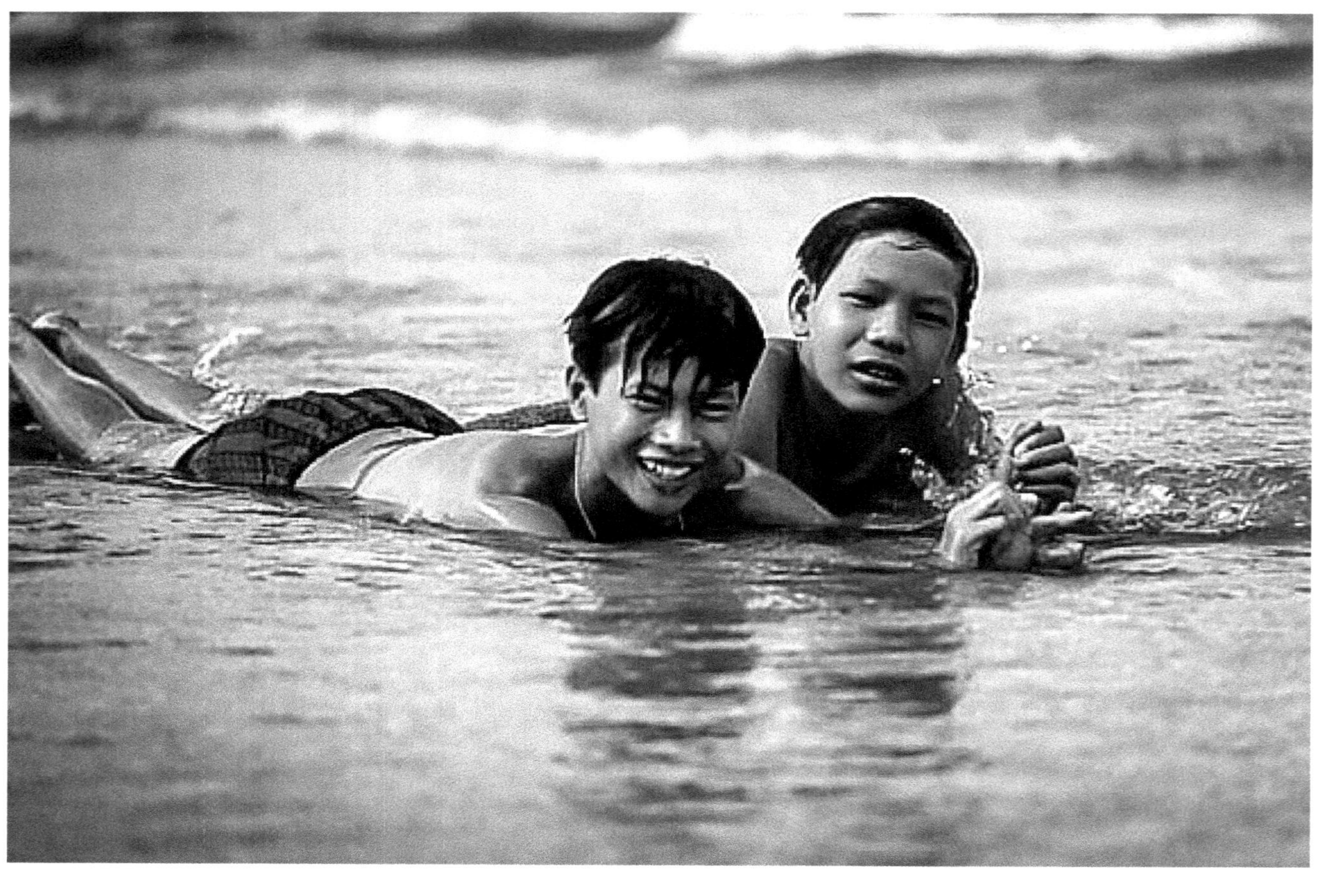

Boys from the Sacred Heart Orphanage attend a picnic we sponsored at China Beach. 1967

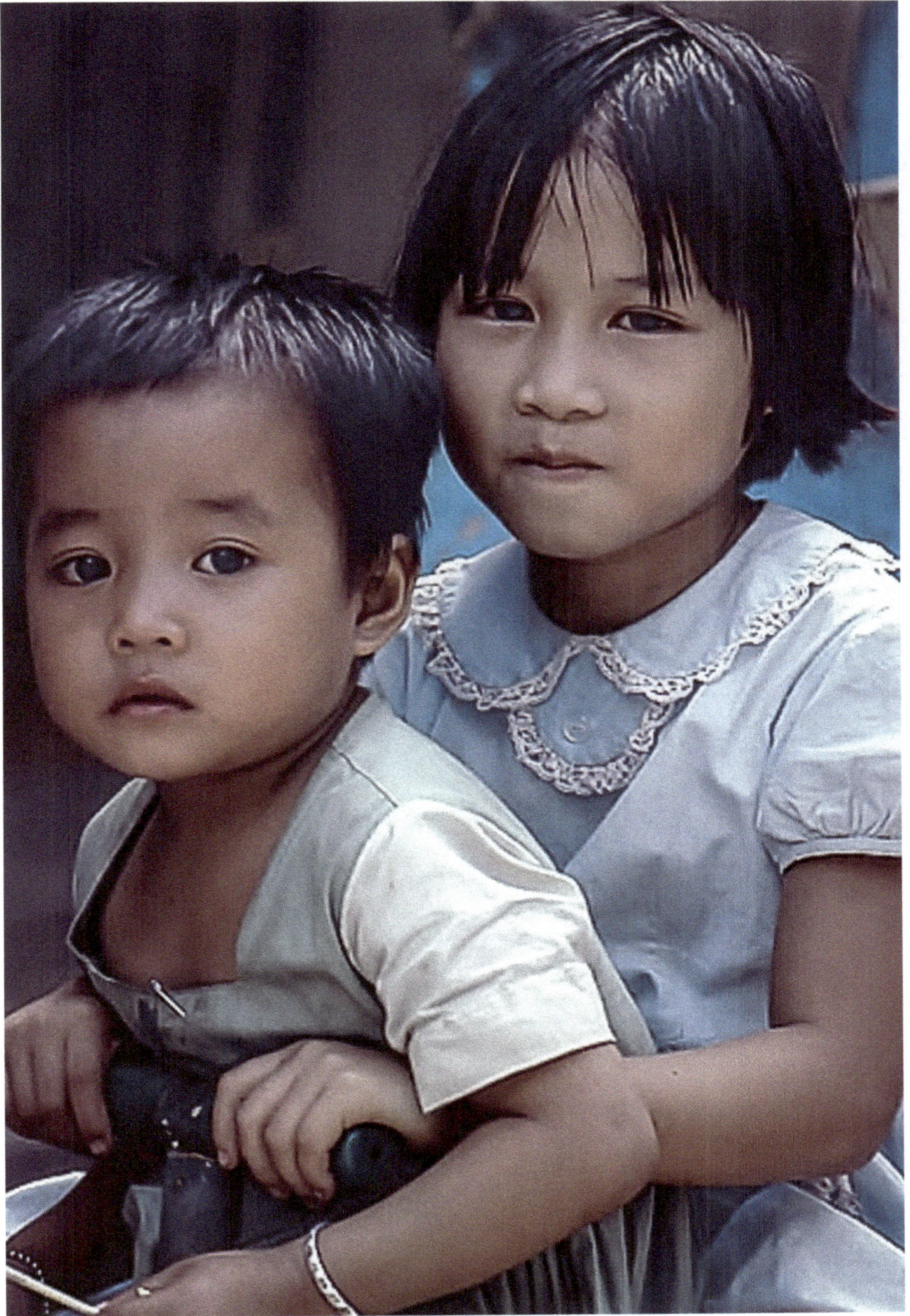

The children in the orphanage were clean and well-dressed. They did not have skin infections that we found with children in the rural areas. 1967

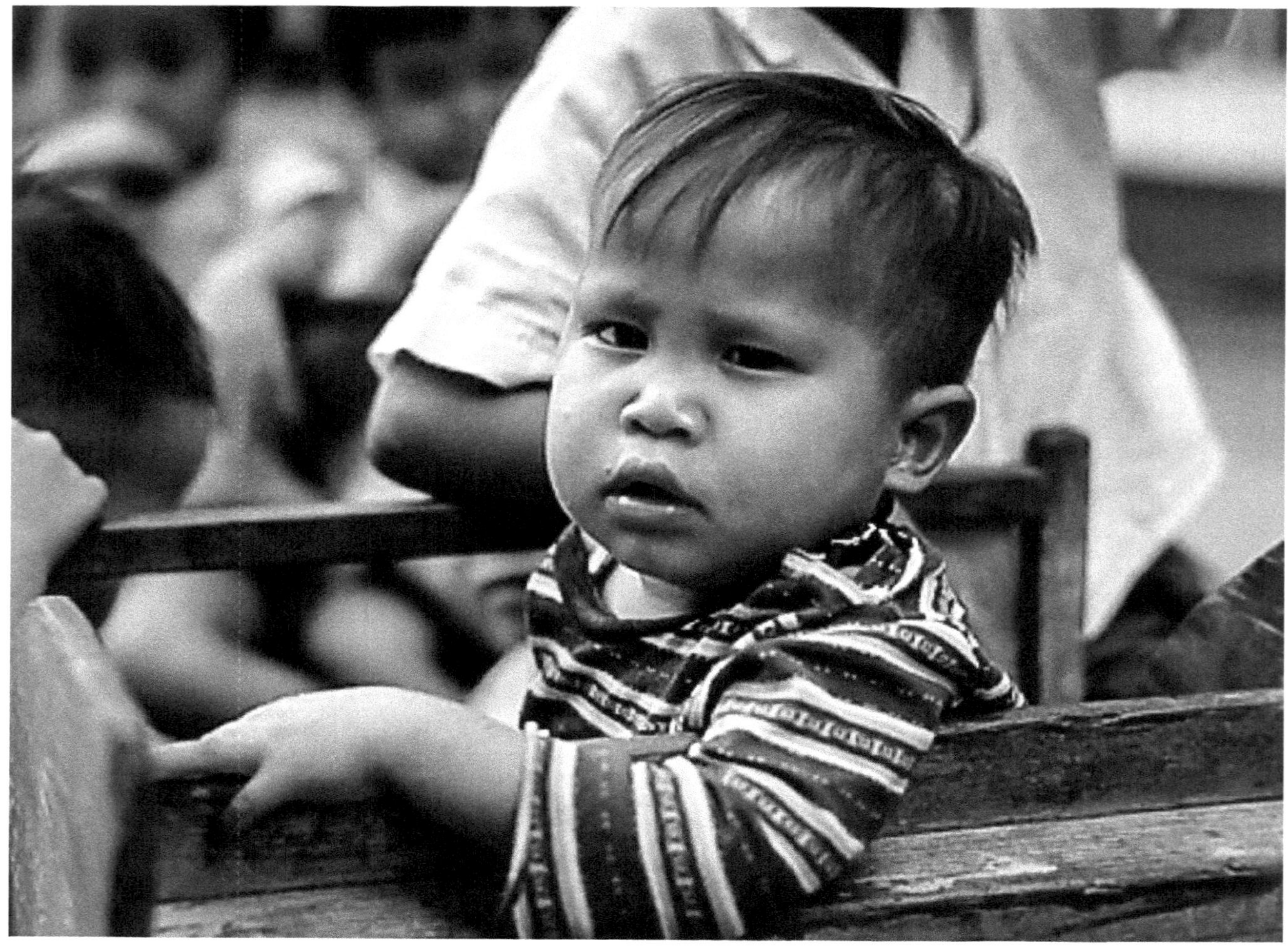

Sacred Heart 1967

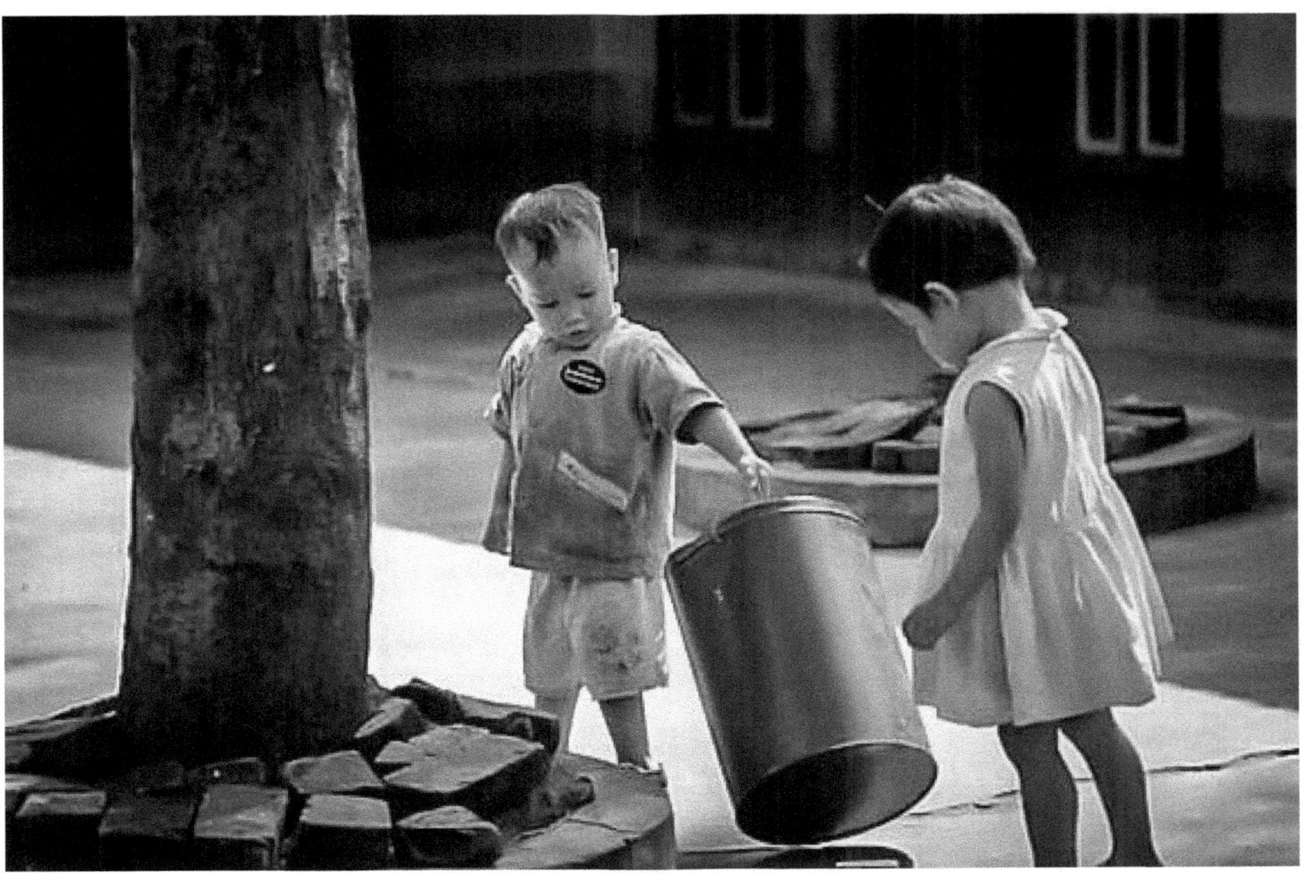

Sacred Heart 1967

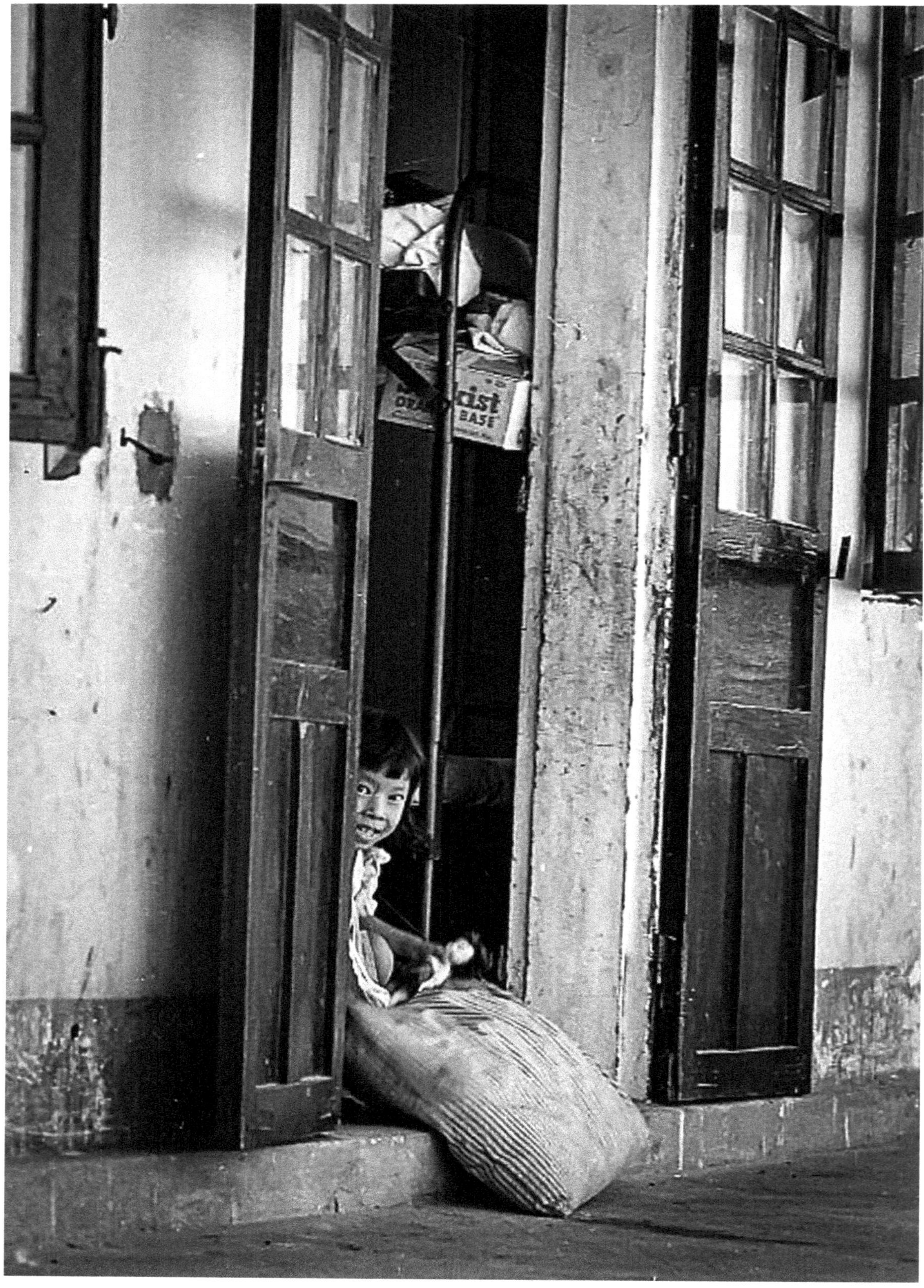

The ever- present universe of play. Sacred Heart

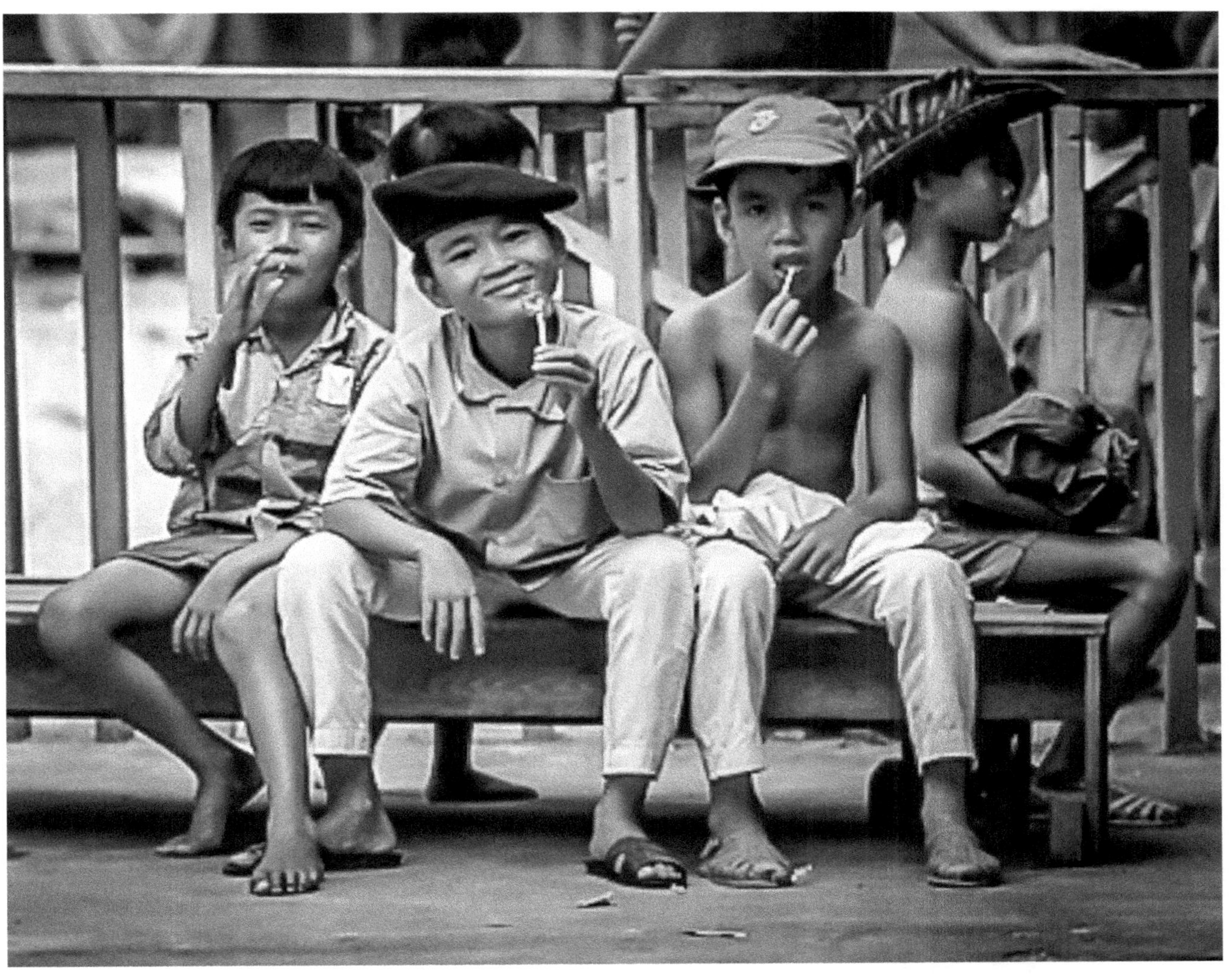

The children were protected and well cared for by the Sisters of Sacred Heart. 1967

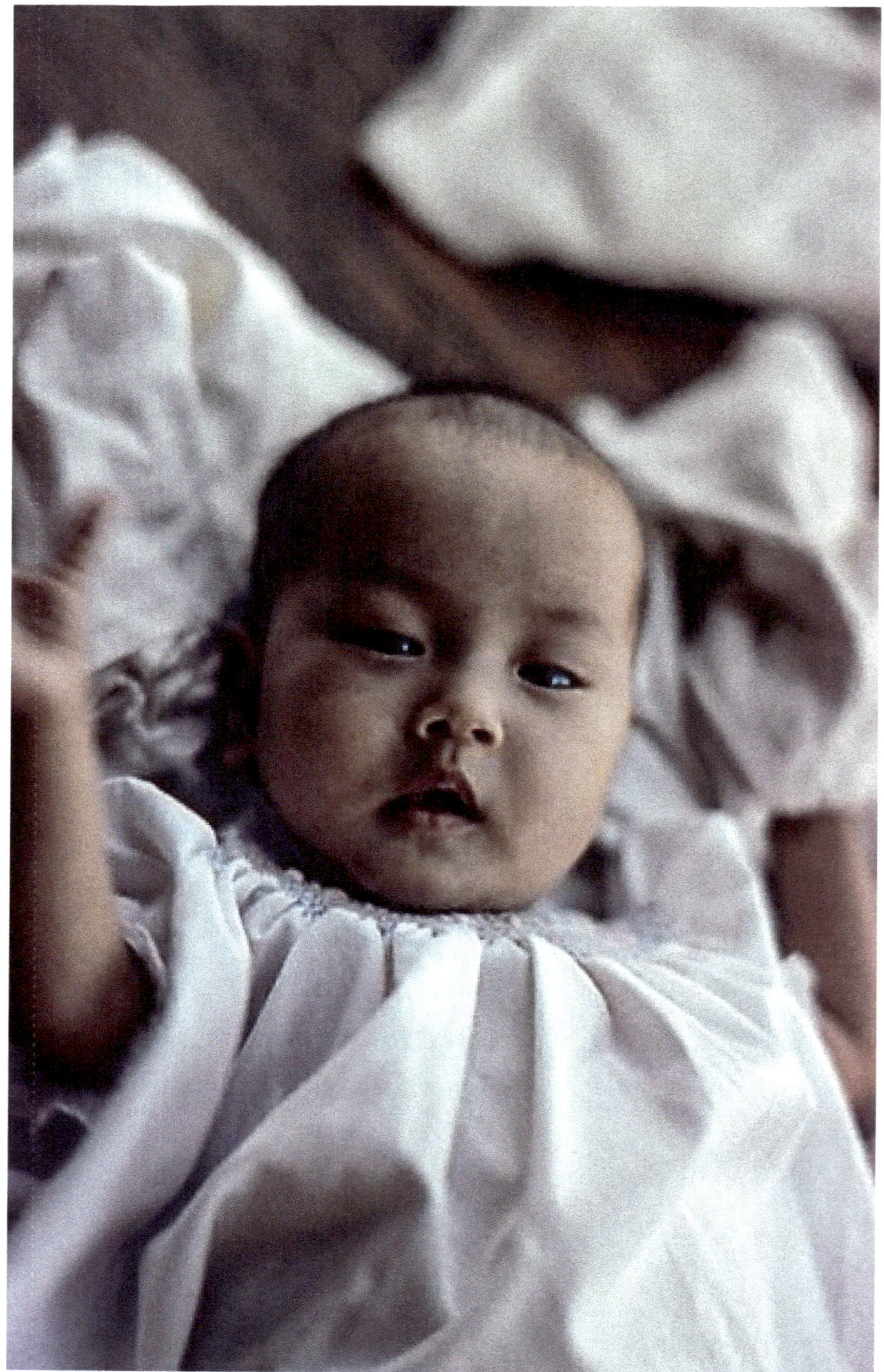

Orphaned by the war, Sacred Heart Orphanage, 1967

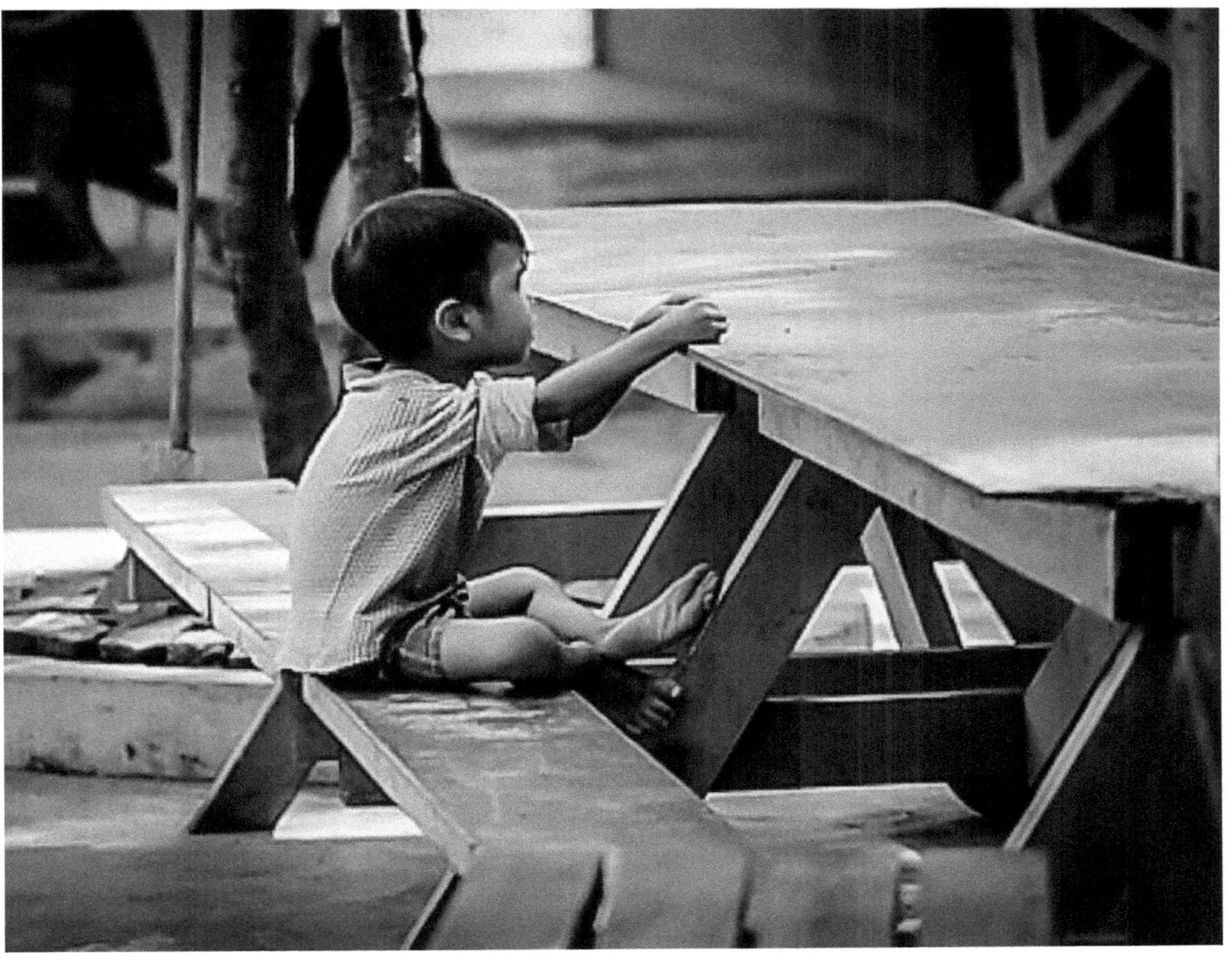

A recent arrival to the orphanage, the emaciated limbs of this young boy show the physical effects of malnutrition.

Sacred Heart 1967.

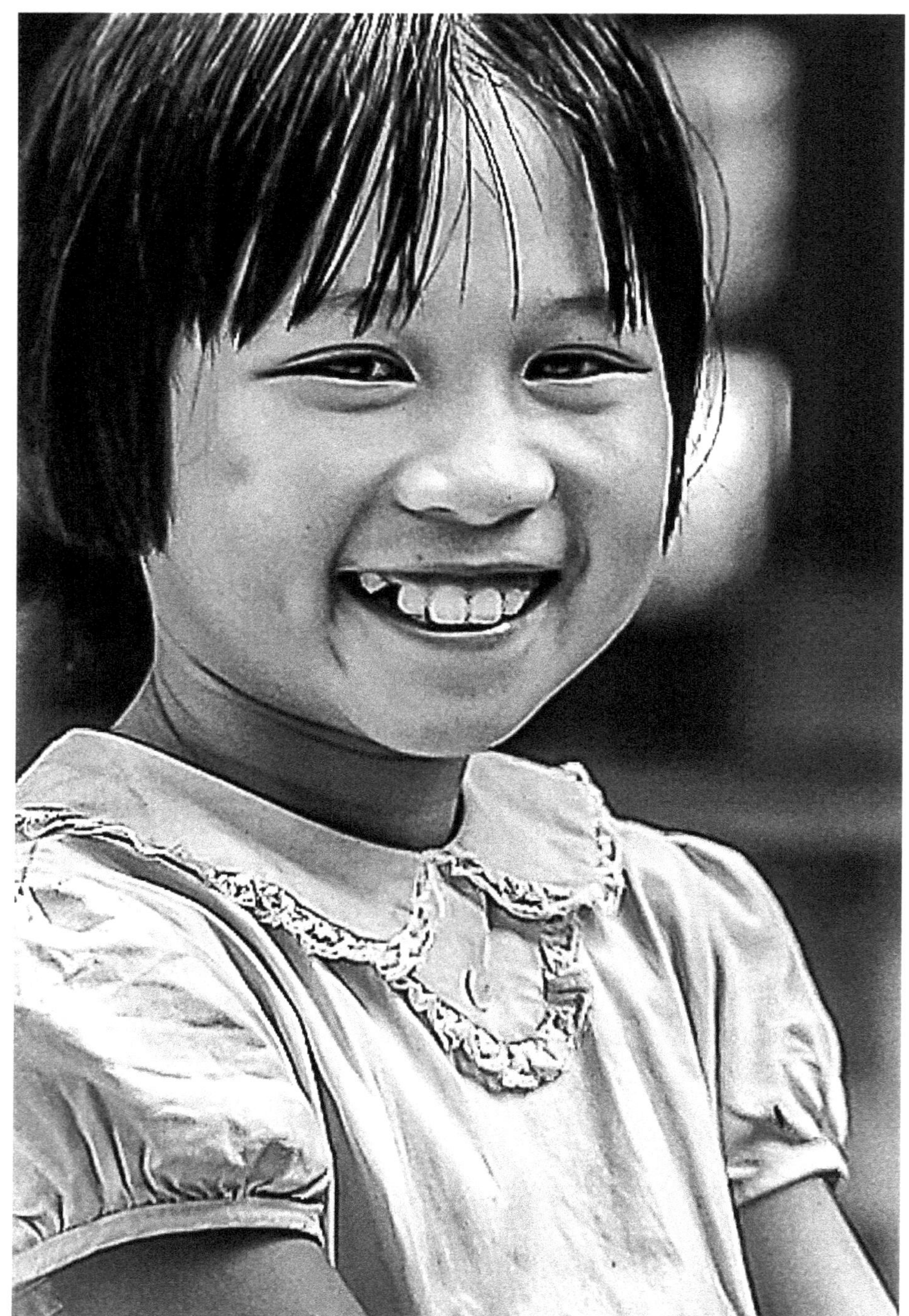

Sacred Heart

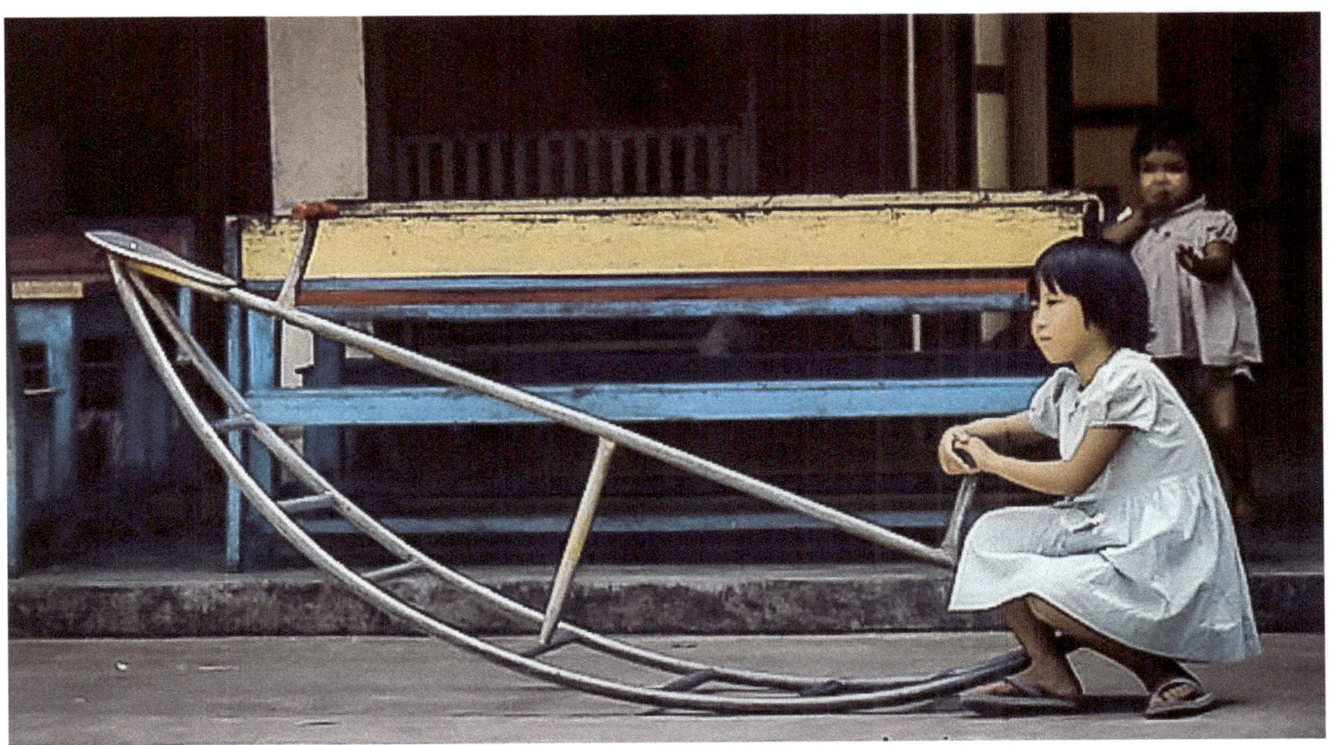

Sacred Heart

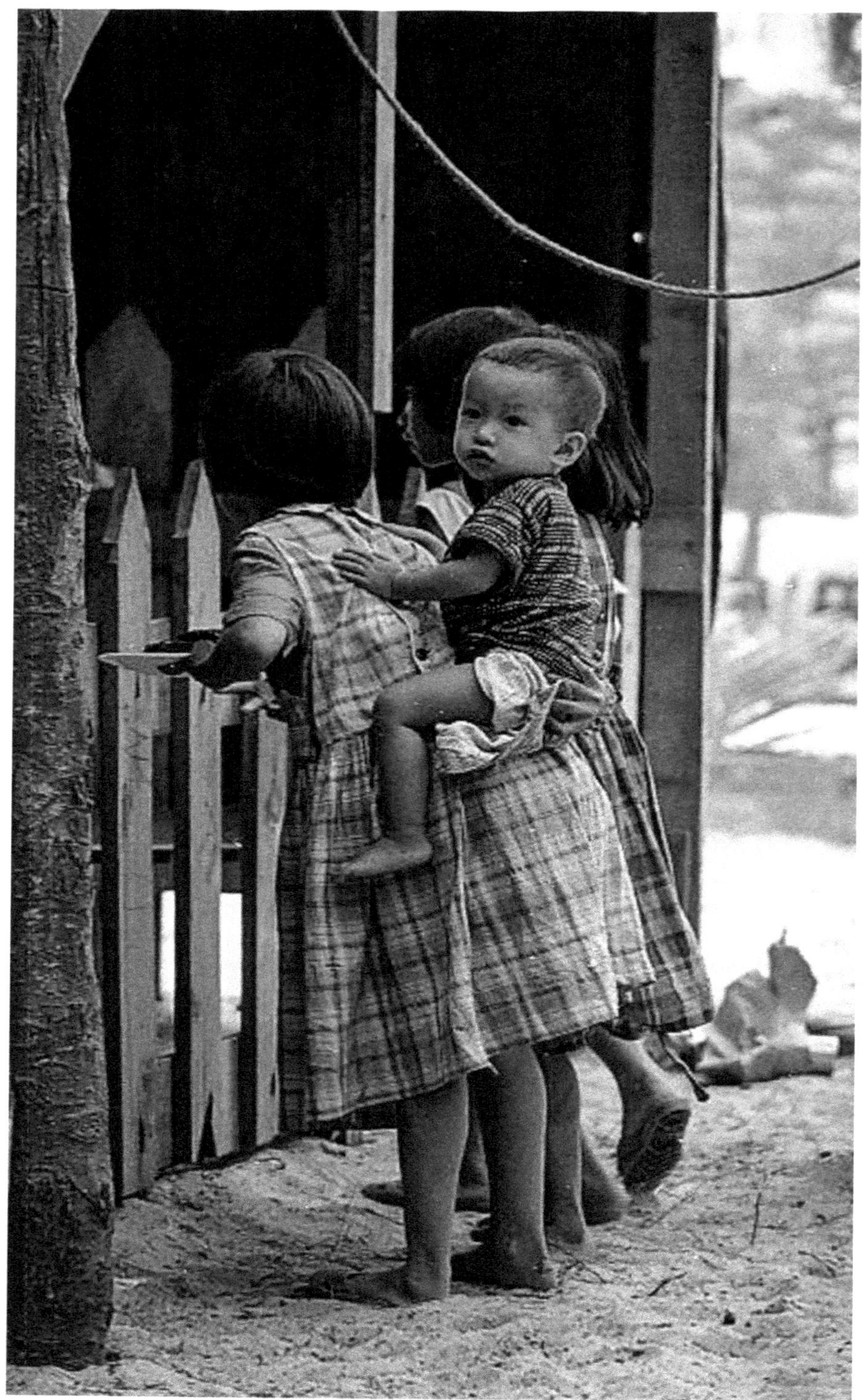

Sacred Heart Picnic at China Beach

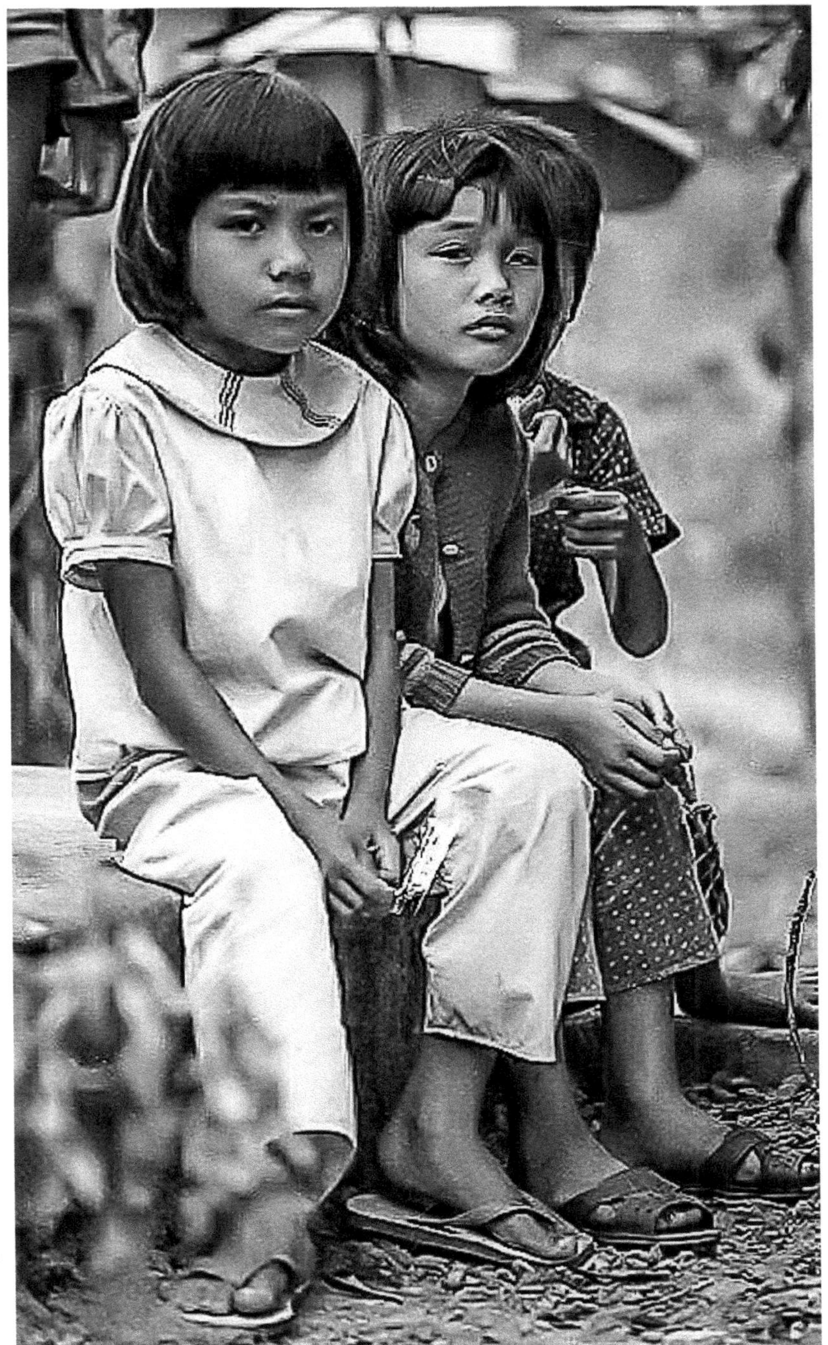

Young girls have yet to adjust to both living at Sacred Heart and circumstances that brought them here. 1967

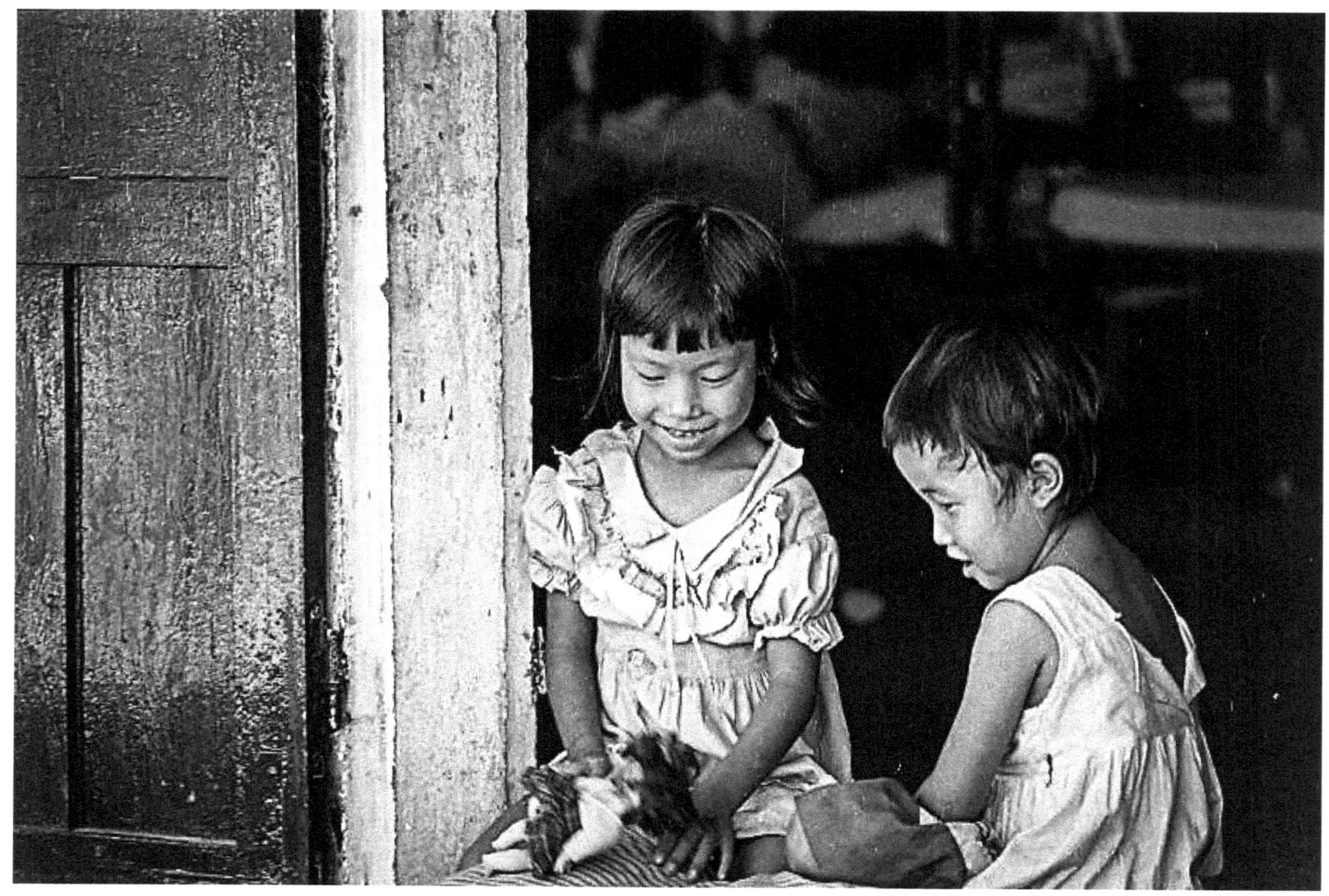

Sacred Heart

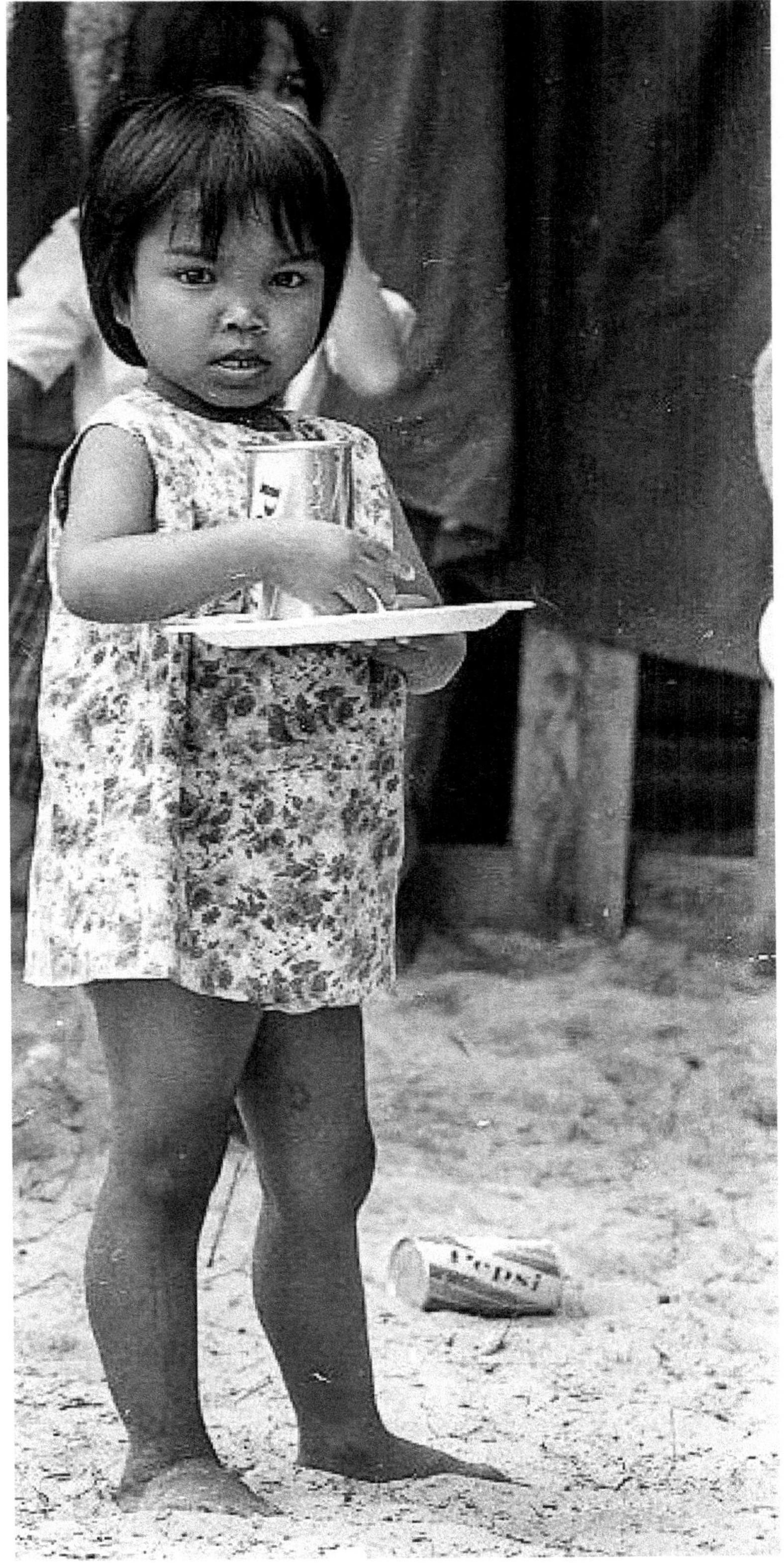

Sacred Heart Picnic at China Beach.

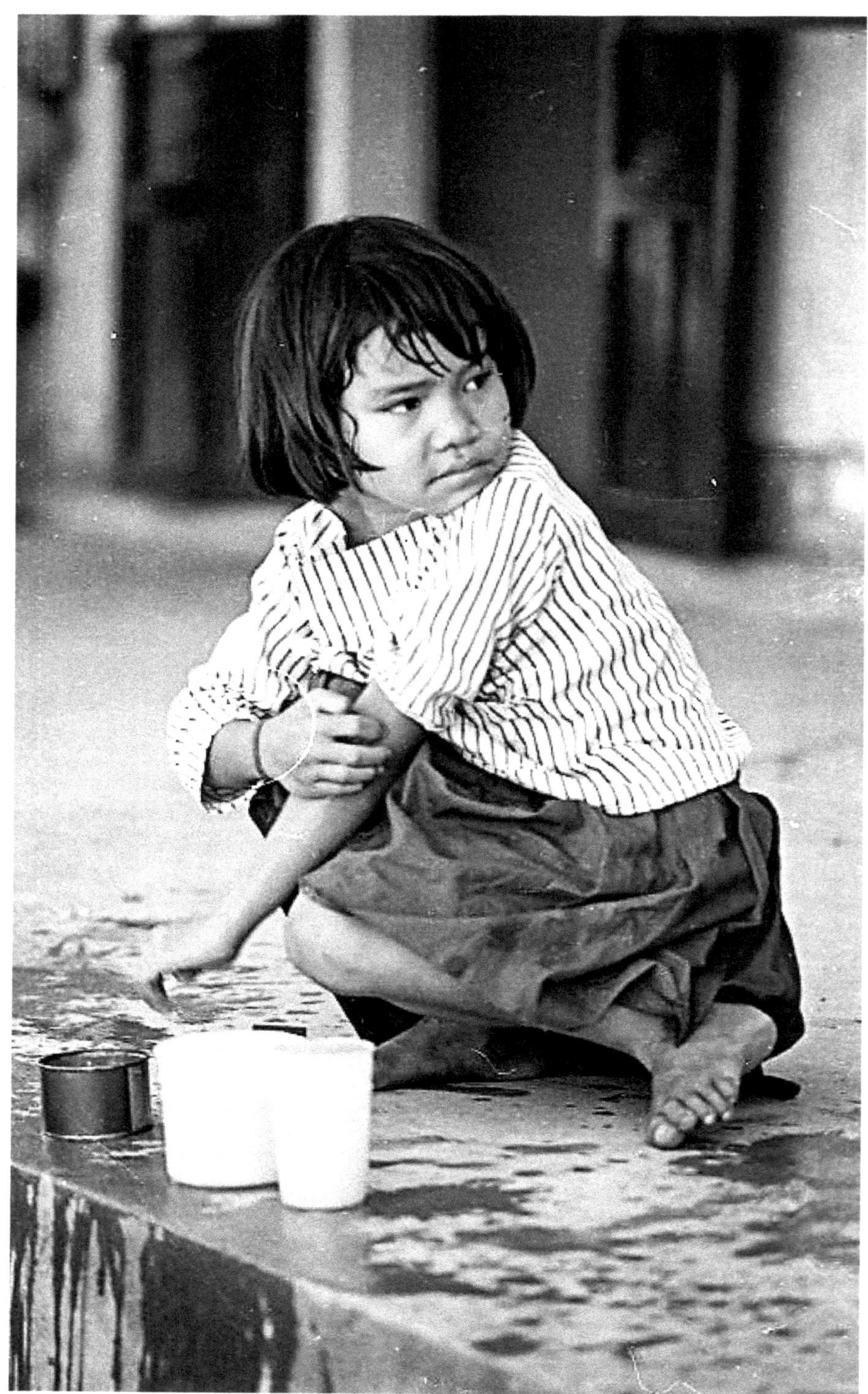

Sacred Heart

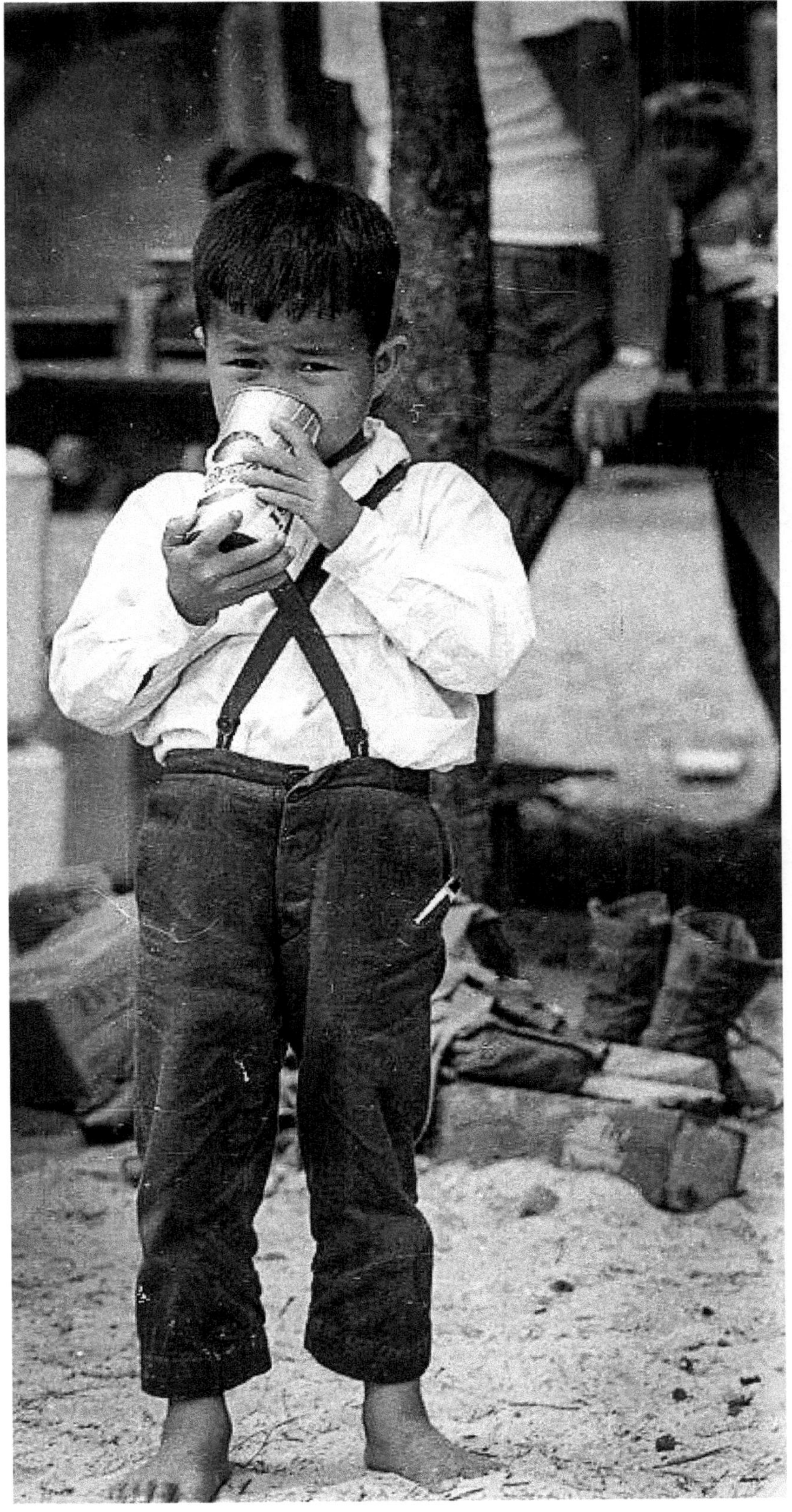

Picnic at China Beach

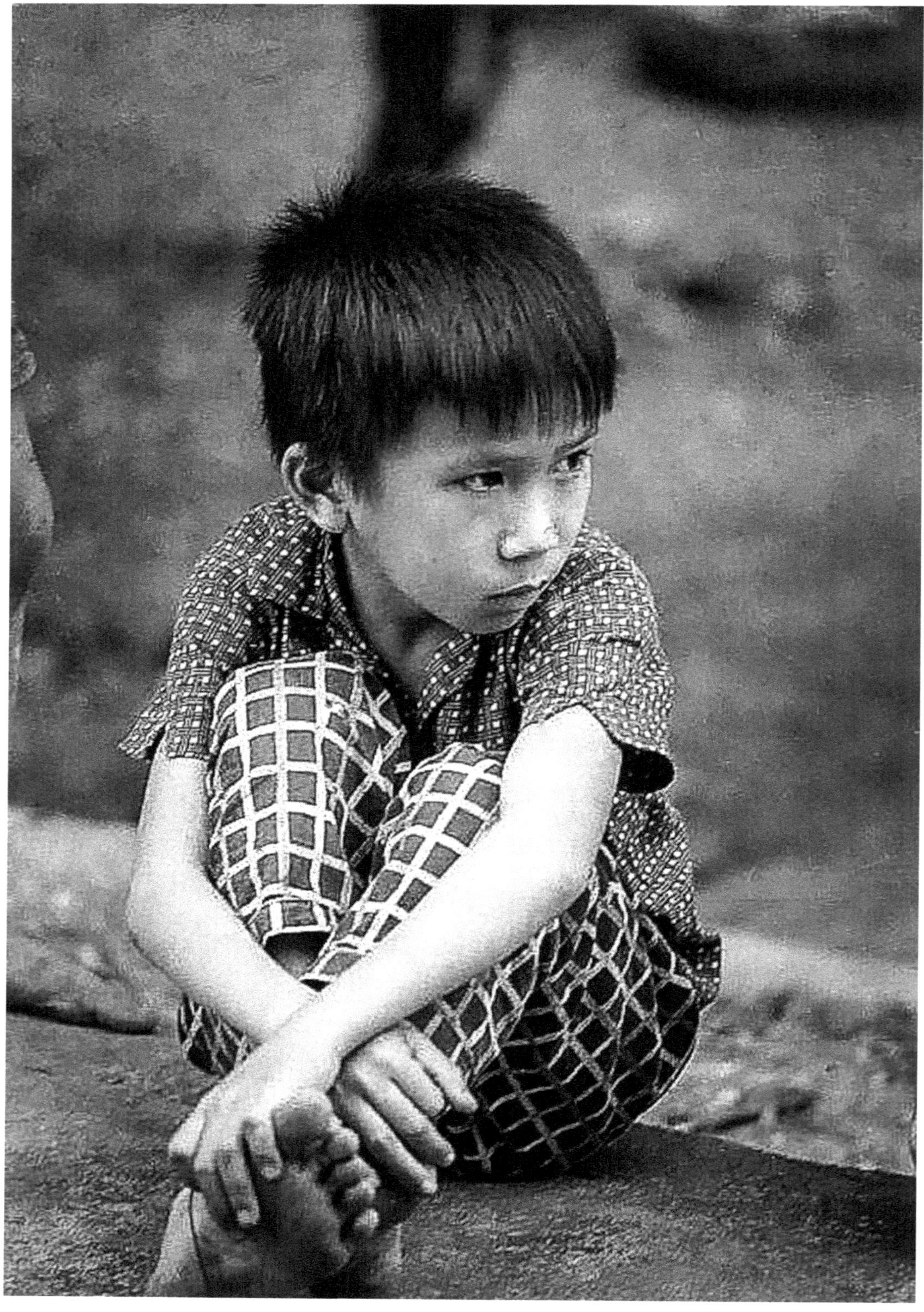

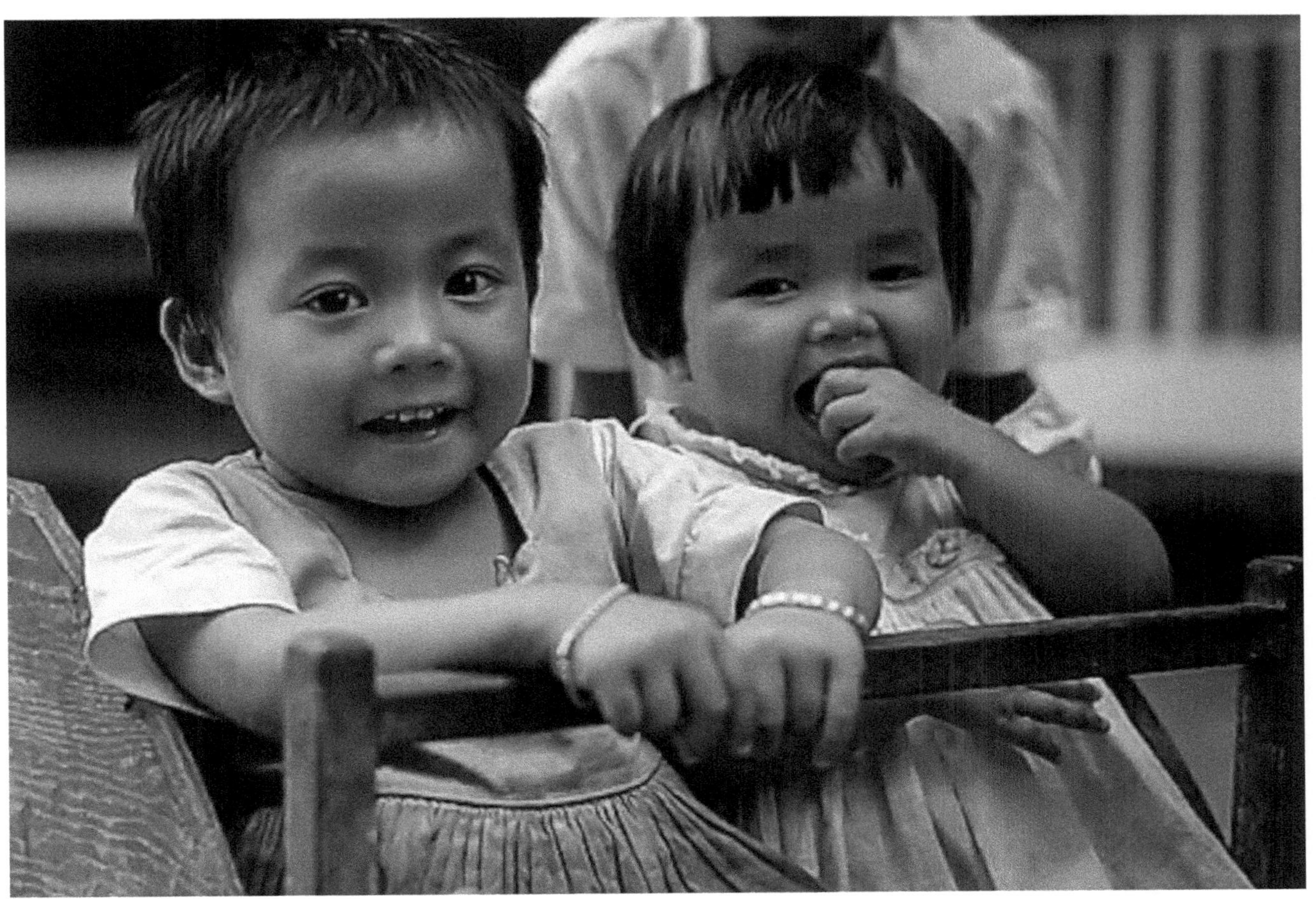

Sacred Heart Orphanage

Da Nang

Da Nang is located at the mouth of the Han River between mountains to the west and the South China Sea to the east, and has one of Viet Nam's largest ports. During the Viet Nam war, U.S. and allied forces used the large Da Nang airfield located here to support ground troops throughout the northern part of South Viet Nam.

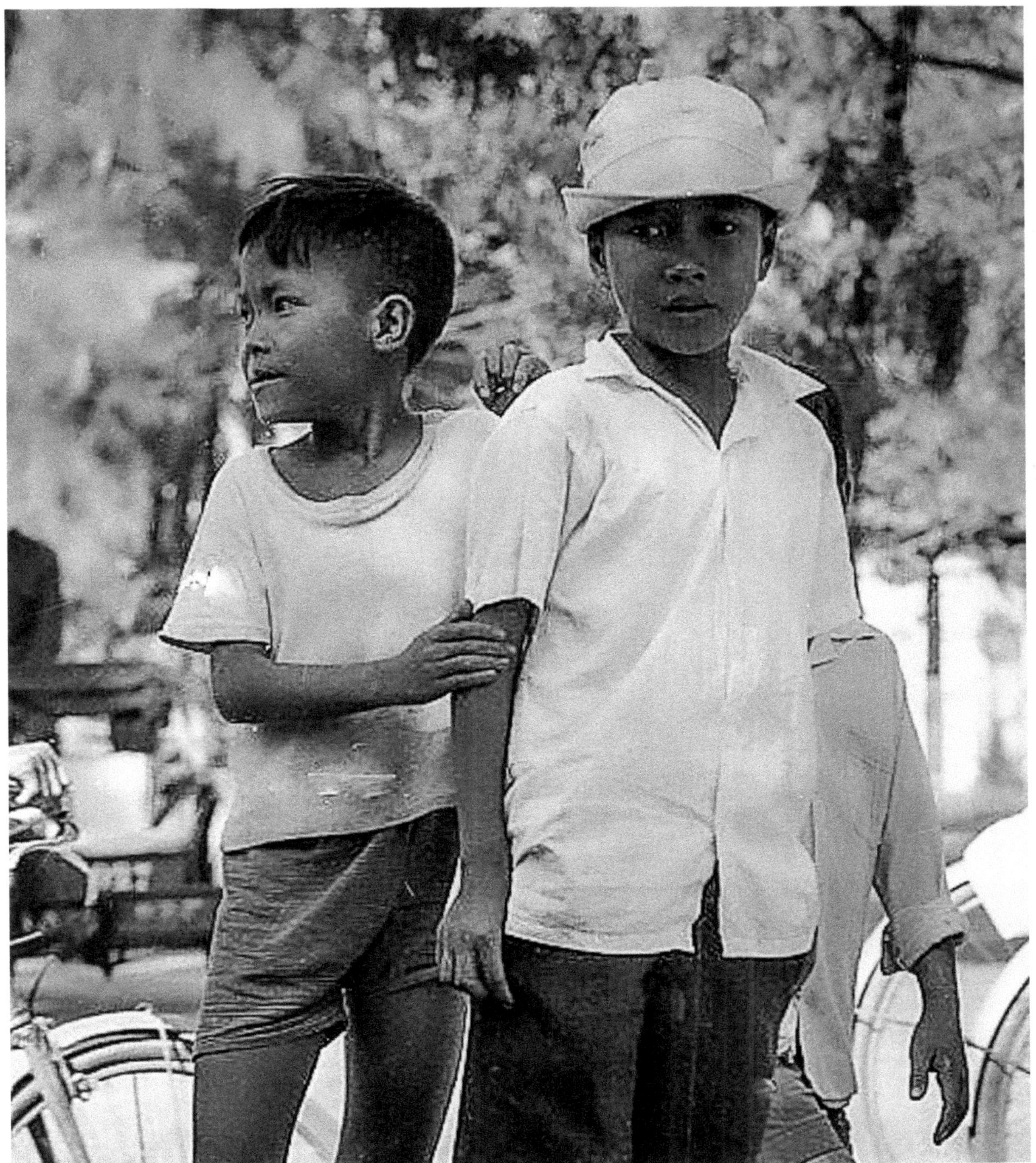

Two friends wander about the streets in Da Nang. 1966

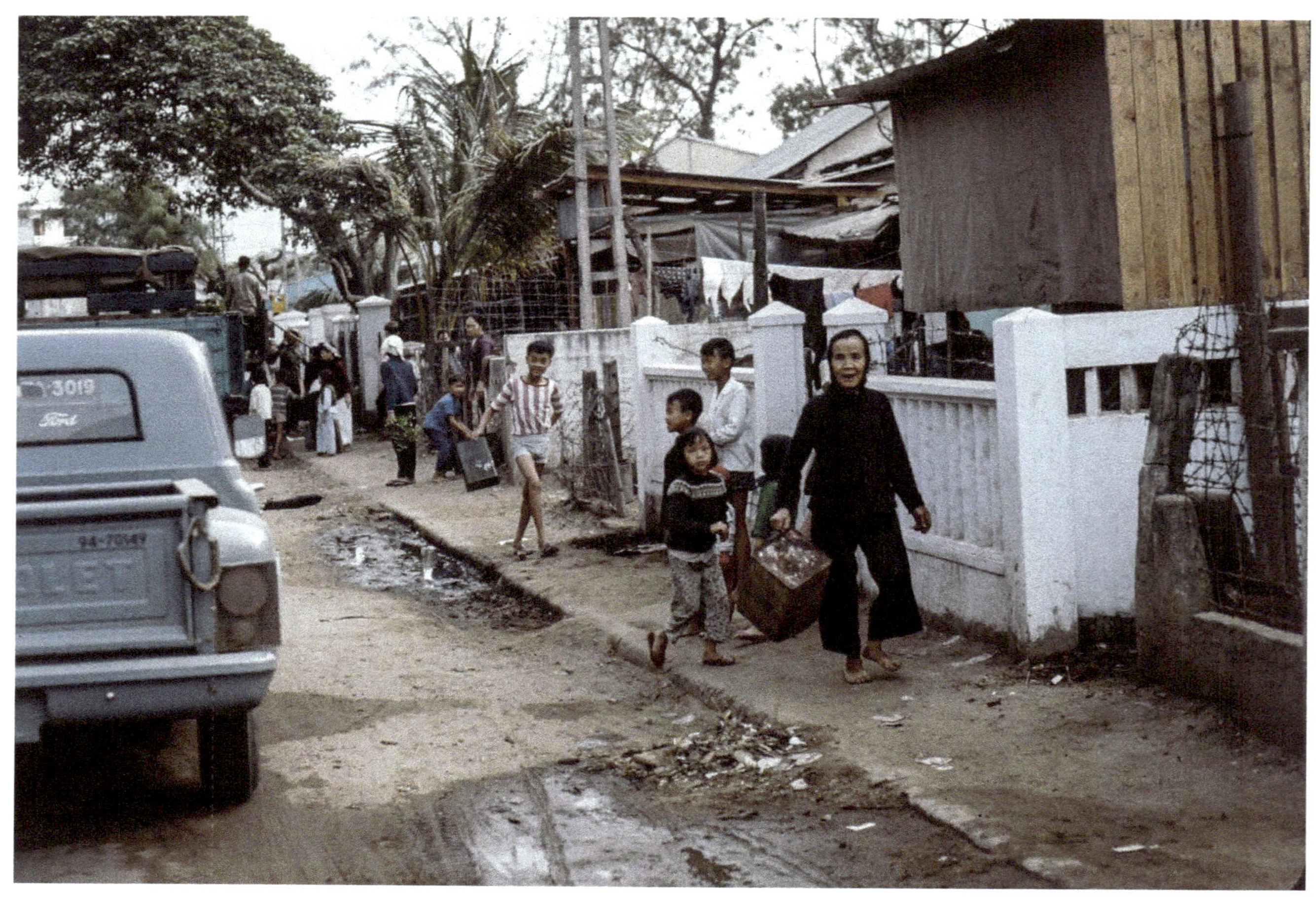

Da Nang City Street, 1966

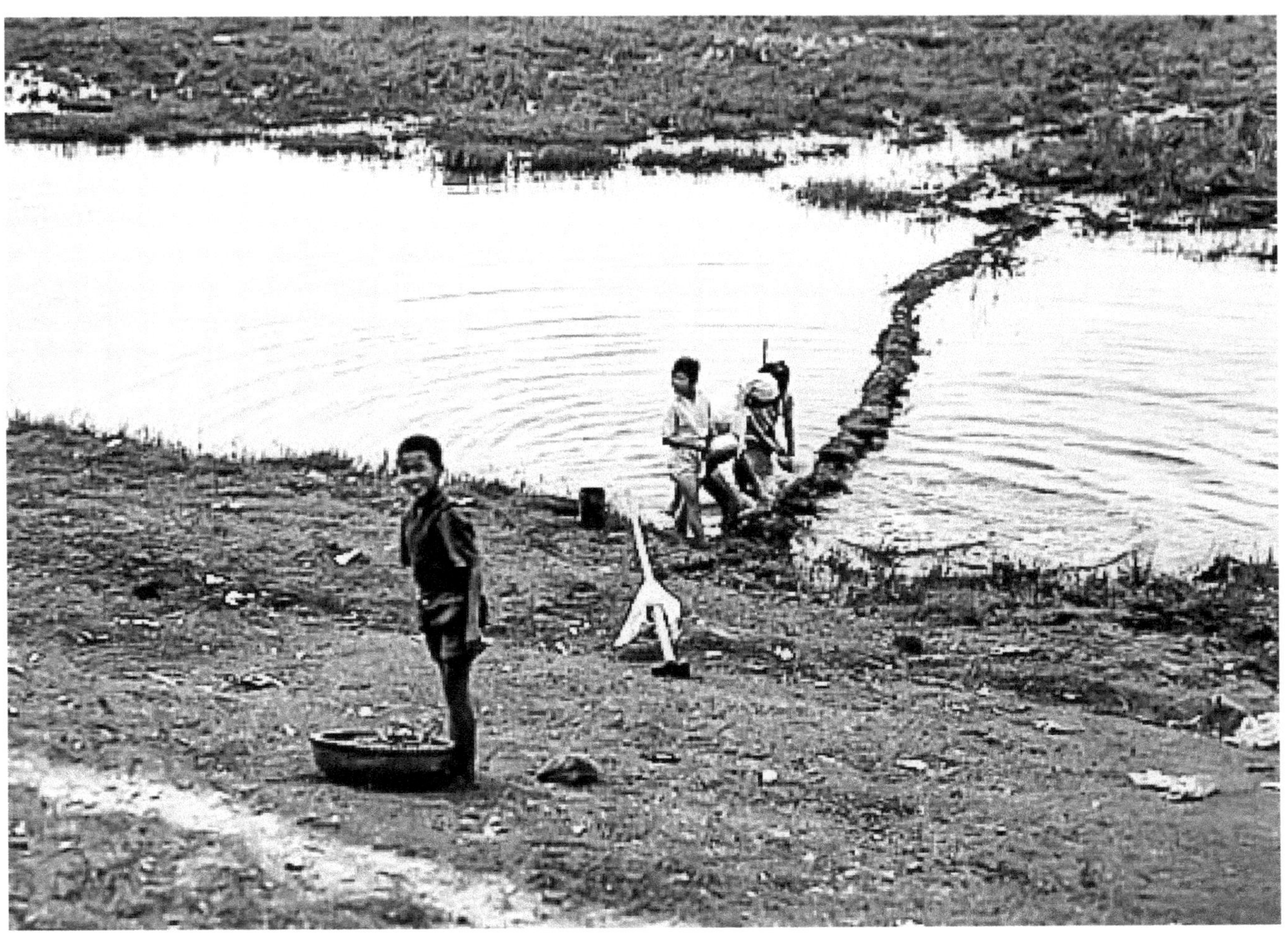

Young boys help their mother build a mud dike for water diversion. Da Nang, 1966.

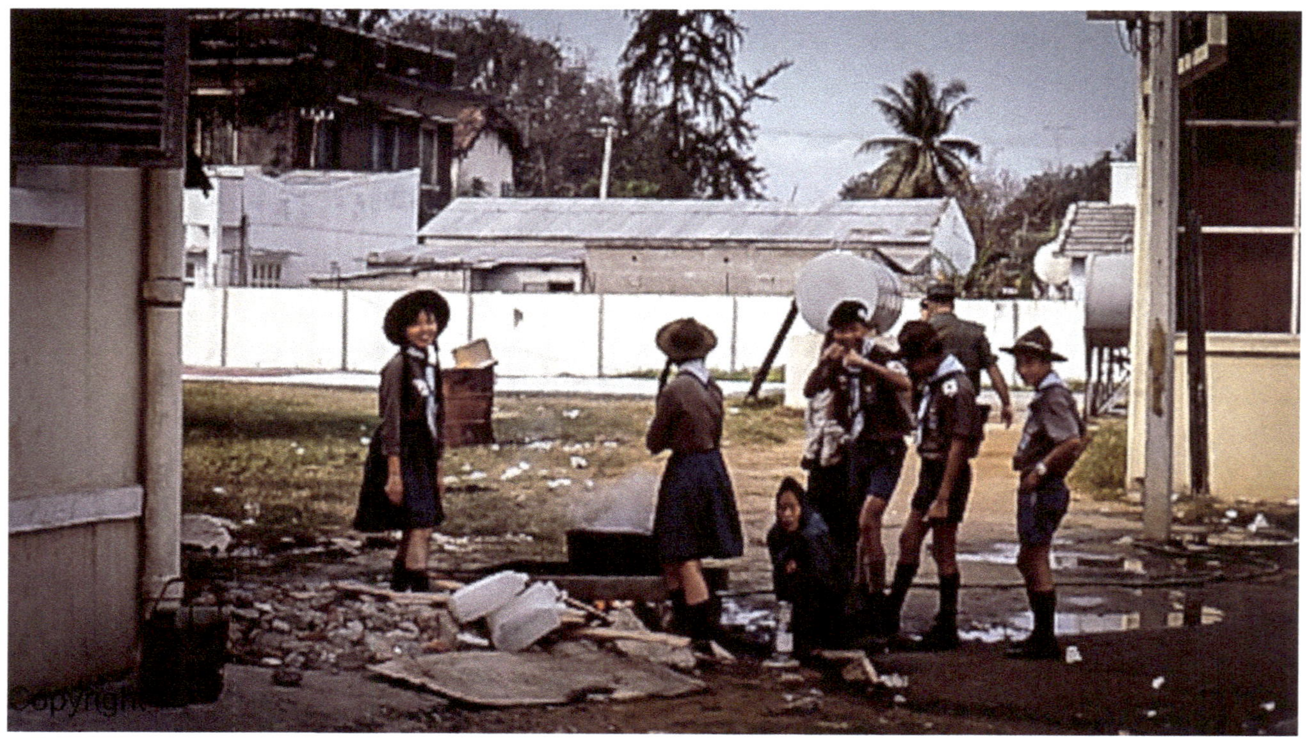

Girl Scouts and Boy Scouts...an activity possible for the children of well-to-do parents in cities, which were more protected from the communist insurgency.

Da Nang, 1967

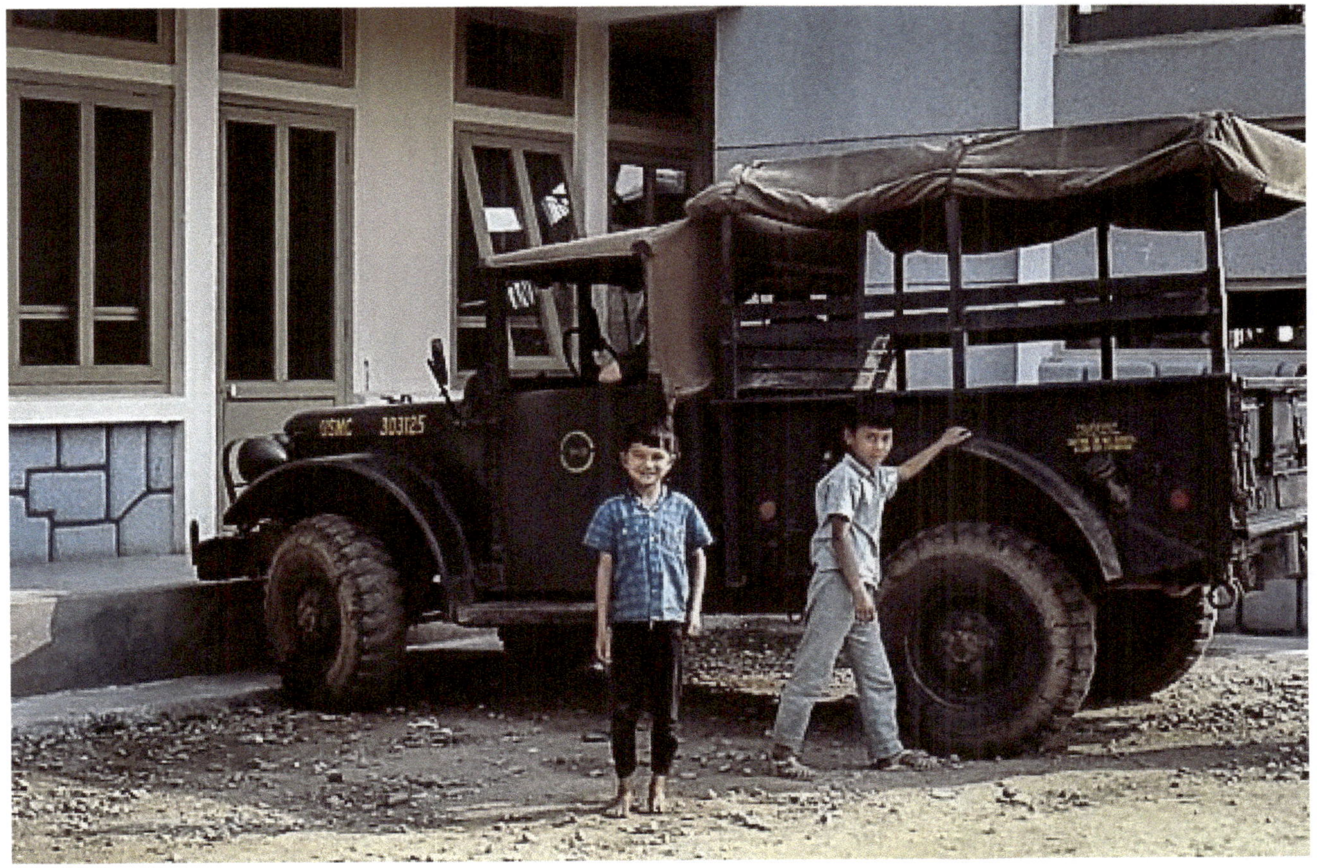

Young boys linger to interact with me at the Quang Nam Provincial Hospital in Da Nang. I was coordinating the transfer of civilian patients we cared for in outlying villages. 1967

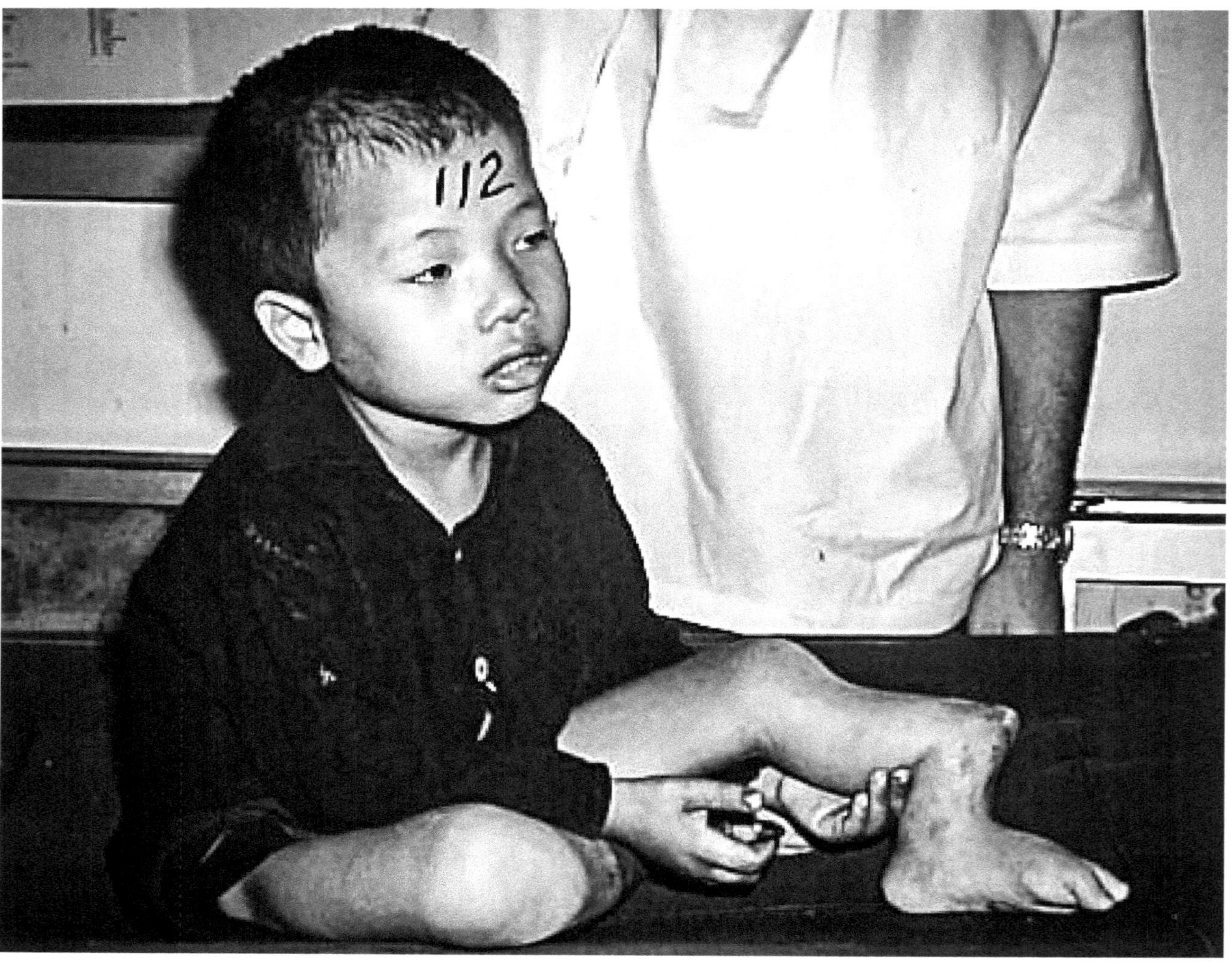

We found this boy crawling with the fractured and deformed leg in a hamlet located southwest of Da Nang. We were told that he injured his leg several months before. He was evacuated to a U. S Navy hospital in Da Nang where surgeons repaired the fracture. 1967

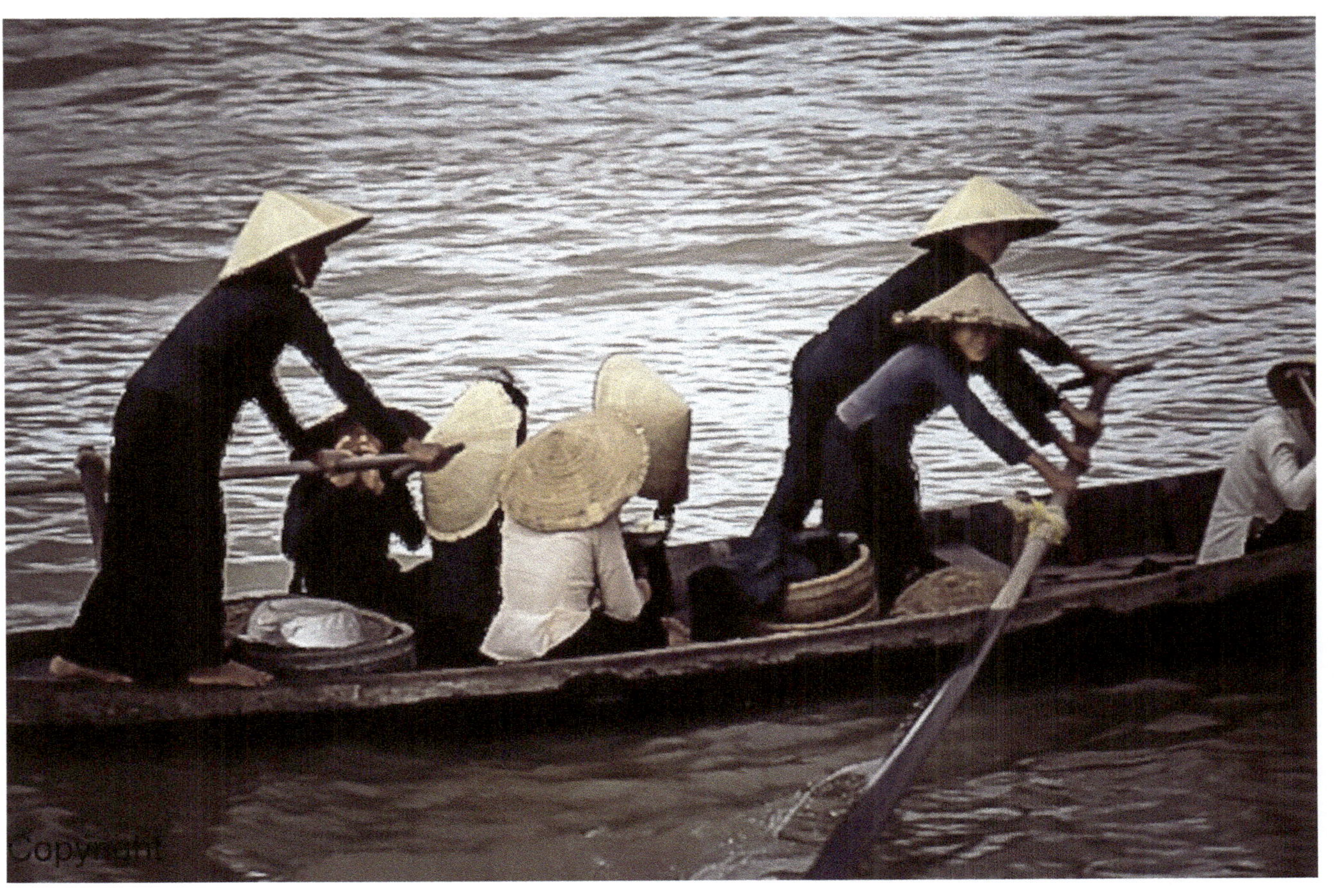

A Young girl assists elders with paddling on the Han River in Da Nang. 1966

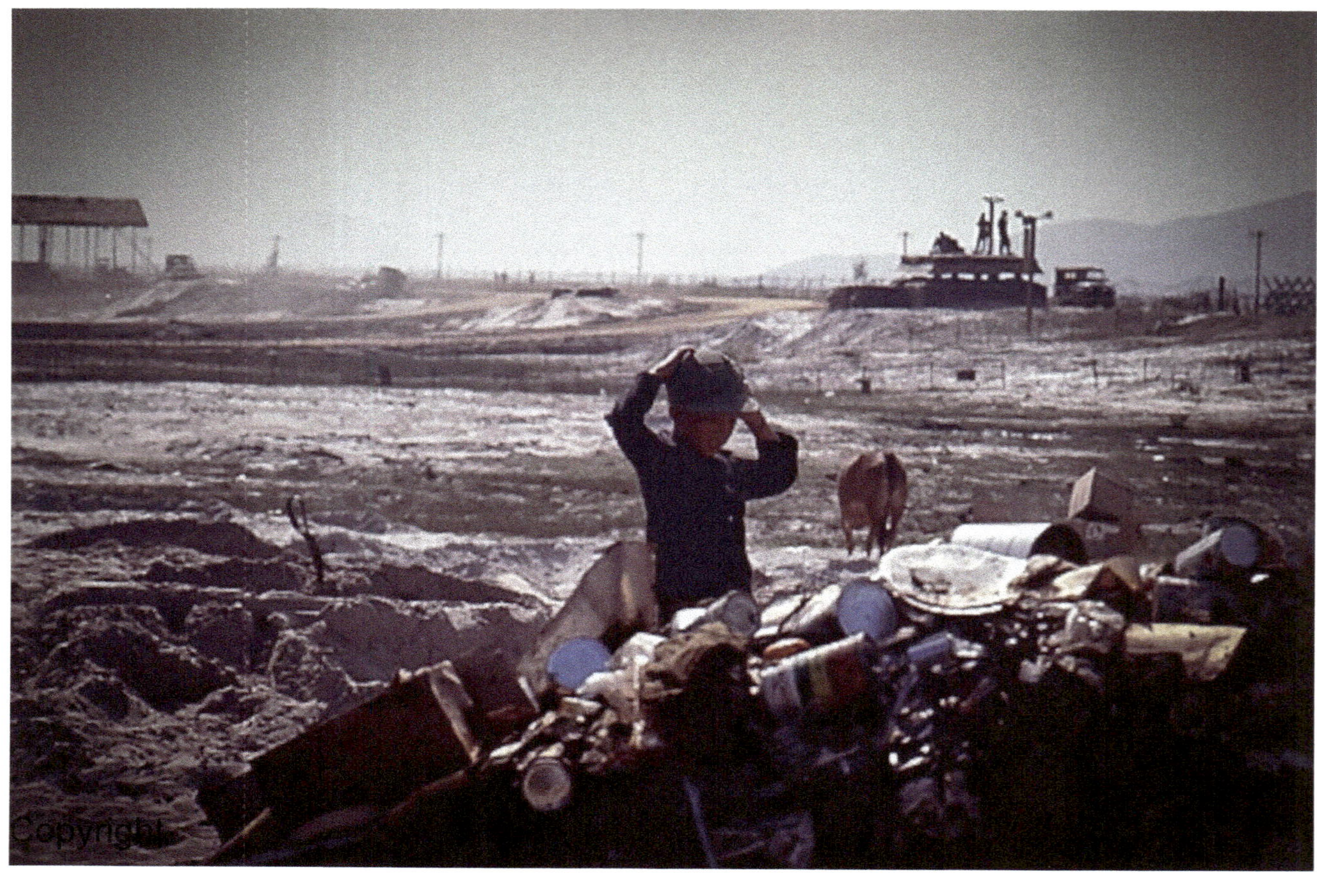

American military bases in Viet Nam produced enormous quantities of refuse and garbage which the Vietnamese found to be very useful in their daily lives. It was common for large groups of people to position themselves at dumping sites waiting for the daily dump to occur.

This young boy is collecting items at this site beyond the perimeter of a military base located in the Da Nang area. 1967

Excerpts from a letter home…Wednesday 28 June 1967.

During an operation with the 2nd battalion 3rd Marines in communist held territory south of Da Nang in the coastal area east of the Truong Giang River.

"The battalion CP was set up along a tree line and extended several hundred meters into a sparsely populated area. Many old stucco and thatched buildings, bearing the scars of gunfire, had been abandoned. Even though buildings had been abandoned, every available foot of tillable land had crops. Vegetation was plentiful and offered sufficient protection from the sun's searing glare. This did not however, alleviate the stifling heat. Sweat from my forehead trickled into my eyes…the salinity burned.

By noon the heat would be so intense it would be foolhardy to attempt anything but idleness…and then one spends his time swatting at the hoard of insects. It must be pure agony to fight in weather such as this. The Vietnamese have a siesta also, two to three hours, when the sun is high overhead. Even the pigs and chickens relent. Our first morning of sick-call brought only 28 people seeking care. Young babies, carried by their mothers with systemic skin infections, were the most common of diseases seen on this or any other day. Old women, teeth stained black by betel (an opiate chewed as tobacco), and backs bent by many years of hard labor, came with the real or imaginary afflictions. Many of them suffered with tuberculosis. Old men were seen less frequently. there were no young men, not one, they are either fighting to topple the government, or save it. All were impoverished, hardened by the near-primitive life they live. All were respectful towards us, offering two palms upraised and held together bowing slightly with a smile, in gratitude. Most humble indeed and impressive to each of us. The small number of people for our first sick-call can be attributed to several things. One; we are in Viet Cong territory and the VC forbid the people to associate with us…with threats of harm. Two; the VC have taught the people to fear us. Three; word has not gotten out to the more distant villages, that we are here to help them. Our second sick-call saw 55 people, an improvement we were happy to accept."

During the ten-day period we were in this area the Marines suffered 123 heat casualties and 13 KIA (killed in action).

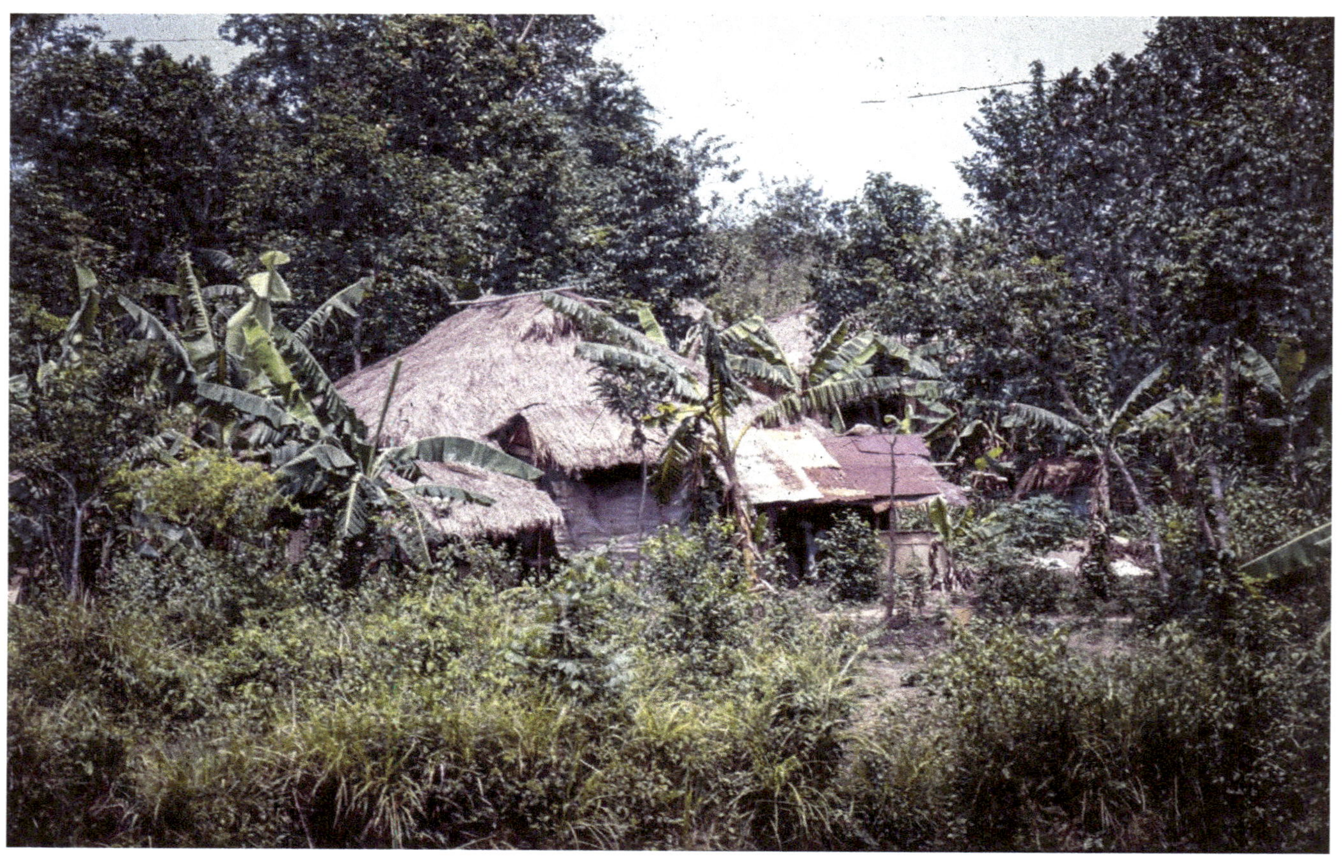

Vietnamese peasant home in a Viet Cong controlled area east of the Truong Giang River.
1967

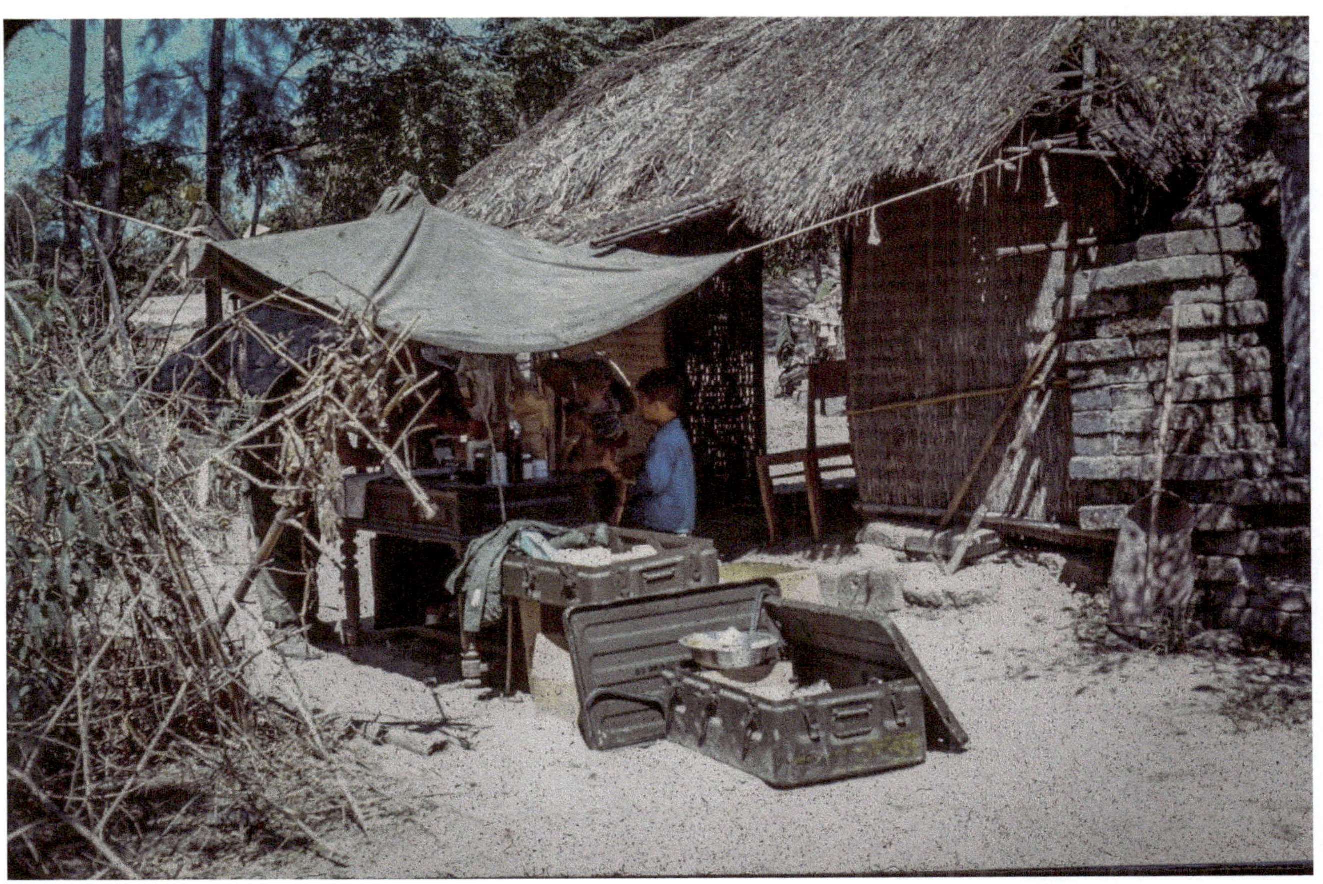

The son of a Vietnamese family is shaded by a poncho liner we have attached to the front his home where we were providing care. VC territory, east of the Truong Giang River, south of Da Nang.

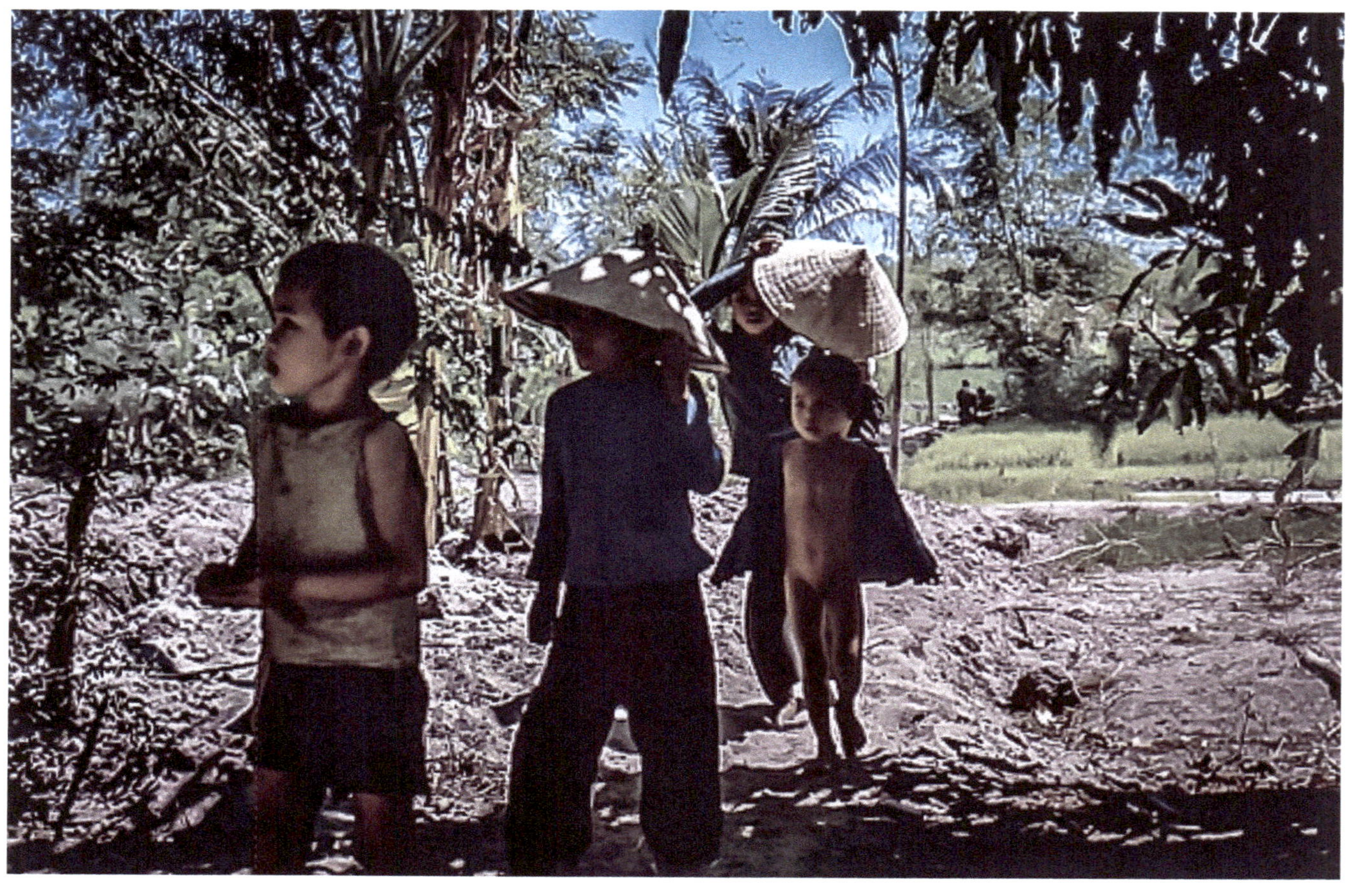

Children who passed through our perimeter walk towards the medical treatment area.

Thua Thien-Hue Province

Thua Thien Province is located within the northern-most region of what was South Viet Nam during the war, with Quang Tri Province to the North and Quang Nam Province to the south. The old Imperial Capitol of Viet Nam is in Hue, which was occupied by Viet Cong and the North Vietnamese Army during the Tet Offensive of 1968. The coastal areas are densely populated and the inner mountainous area is sparsely populated by the indigenous Montagnard People.

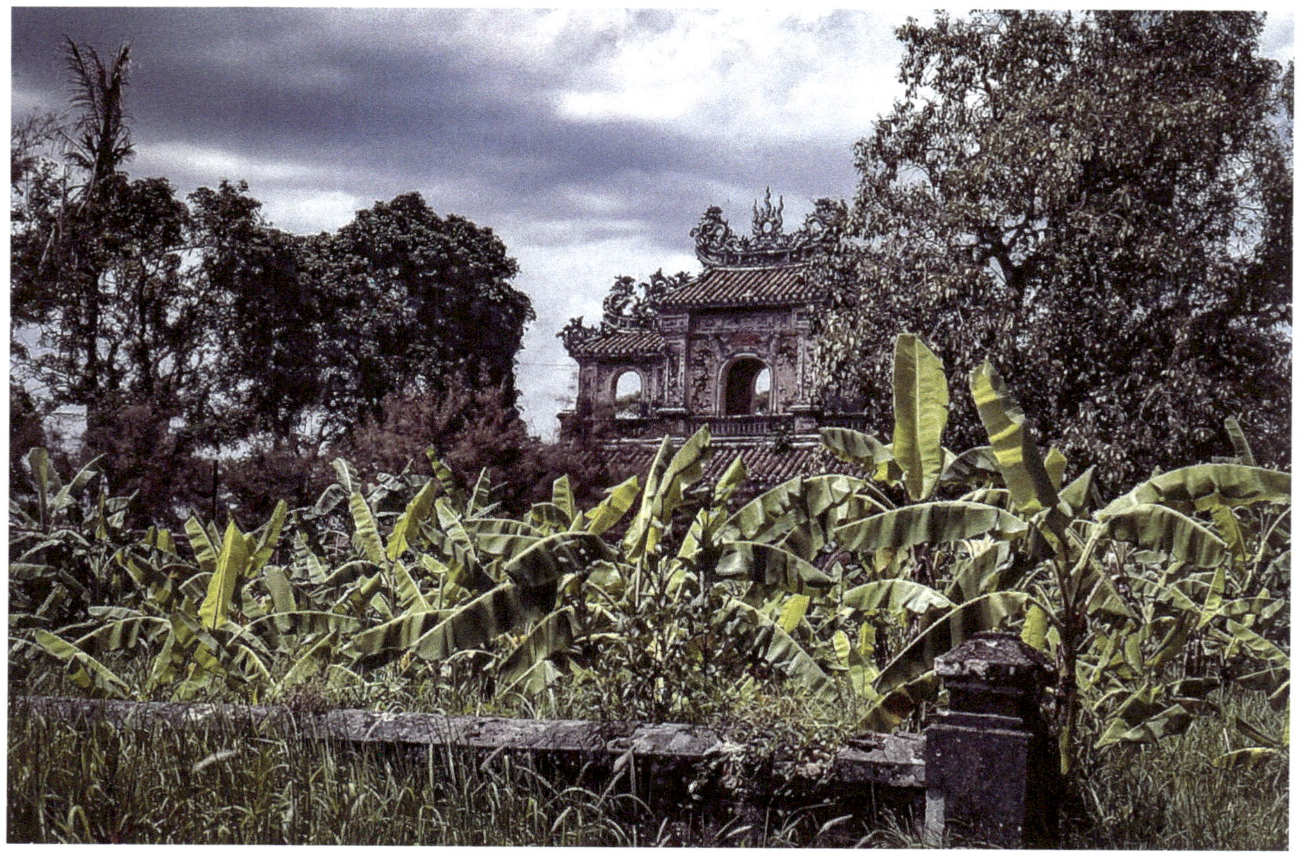

Ornate gate within the Citadel which served as the old Imperial Capitol of Annam during the French Indochina period.

Bitter fighting for control of the Citadel and Hue occurred during Tet in 1968 when the Viet Cong and North Vietnamese Army invaded the city and occupied the citadel. 1968

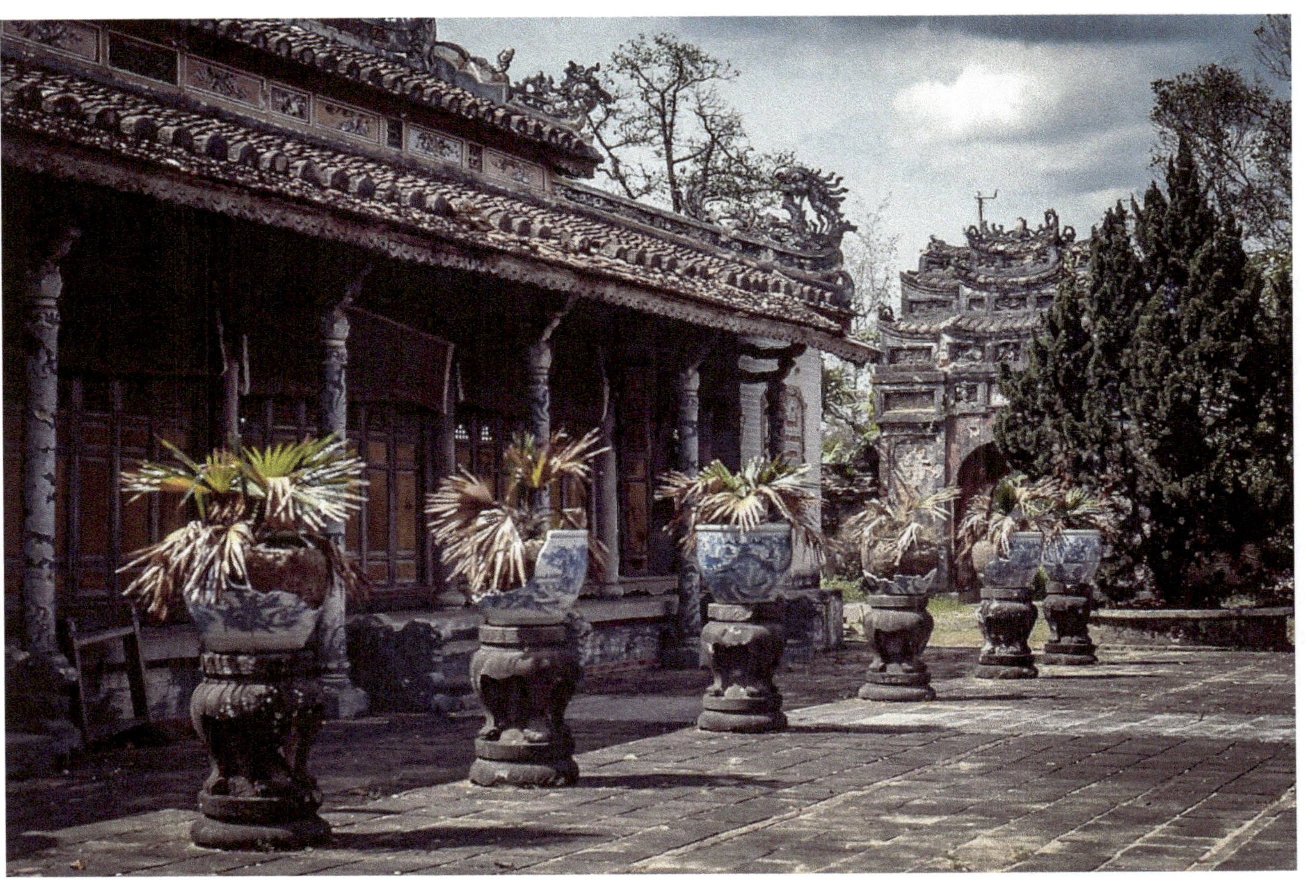

Ornate inner courtyard of the Hue Citadel. The palace roof and centuries-old planter crockery was damaged by the violent fighting that occurred here. 1968

Excerpt from a Letter Home,

Wednesday, 15 May 1969, Phu Bai, RVN

"It is about 5:30 p.m. At this time. It has just begun to rain. This of course is welcome, for the heat has been tremendous. I do not know what the exact temperature was today, but I would estimate that it reached at least 115 (degrees Fahrenheit). It rained last evening; I would say about 4 inches. Soon after it began raining we were slopping around in mud. Today at 4: 00 p.m., there was nothing but fine dust everywhere except for a few mud puddles.

We have been notified by intelligence that our area of responsibility will be quite dangerous this month. They have advised us not to penetrate the village area too deeply until after the first of June. Sunday evening an assassination squad (Viet Cong) numbering 14, murdered a National Policeman adjacent to the Catholic church, which is in Phu Tay Hamlet. Just about every evening VC Cadres enter our area and the tax the people heavily in the form of rice.

Even though we are presently restricted somewhat in our activities within the village area, we are attempting to carry on a program of civic action on a minor scale until we are given the okay to penetrate the area more deeply. We are currently holding Medcaps (medical civic action program) in Phu Tay Hamlet, and conducting research on the entire area (about ten miles square) to determine possible courses of action for our program. We have spent several days in counsel with the Village and Hamlet Chiefs discussing the various problems that exist within their respective areas. I have visited District Headquarters (the next higher seat of government beyond the village level) and have talked with the various heads of departments concerning the village's status. I am very much motivated by the work, the area, and the realization of the good we could accomplish with these people."

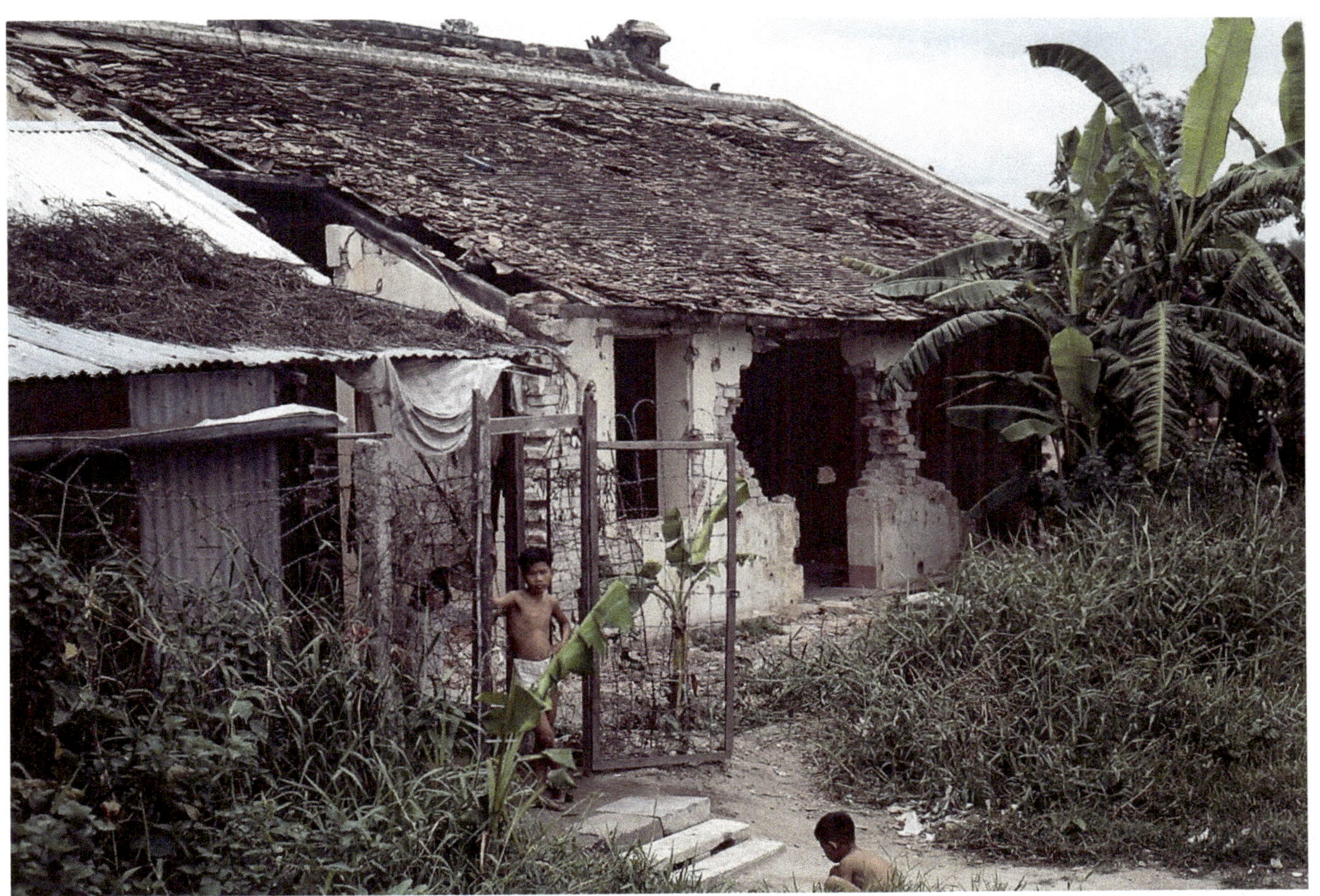

Vietnamese boy stands outside his war damaged home in Hue as his younger brother plays in the yard. The Viet Cong and North Vietnamese Army invaded Hue during the Tet Offensive of 1968 and occupied a large part of the city as well as the Citadel. The battle to retake the city resulted in widespread damage and destruction to homes such as this, as well as a considerable loss of life within the civilian population. All were innocent victims. 1968

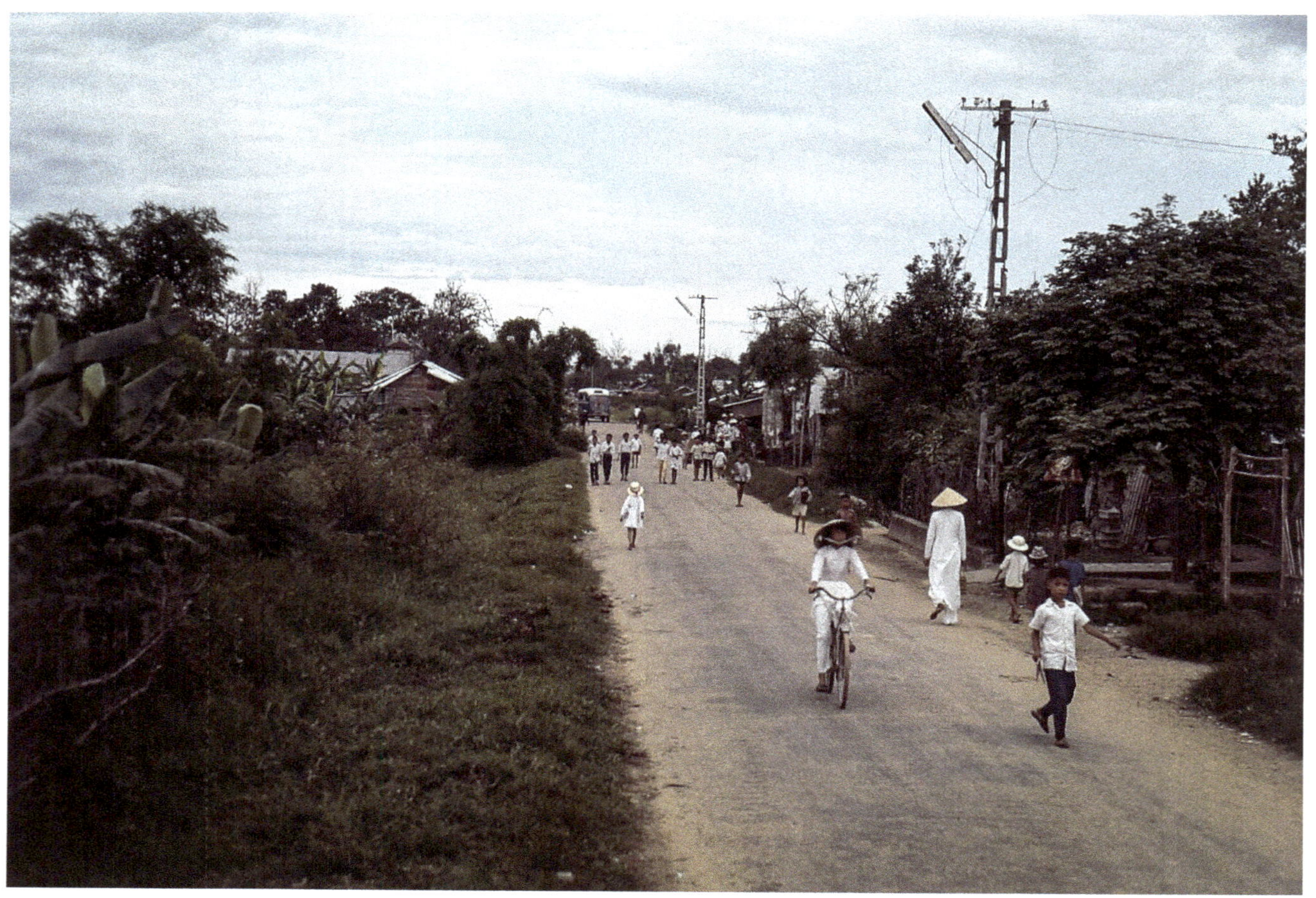

The battle for Hue City concluded and debris of war cleared from the streets, Vietnamese children emerge from their homes in the aftermath of the Communist Tet Offensive. 1968

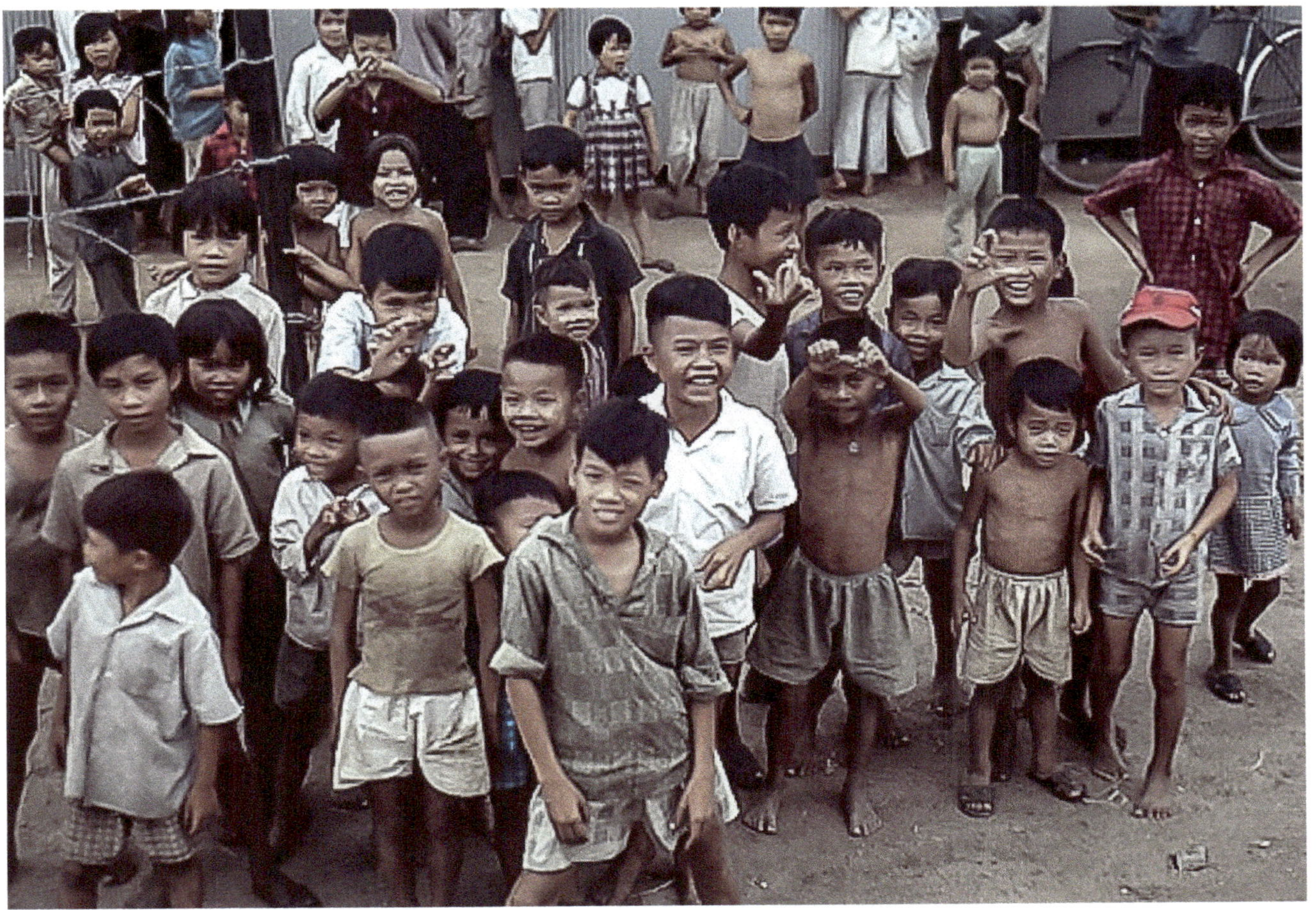

The children of Hue City after the Communist Tet Offensive. Thua Thien Province,1968

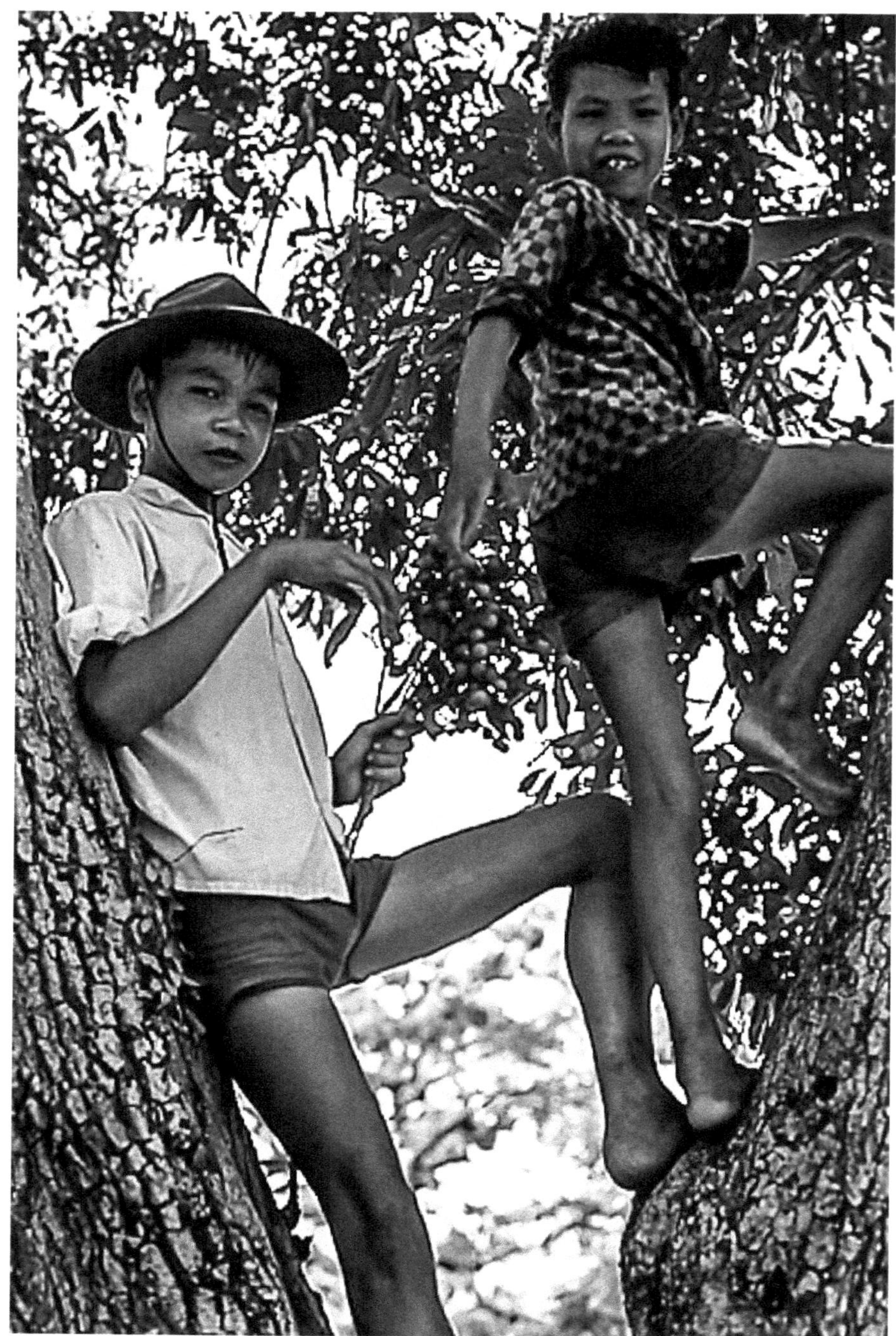

Hue City, 1968

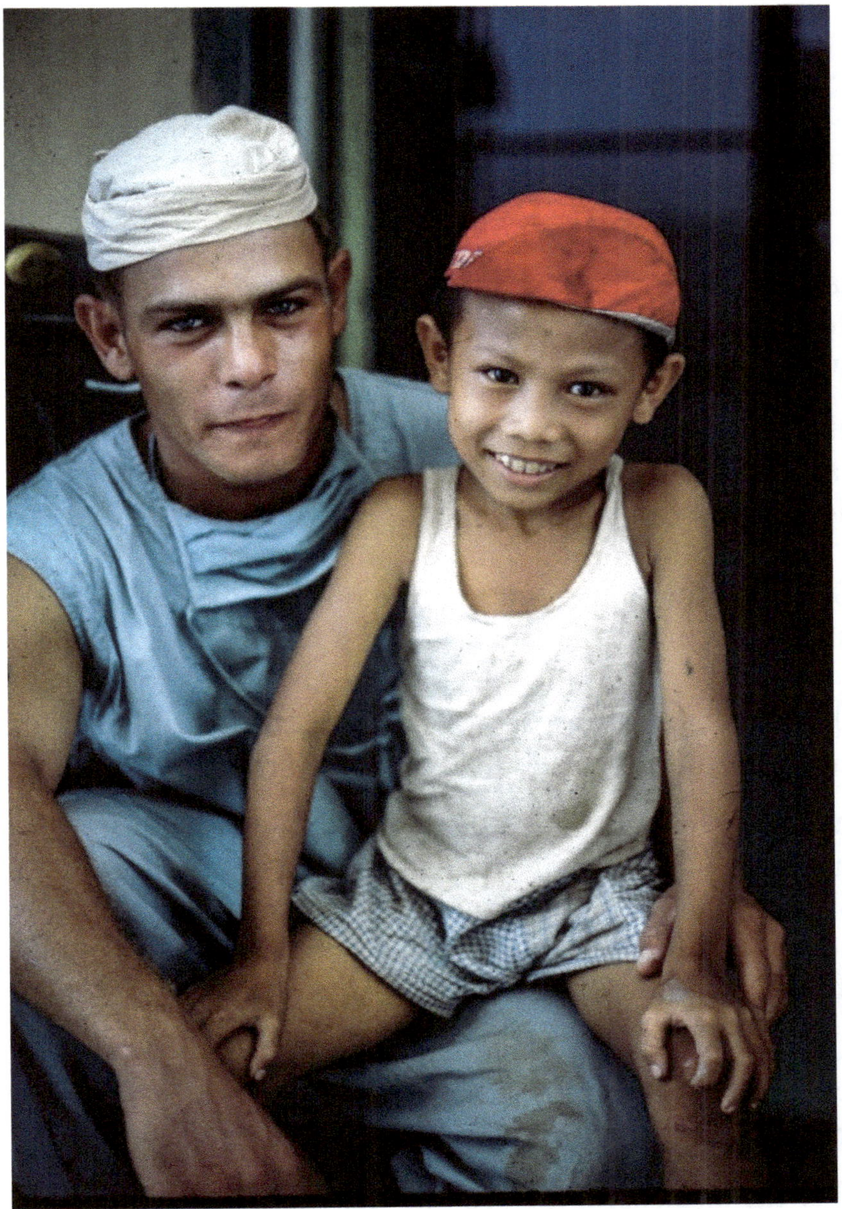

My newly found friend at the Provincial Hospital in Hue. The Viet Cong and North Vietnamese Army murdered Vietnamese physicians and surgeons at this hospital during the Tet Offensive of 1968. In an effort to cover for the loss of the Vietnamese surgeons, I and two of the Medical Battalion's surgeons, traveled to the hospital from the Phu Bai combat base over a 2- month period of time, and performed emergent and non-emergent surgical cases. All of our surgery at the Hue hospital was performed as an addition to our responsibilities at the medical battalion caring for wounded Marines and performing Civic Action in hamlets and villages.

Excerpt From a Letter home

Sunday, 16 June 1969
Phu Bai Combat Base

"My normal day will begin at 6:30 a.m. at which time I will check out our PC (personnel carrier) from motor transport. I then stop by the office and pick up four empty water cans, take them to the water point and fill them, depending on how hot it becomes.

If there is work to be done in one of the hamlets, or a meeting is scheduled with one of the hamlet or village chiefs, we leave as soon as possible. When we go to the Civic Action area, we take no less than a fire team for security. When we visit Phu Nam we take slightly more than a fire team in addition to a radioman. The entire village area (Thuy Chau) is bordered by a VC/NVA domain. Infiltration into our hamlets occurs on a regular basis. For instance; last Thursday evening 30 VC entered Phu Nam, took rice, and coerced the people into giving them shelter for the night. Friday morning, we went to Phu Nam to hold a Medcap, and the hamlet chief informed us what happened during the night. About 3 weeks ago, a VC assassination squad entered Phu Tay and murdered a National Policemen.

One of the hamlets in our area (Loi Nong) is controlled by the VC. Thus far, any attempt to root them out has been unsuccessful. If an allied unit approaches the hamlet, the VC will weigh the possibility of successfully engaging the unit in combat. If they believe they will win they stand and fight. If they believe they will lose they simply melt into the jungle and await the departure of the invading unit.

Monday through Wednesday, I spend my daylight hours working with the hamlets concerning projects, problems that arise, and the various other issues that are important in the civic action program. Thursday through Saturday are Medicap days.

Last Tuesday I spent discussing the preliminary plans for a school in Thach An Hamlet at the hamlet chief's house. Presently, the hamlet has a one-room school suitable for attendance by 30 children, but at least 50 attend classes. There are an additional 300 children in the hamlet of school age who are being deprived of an education because of the lack of sufficient educational facilities. And so, we are attempting to initiate a school construction project for Thach An. In addition, the hamlet wells are drying up, and this requires our immediate attention. We have already repaired one of the wells structurally, but it is assumed that the remainder of the wells (4) will require considerable deepening.

In Phu Tay Hamlet, we are repairing 3 wells and constructing another. The hamlet school was damaged by VC ordnance not too long ago and requires repair. The hamlet does not have any qualified medical personnel or any structure used for medical purposes. In fact, the entire village lacks medical facilities. The village headquarters are located in the hamlet, and it just so happens that district headquarters are also located here. This makes for an ideal situation when one considers that the chain of government goes hamlet to village and then to district. Quite often district is located many miles from the hamlet or village that you are working with.

Phu Tay Hamlet covers about 1 ½ miles of dense jungle and two miles of flat open land on which rice is grown. Thatched and cement buildings are scattered throughout the jungle area. During the extreme heat of a summer afternoon, the jungle area is the only refuge from the sun's penetrating rays, but the heat remains a stifling adversary regardless of where you may be. If while walking through the dark alleyways of the jungle, one should find a path which meanders in an easterly direction, a strong breeze will follow its course offering an unnatural coolness.

The people of Thuy Chau have a singular communion with the nature in which they live; ultimately depend on for their very survival. Here is a world that enthralls me. It is ancient and beautiful, removed from any semblance of 20th century intrusion (except this seemingly interminable war). Here, there is an inexhaustible source of knowledge, a type of knowledge obtainable nowhere else."

Excerpt from a letter home,

Tuesday, August 27 1969. Phu Bai, Thua Thien Province.

"Currently, we (I and my Vietnamese friends in the hamlets) are attempting to keep the steam on developmental projects in all the hamlets. In Thach An. we are building a school and a dispensary (have completed repairing the wells here). In Phu Tay we are building one well and repairing the school which was damaged by VC ordinance (have repaired two wells here already). In Phu Nam we are repairing two wells and are building another (or is it digging?) In addition, we are attempting to resettle 100 families who were refuged from Loi Nong. The communists, in their war of liberation, succeeded in destroying their homes for no apparent reason. Also; I must plan and coordinate (from the bottom up) Medcaps to these hamlets once per week, and treat the people. The planning stage involves such basic things as insuring that I have proper medications to checking on intelligence reports (so that we don't walk into an NVA Battalion, or the VC…an impossible thing to do). Finally, I have to organize the security element which accompanies us for protection. I drive the vehicle, I interpret (although I have a trusted Vietnamese who also interprets), and I treat sick people. If something goes wrong-it's my neck, particularly if I am negligent in arranging security and its deployment. People's lives are valuable. Then when the field work is completed, there is an entire family of reports to substantiate "work completed" …projects underway, people treated, etc. I may leave my workspace before 8:00 pm. But in spite of it all, the work is rewarding, beneficial to me and other people.

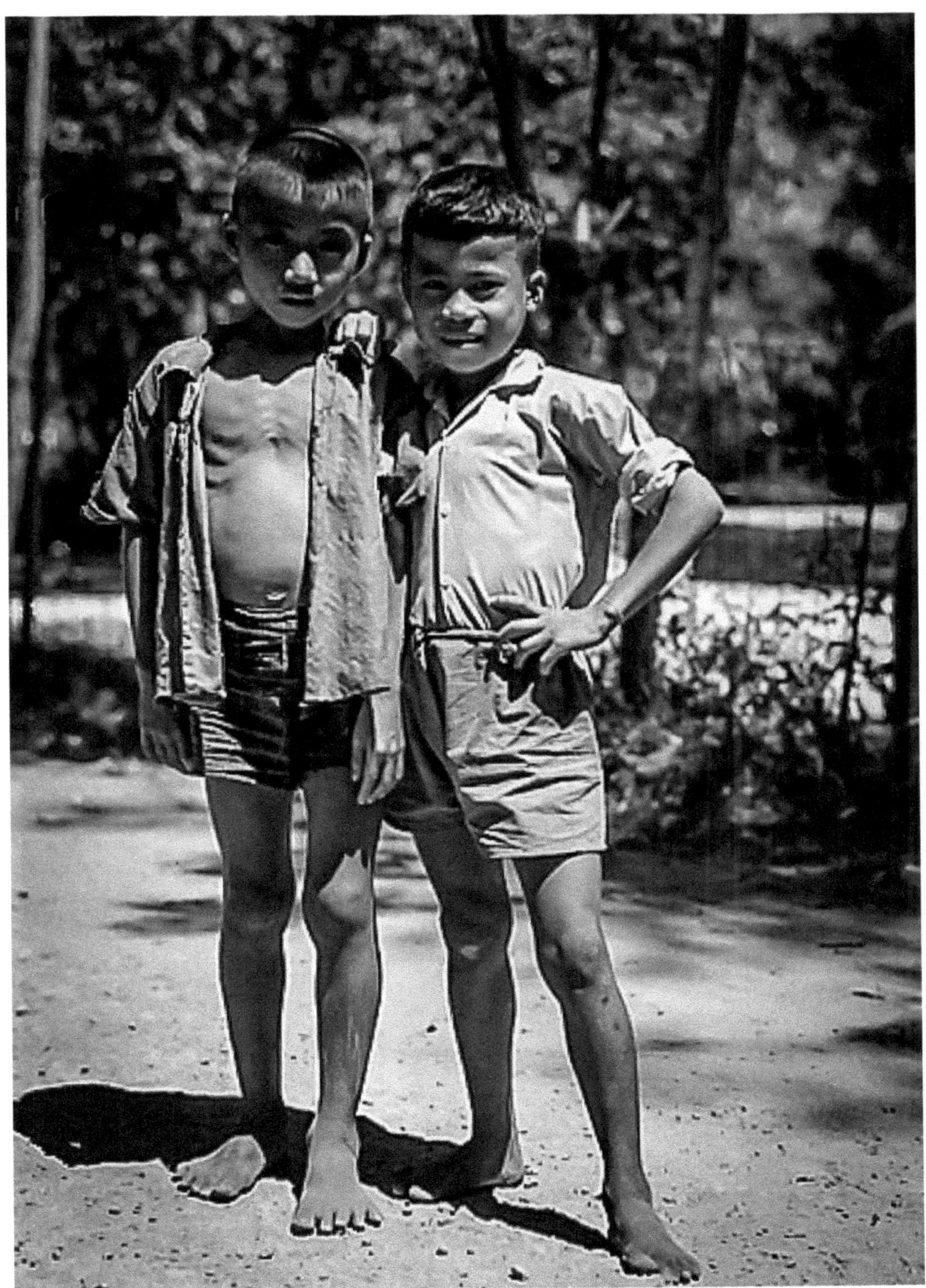

We set up our medical gear under the awning of a hamlet home in Loi Nong. The hamlet is controlled by the Viet Cong at night. As I talk with these boys I hear automatic weapons fire and explosions in the adjacent hamlet. The boys did not seem to be disturbed. This is normal for them. 1969

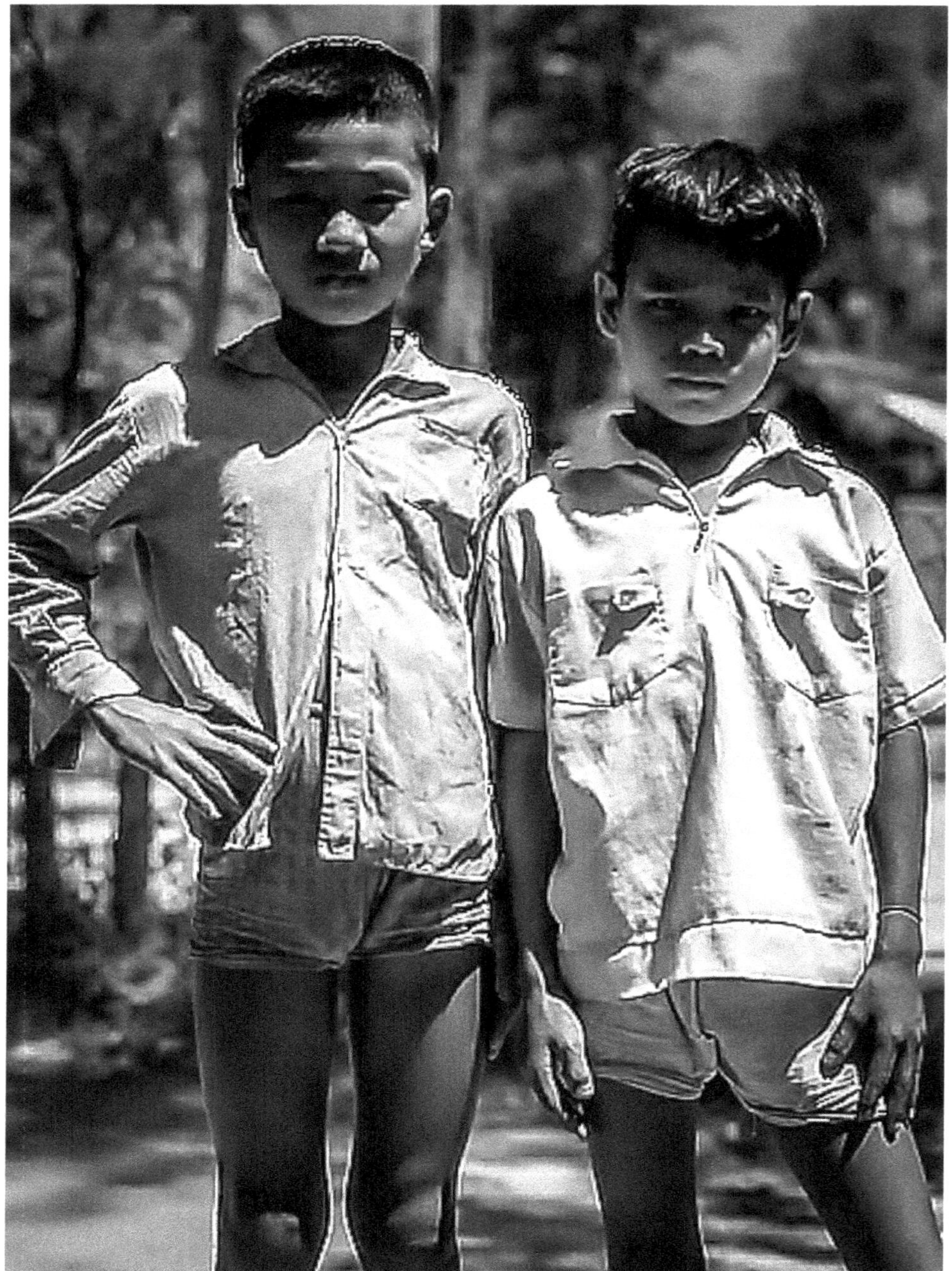

Loi Nong Hamlet is their home and it is controlled by the Viet Cong at night.
I wonder what they must they do to live and survive here with their families. 1969.

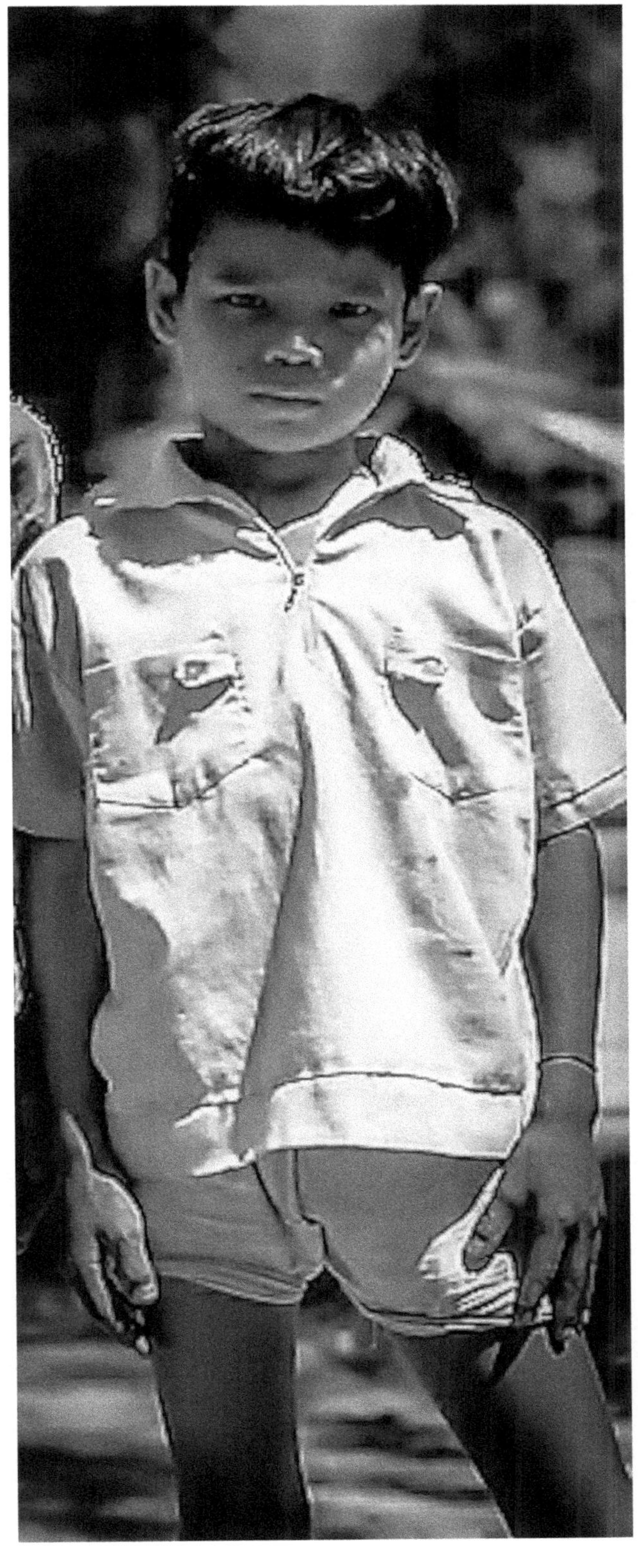

Loi Nong Hamlet

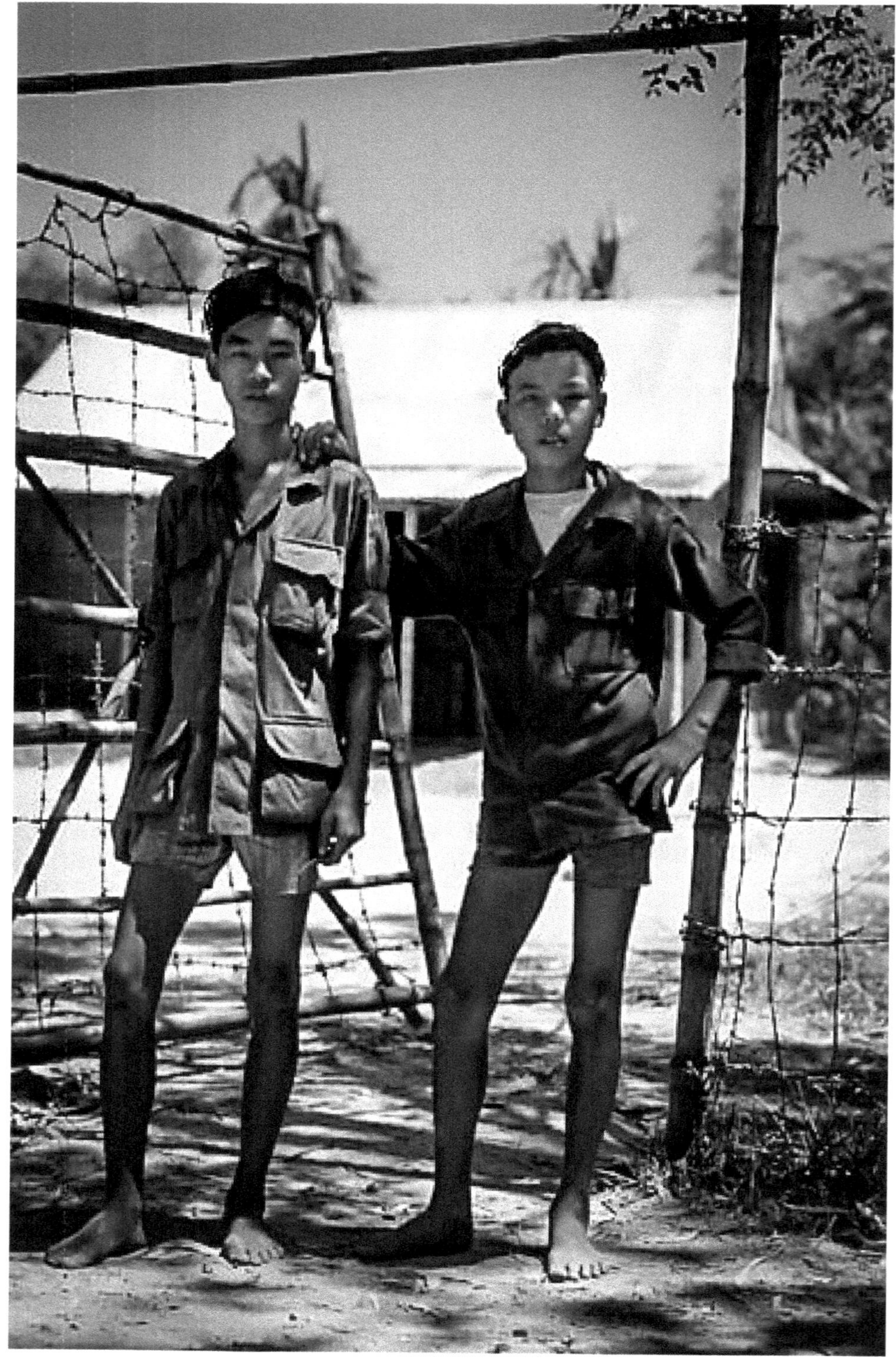

Adolescent boys presenting for care were a rarity in Loi Nong. 1969

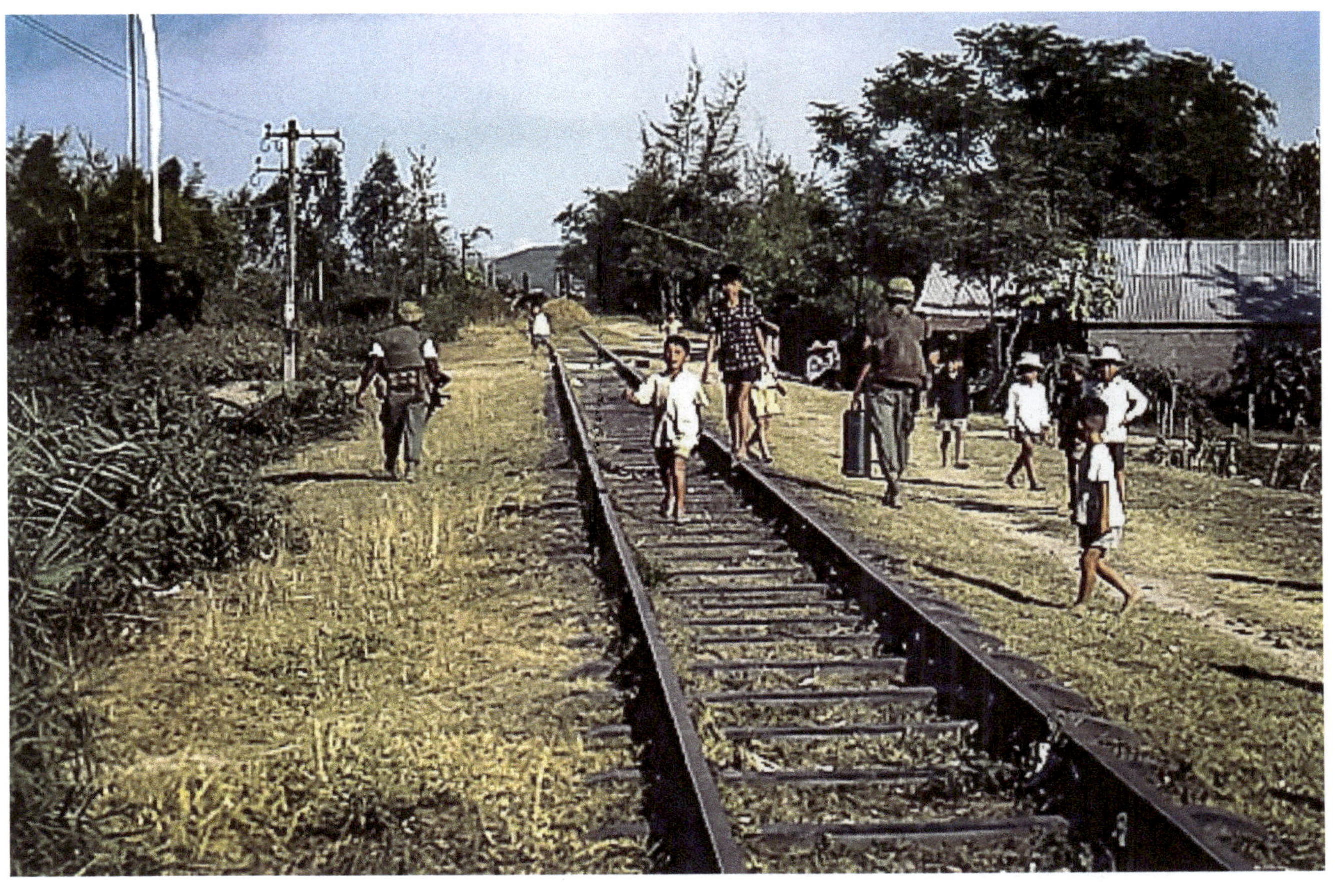

The children come to greet us as we walk toward

Thach An Hamlet, Their presence indicates that there is less chance of an ambush in this largely Viet Cong controlled area. The railroad stretched from Saigon (Ho Chi Minh City) to Hanoi, but was not in use because of repeated sabotage by the Viet Cong. 1969

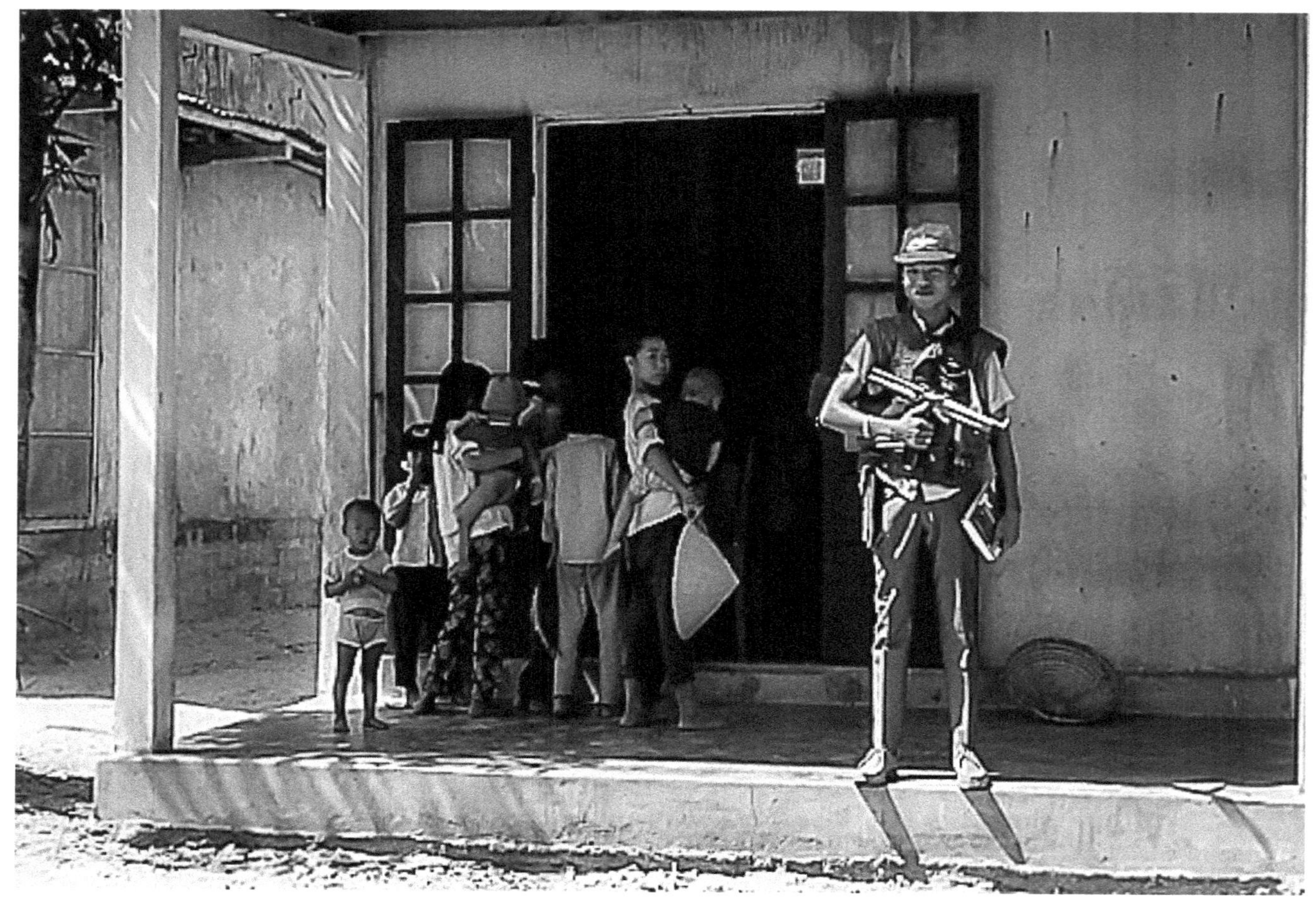

Thach An School

Children wait for medical care outside their school. Vietnamese interpreter and my friend, cradles a weapon for personal protection. The absence of older males presenting for care is notable. 1969

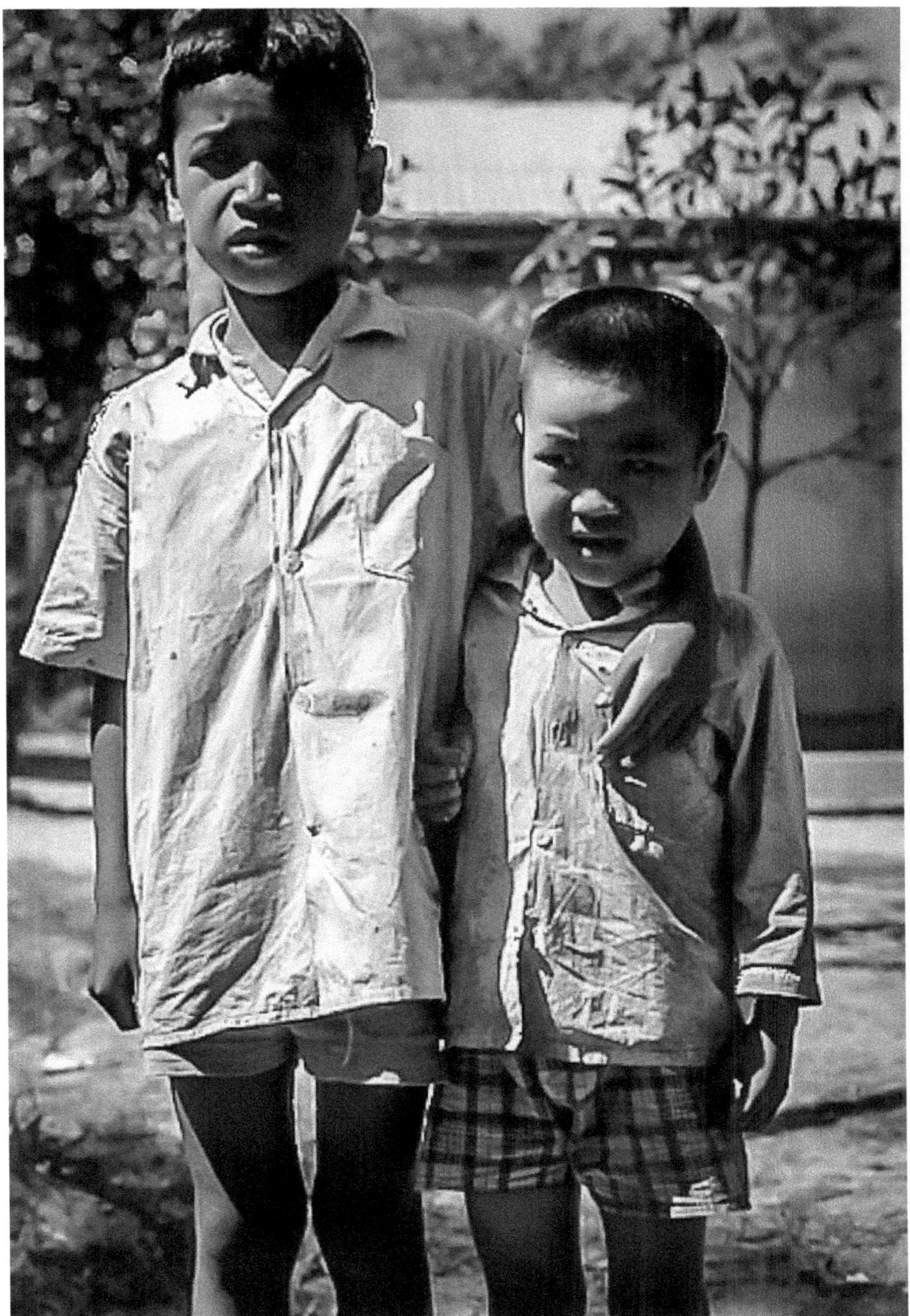

Boys of Thach An Hamlet, 1969.

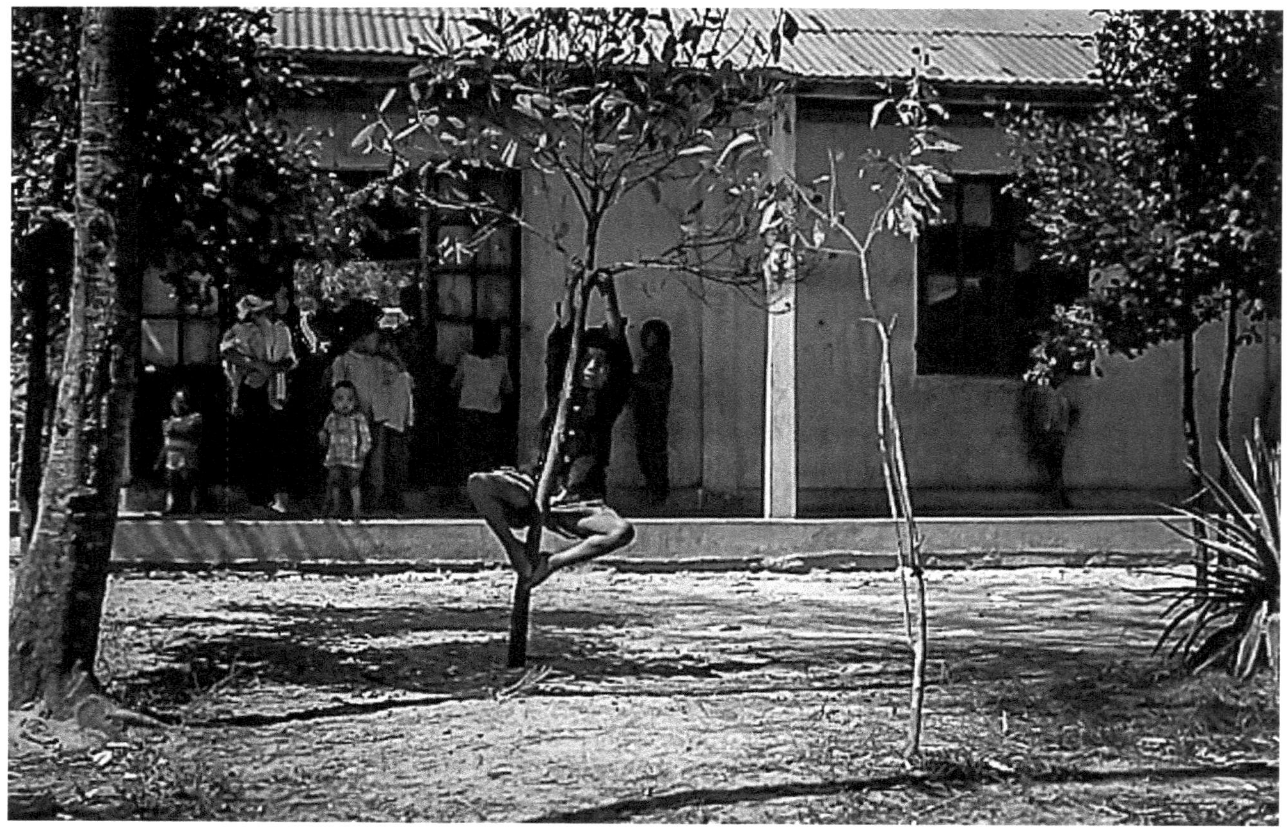

We would schedule Medcaps (medical civic action) with the hamlet and village chiefs who would in turn notify the local populace by word of mouth. Care was usually provided in the local school, or if there was no school or it had been destroyed, we would use someone's home.

Thach An Hamlet School 1969.

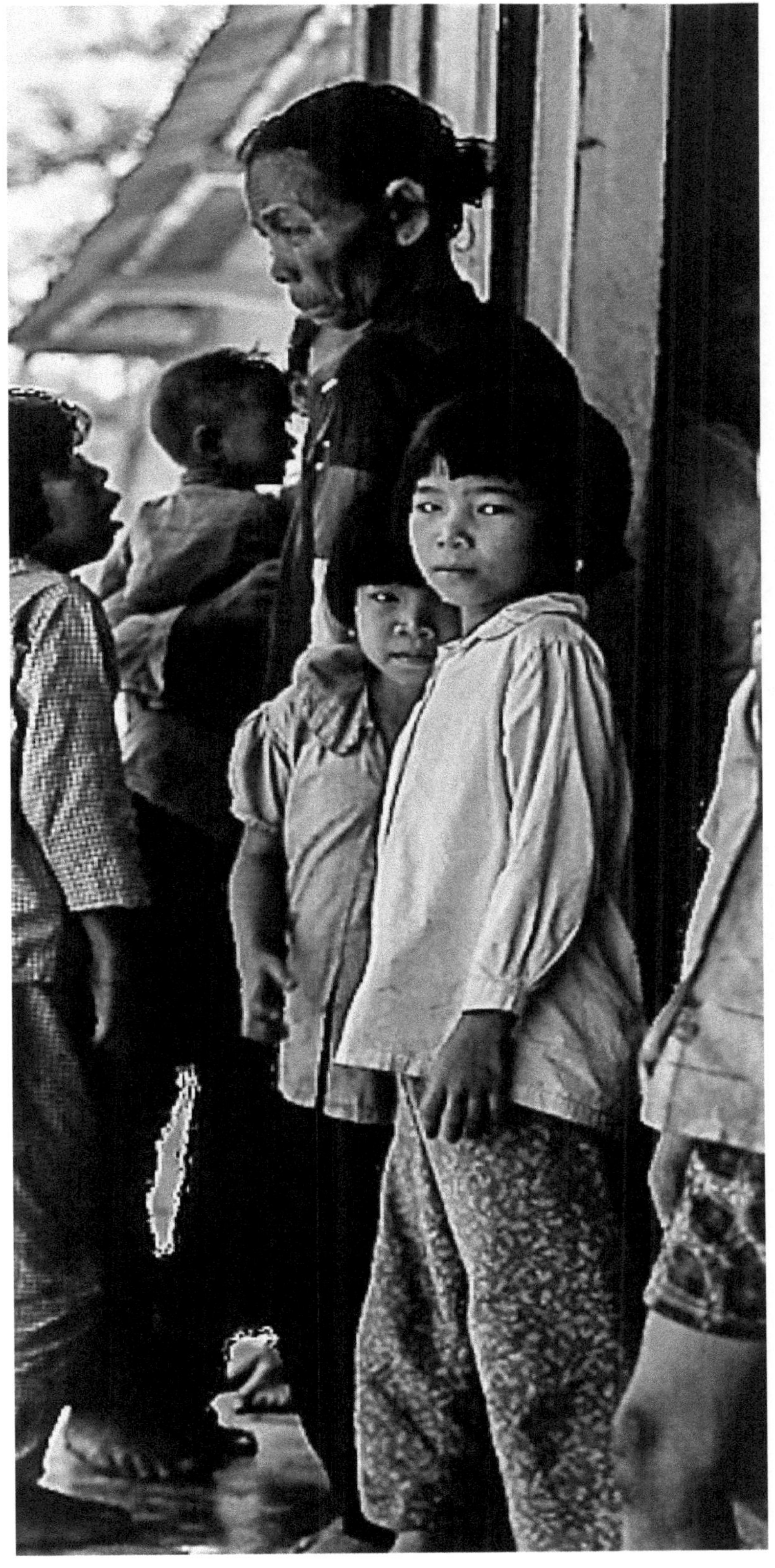

Children wait in line with an elder for medical care outside the Thach An School. 1969

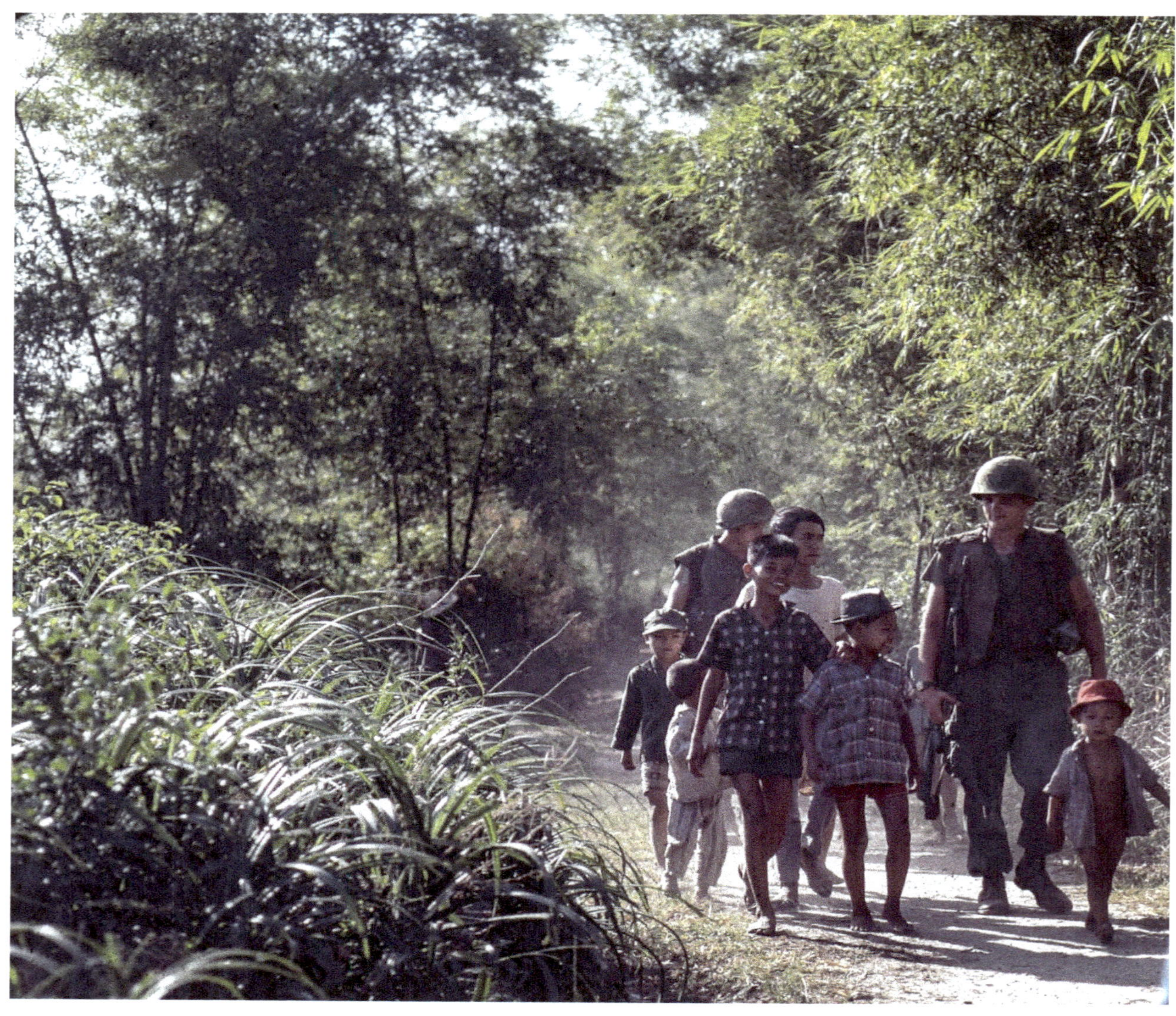

Children from Thach An have become our trail companions on this visit.

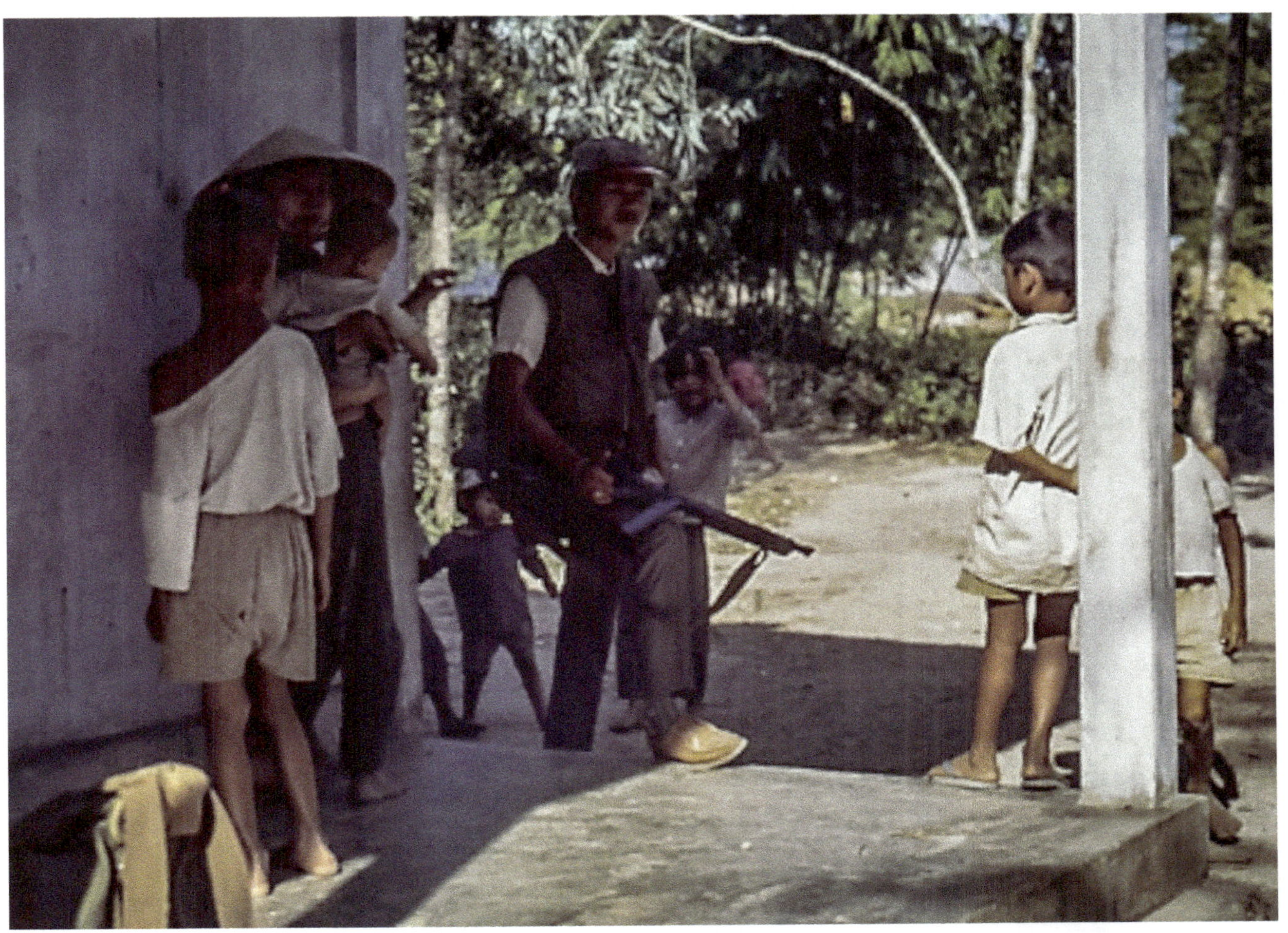

Our Vietnamese interpreter talks with children at the Thach An School. 1969

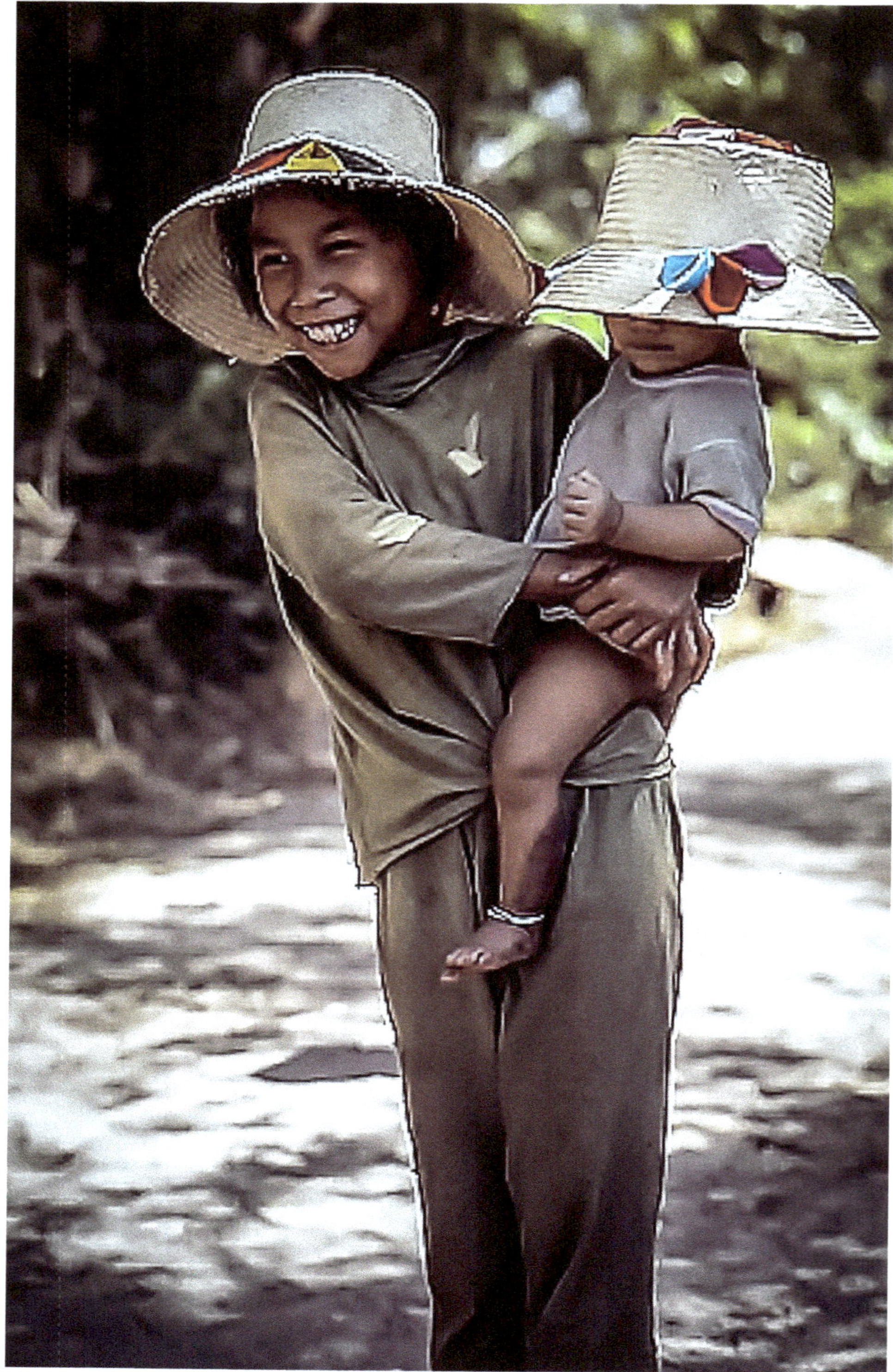

Hue-Thua Thien Province1969.

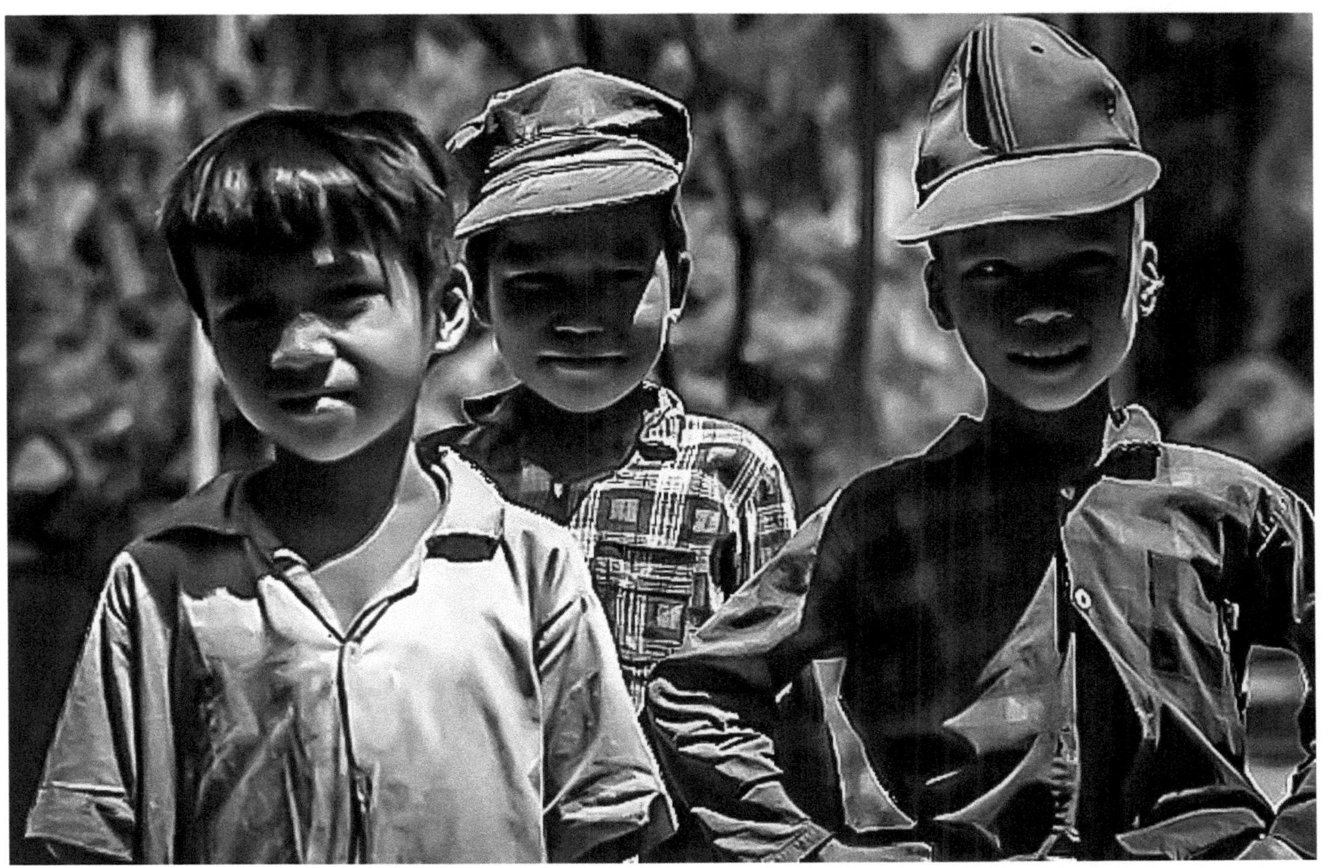

The boy on the right wears a US Army hat,
the boy in the middle wears a Marine hat. 1969

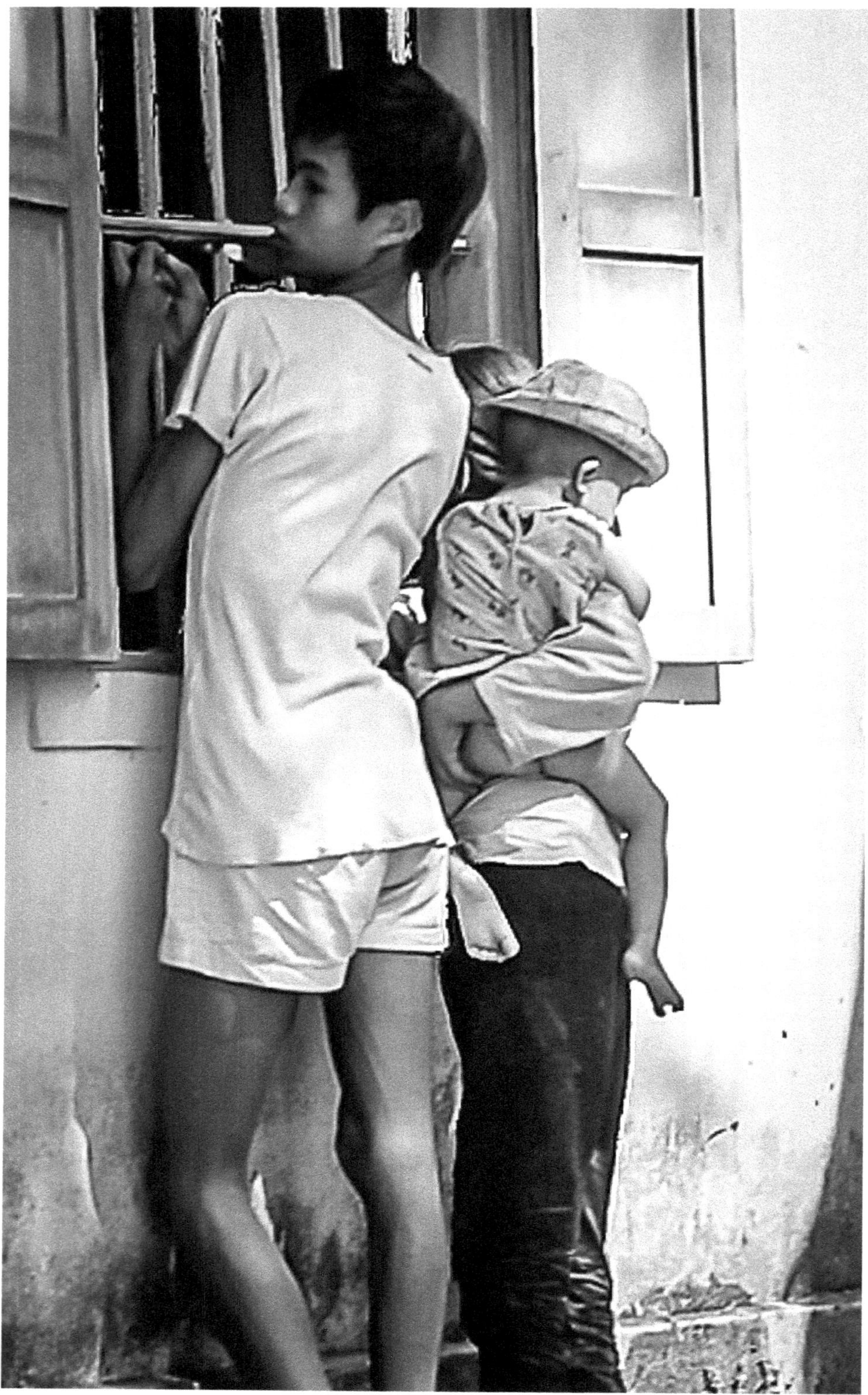

Waiting for care. 1969

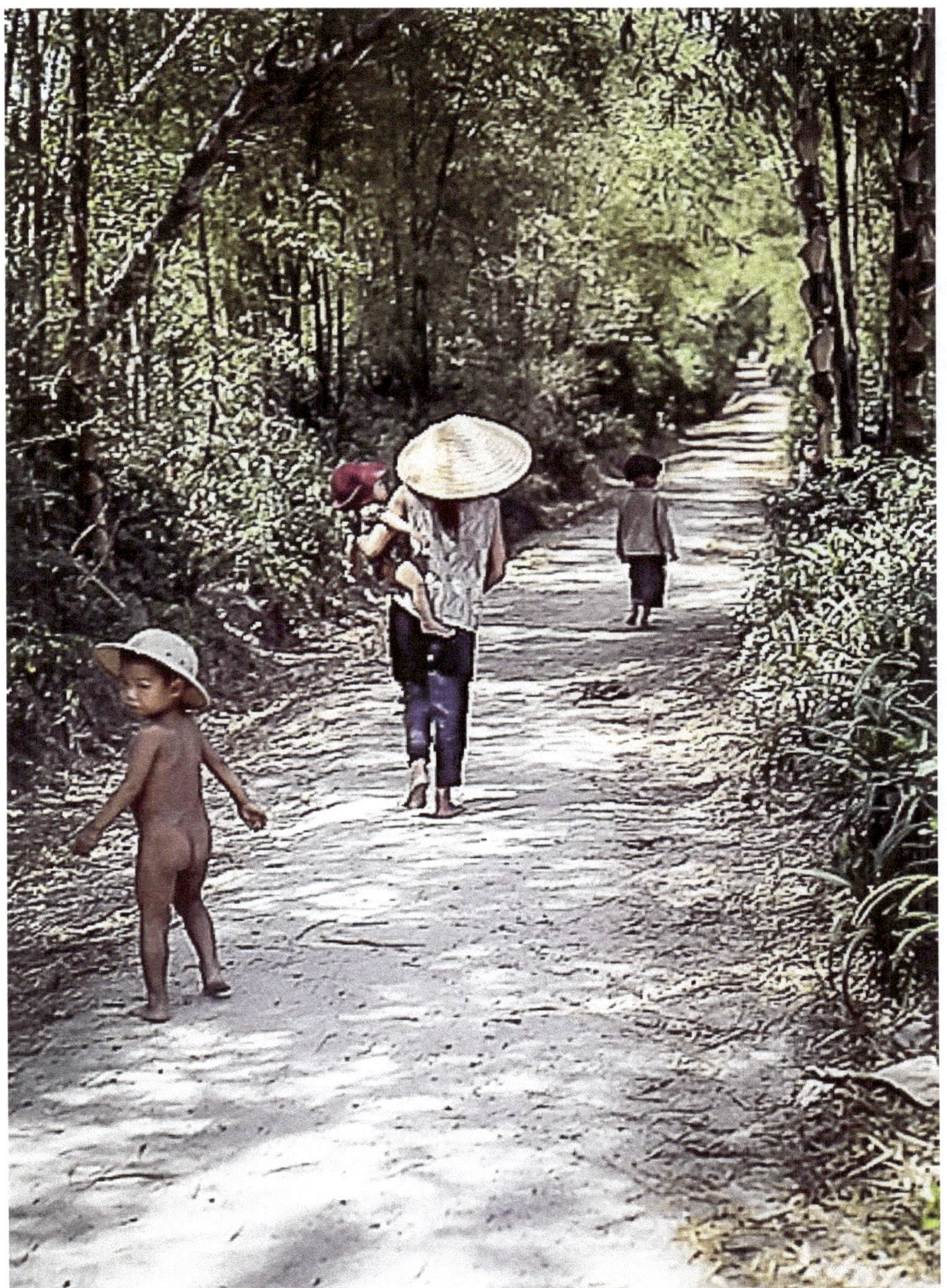

The path home.

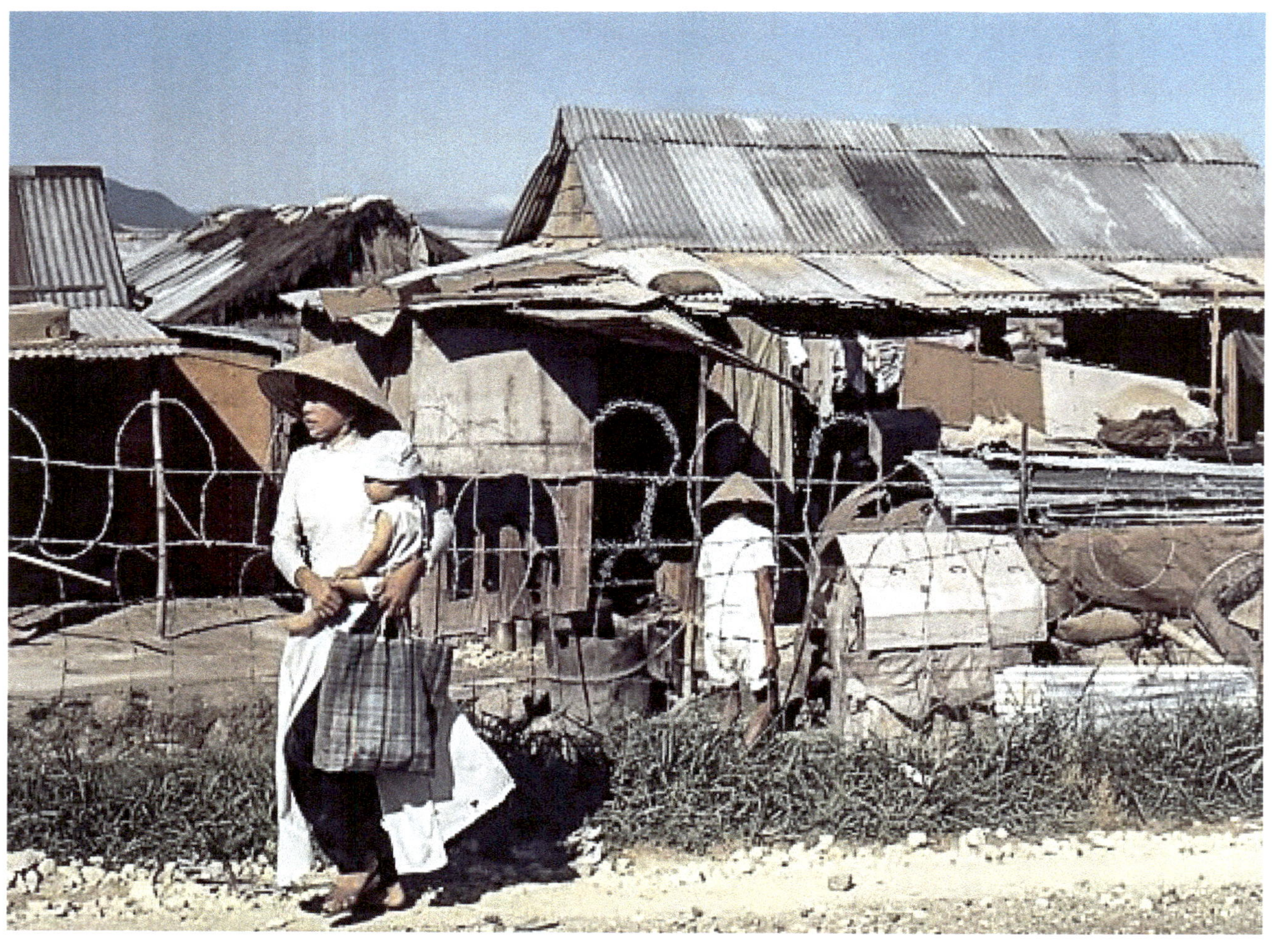

A mother carries her infant son on Route 1 outside the Phu Bai combat base past a crowded lean-to encampment constructed by war refugees. 1969

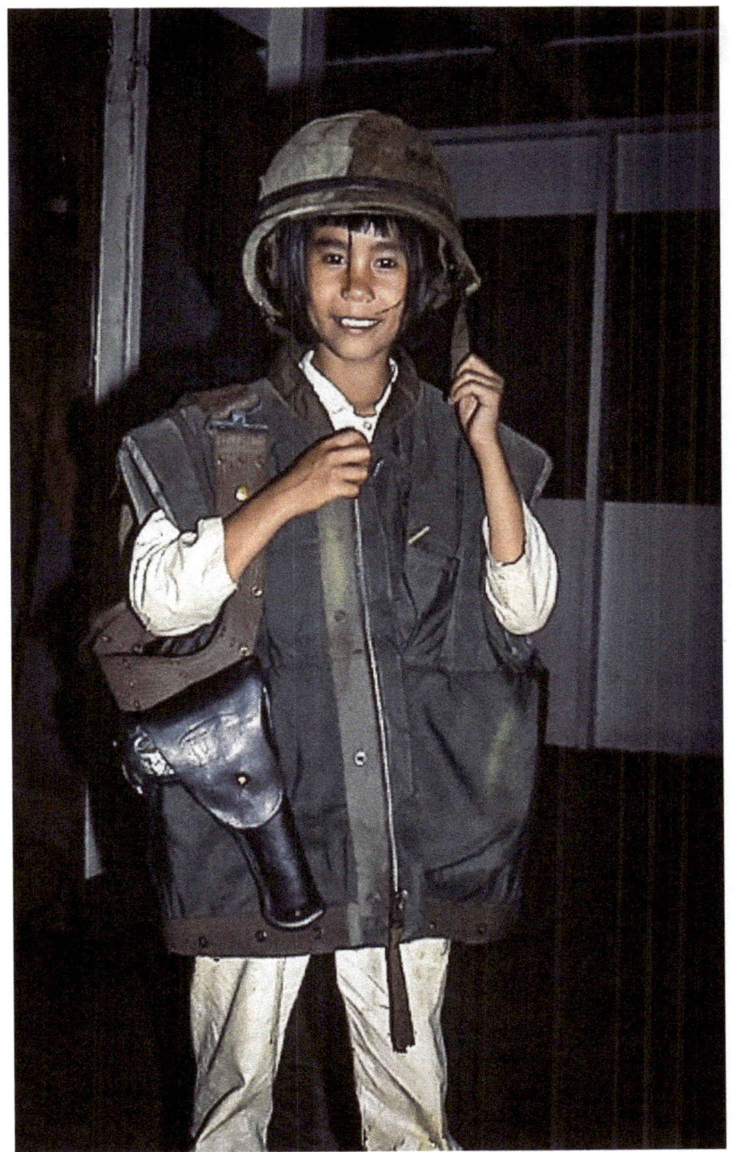

Stranded at the field hospital in Phu Bai after a Viet Cong mortar attack on the adjacent airfield, she donned a flak jacket and helmet and wantedher picture taken. 1969

The Children of Happy Valley

lived in a broad valley that served as a major Viet Cong stronghold and infiltration route from Laos and the Ho Chi Minh Trail. The people lived a largely agrarian and impoverished life. The valley was covered in dense jungle and elephant grass.

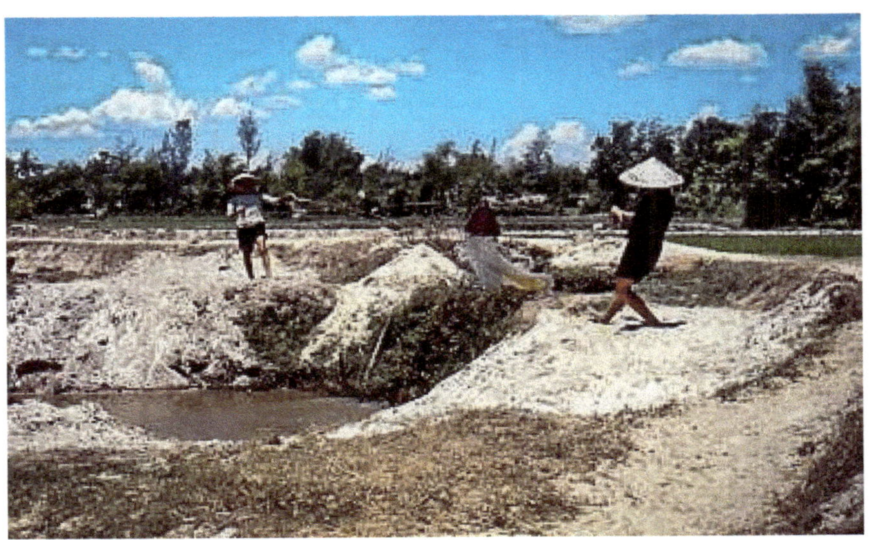

An ancient method of field irrigation. Happy Valley.

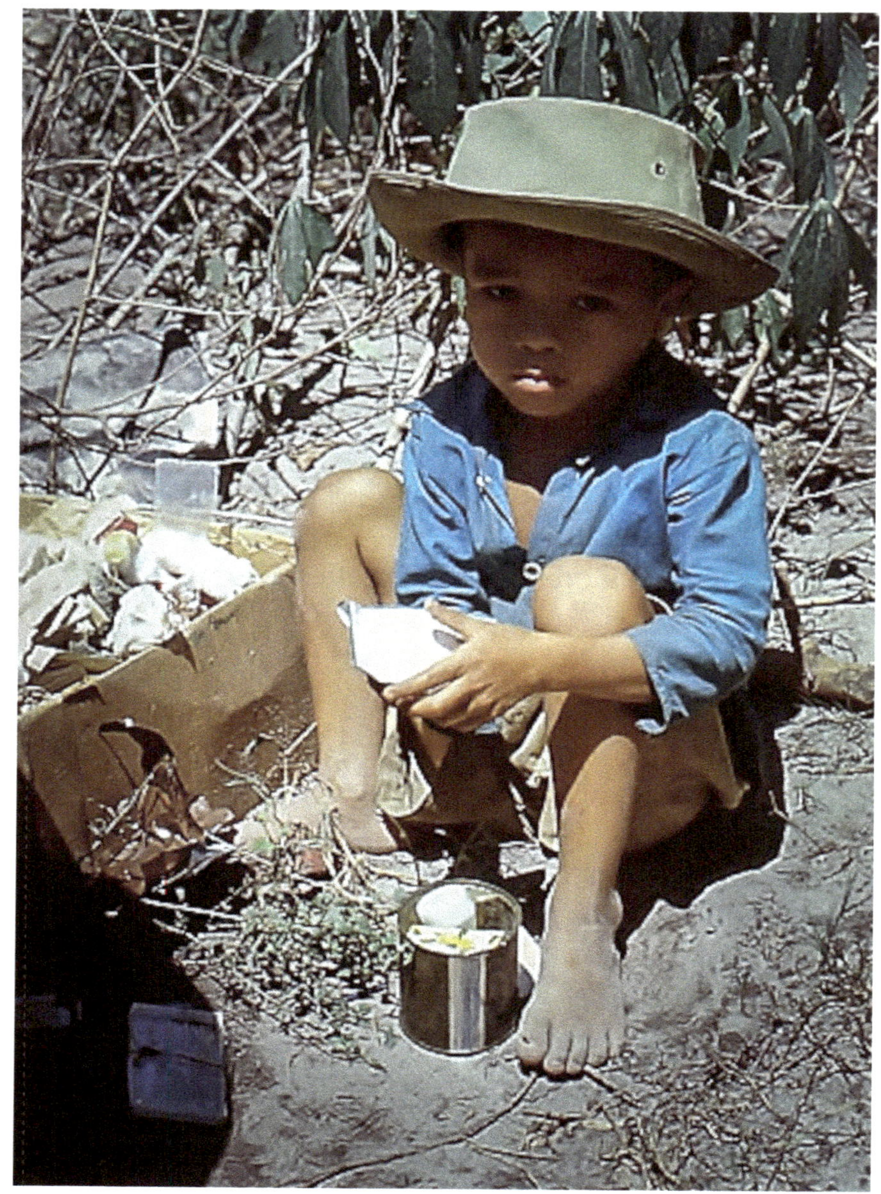

C-rations…we shared them with the children when possible.

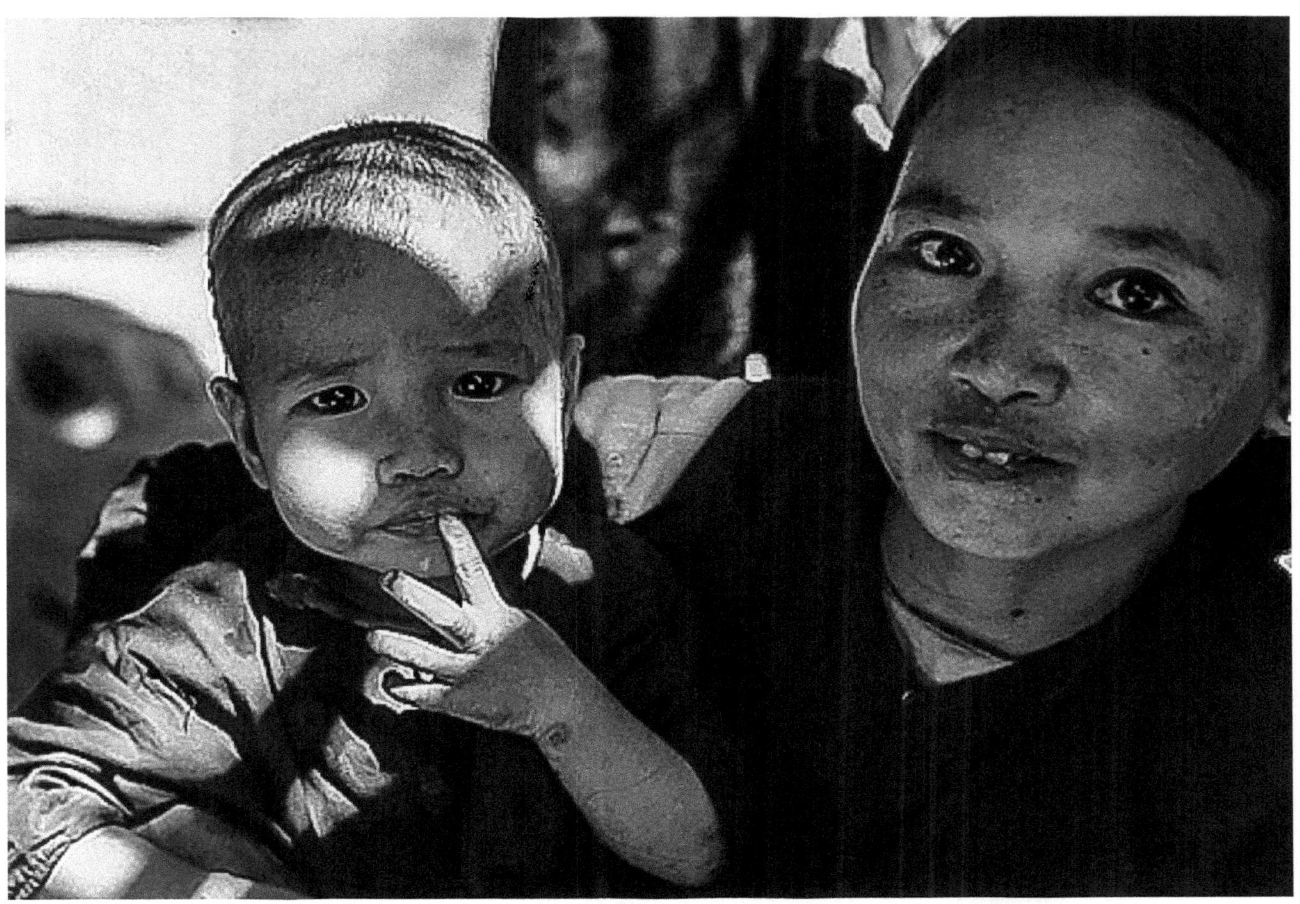

Happy Valley, 1967

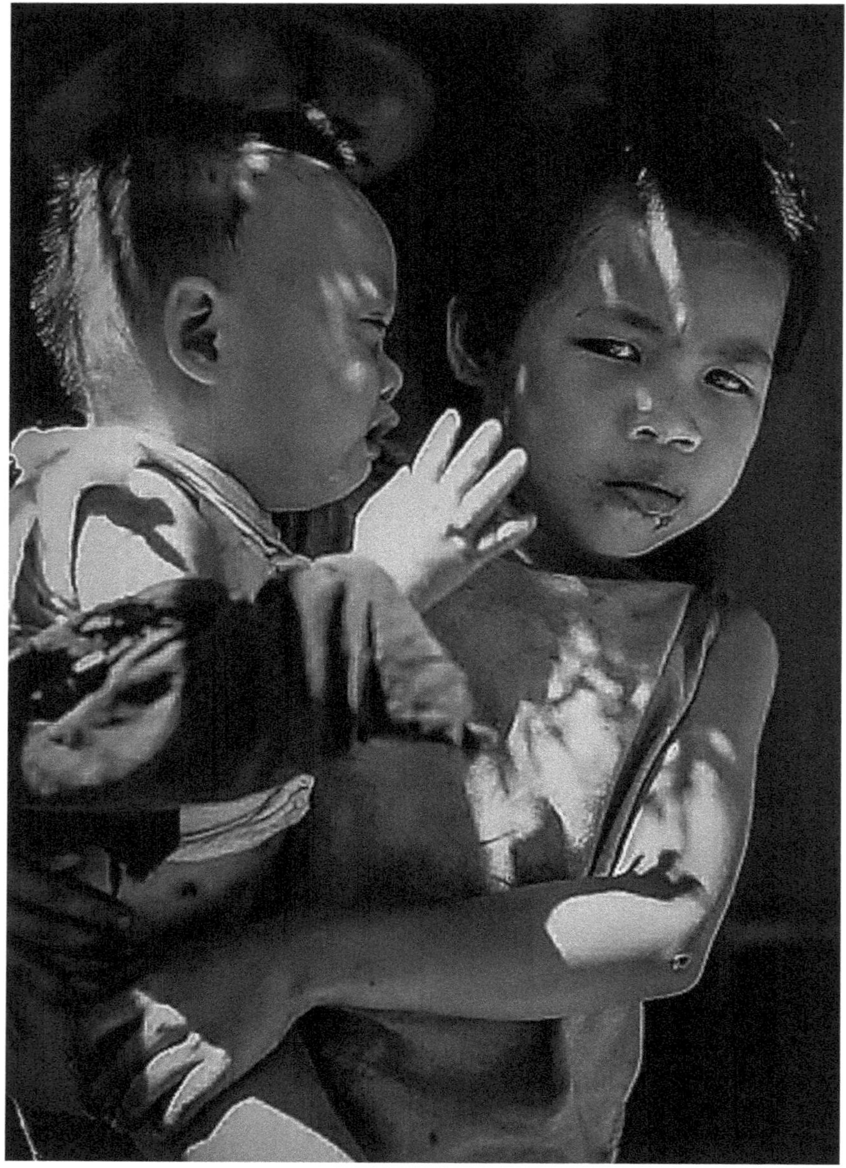

Happy Valley

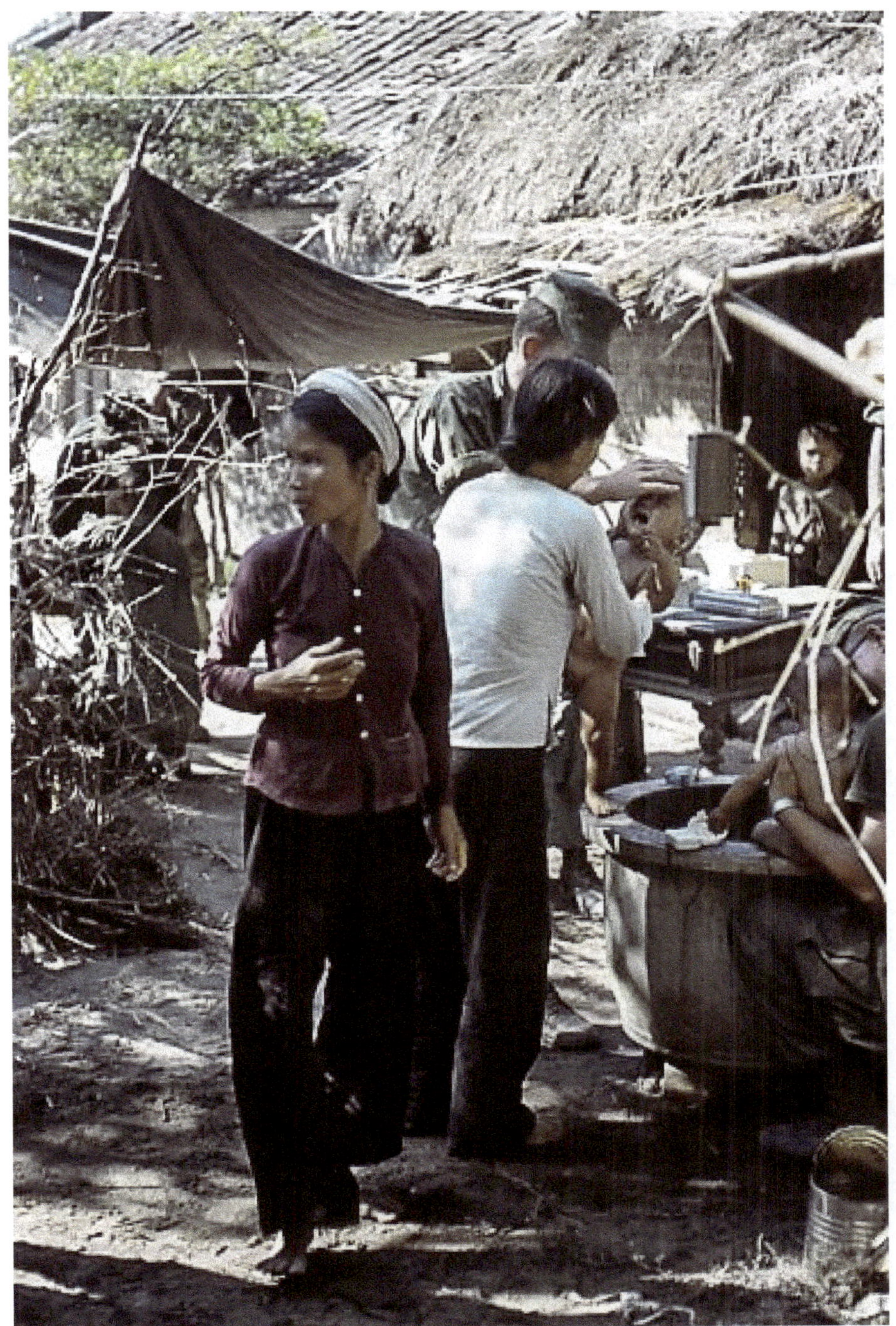

Corpsmen instructing mothers on the fundamental hygiene task of bathing their infant children. Skin infections of children were common and the result of infrequent bathing and the absence of clean water. Happy Valley, 1967

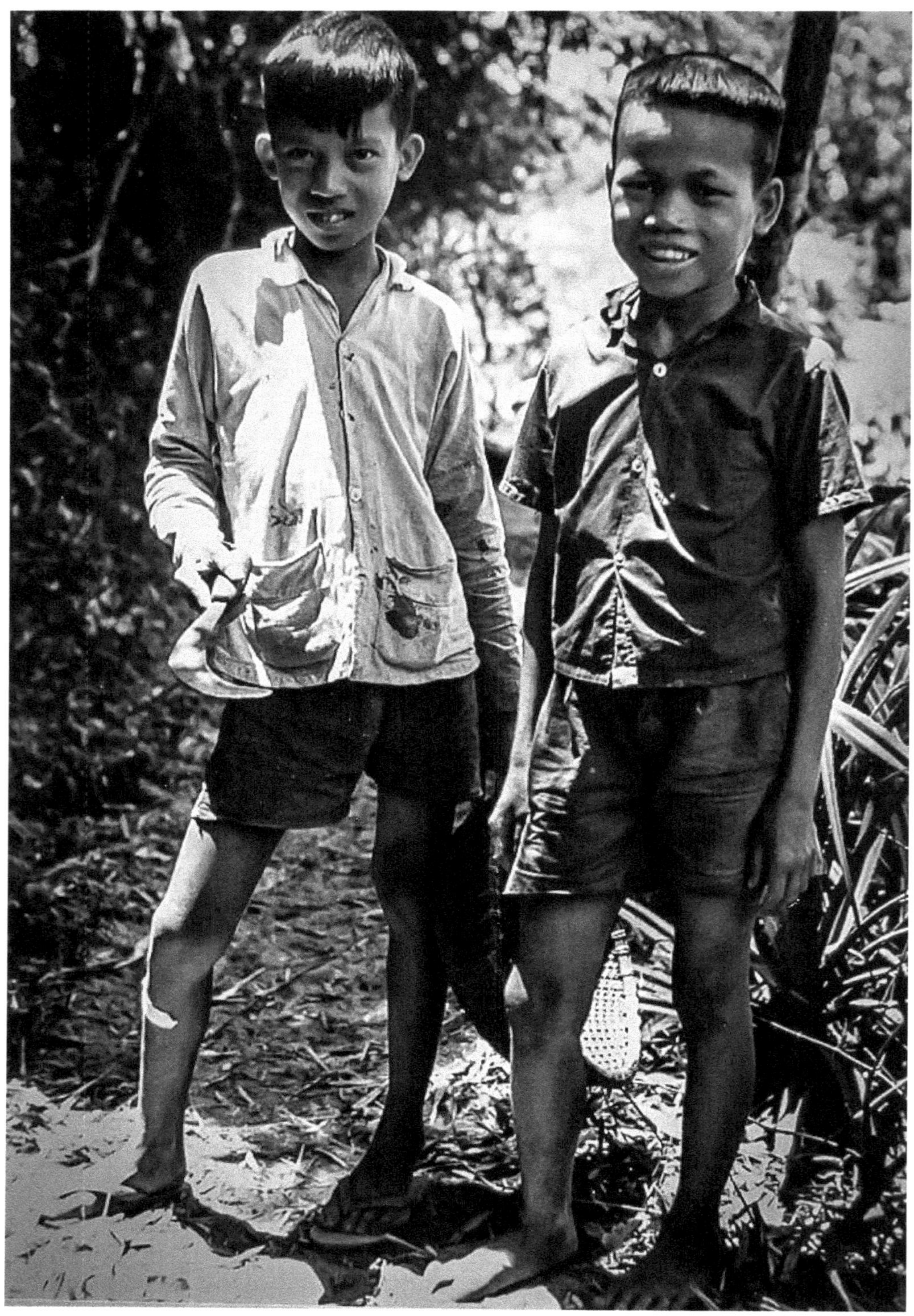

On the way to harvest rice, in the extreme heat of mid-day in temperatures of 115 to 120 degrees Fahrenheit. Happy Valley 1967.

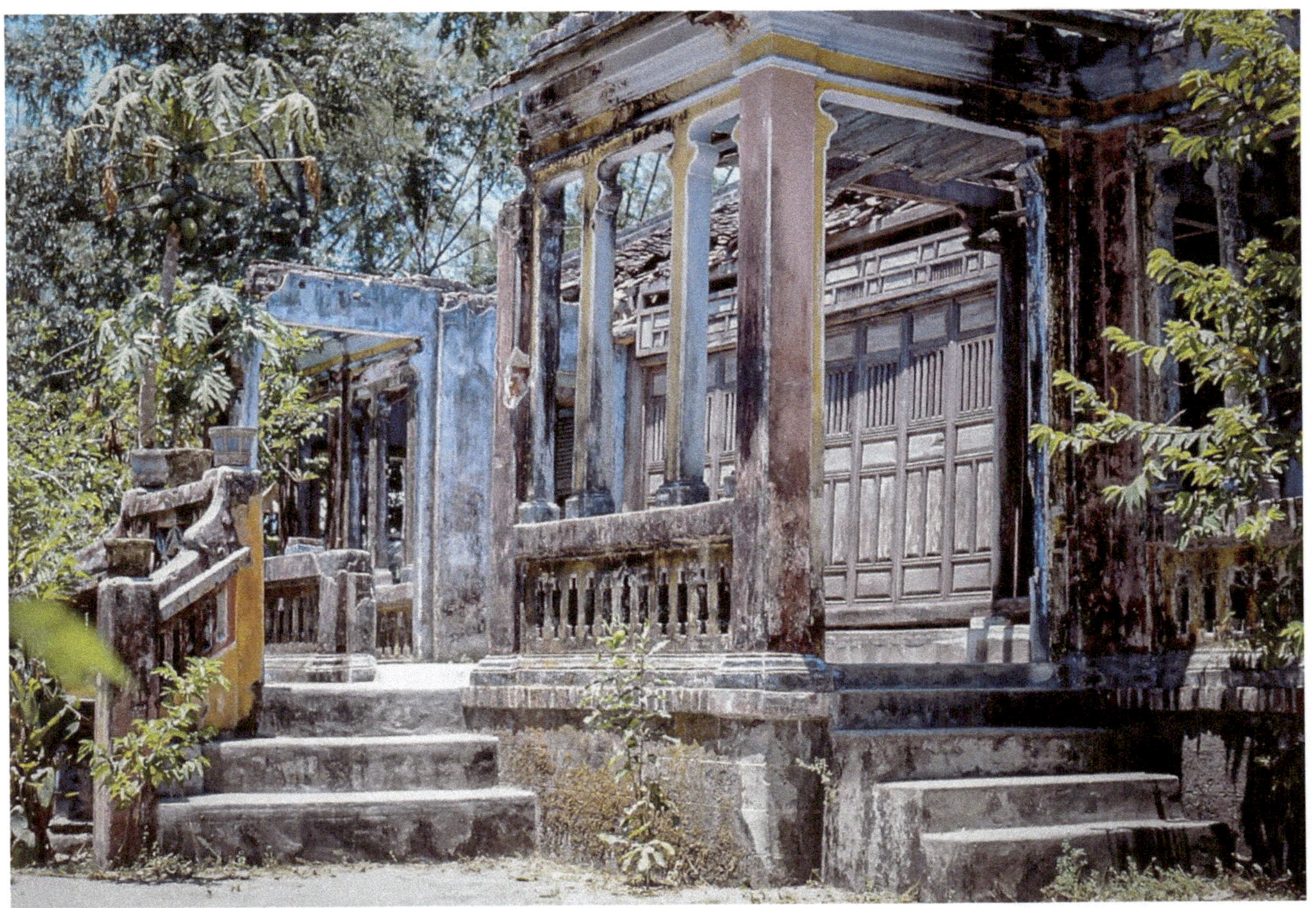

Abandoned estate in a Viet Cong controlled area within happy Valley. 1967

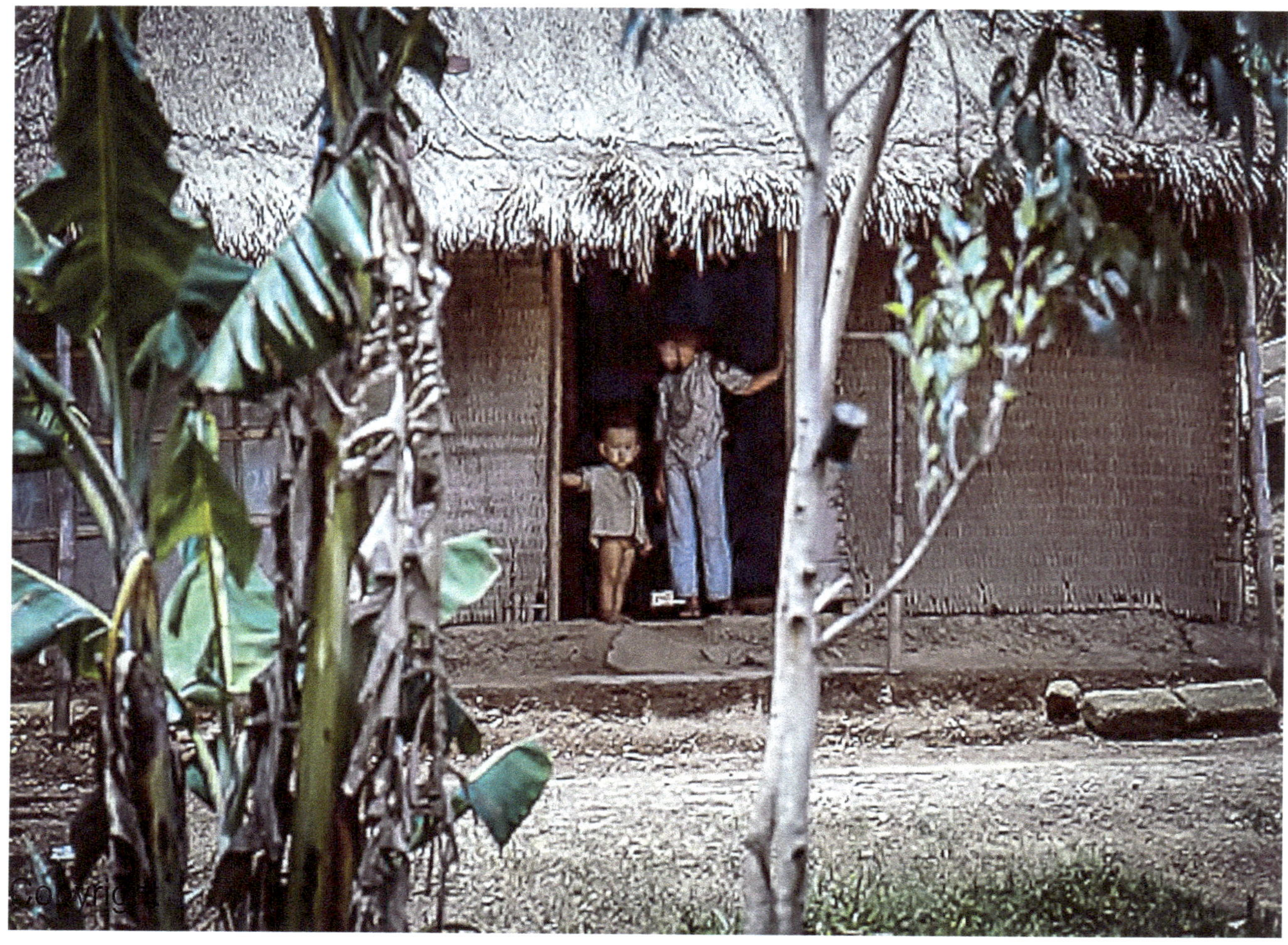

The typical rural thatched home also had a bunker to protect the family. The war was fought mostly in rural areas such as this, which invariably resulted in the destruction of individual homes or entire villages. Happy Valley 1967.

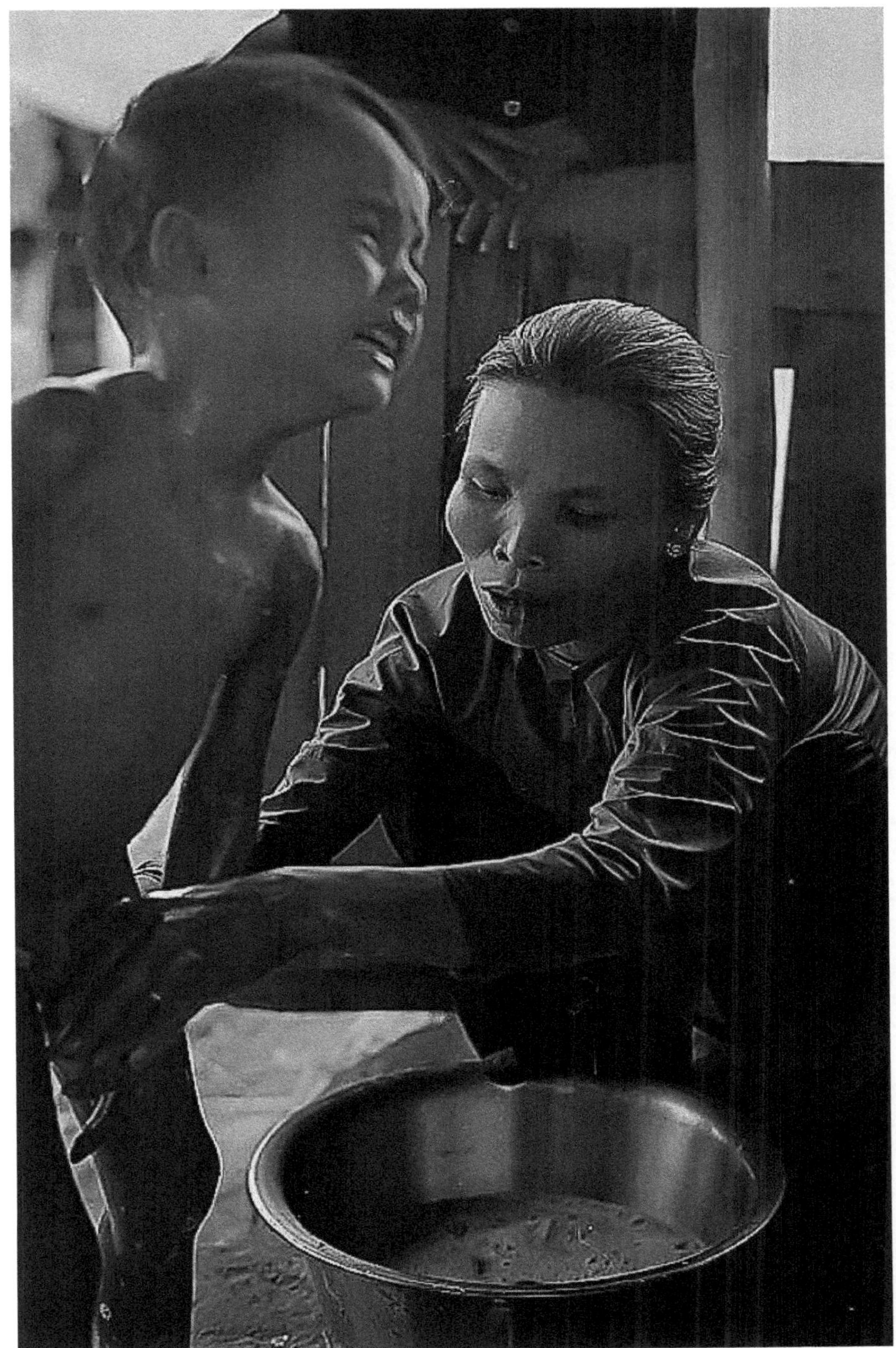

Hygiene Classes were always a priority in The effort to lower the incidence of skin infections in children. 1967

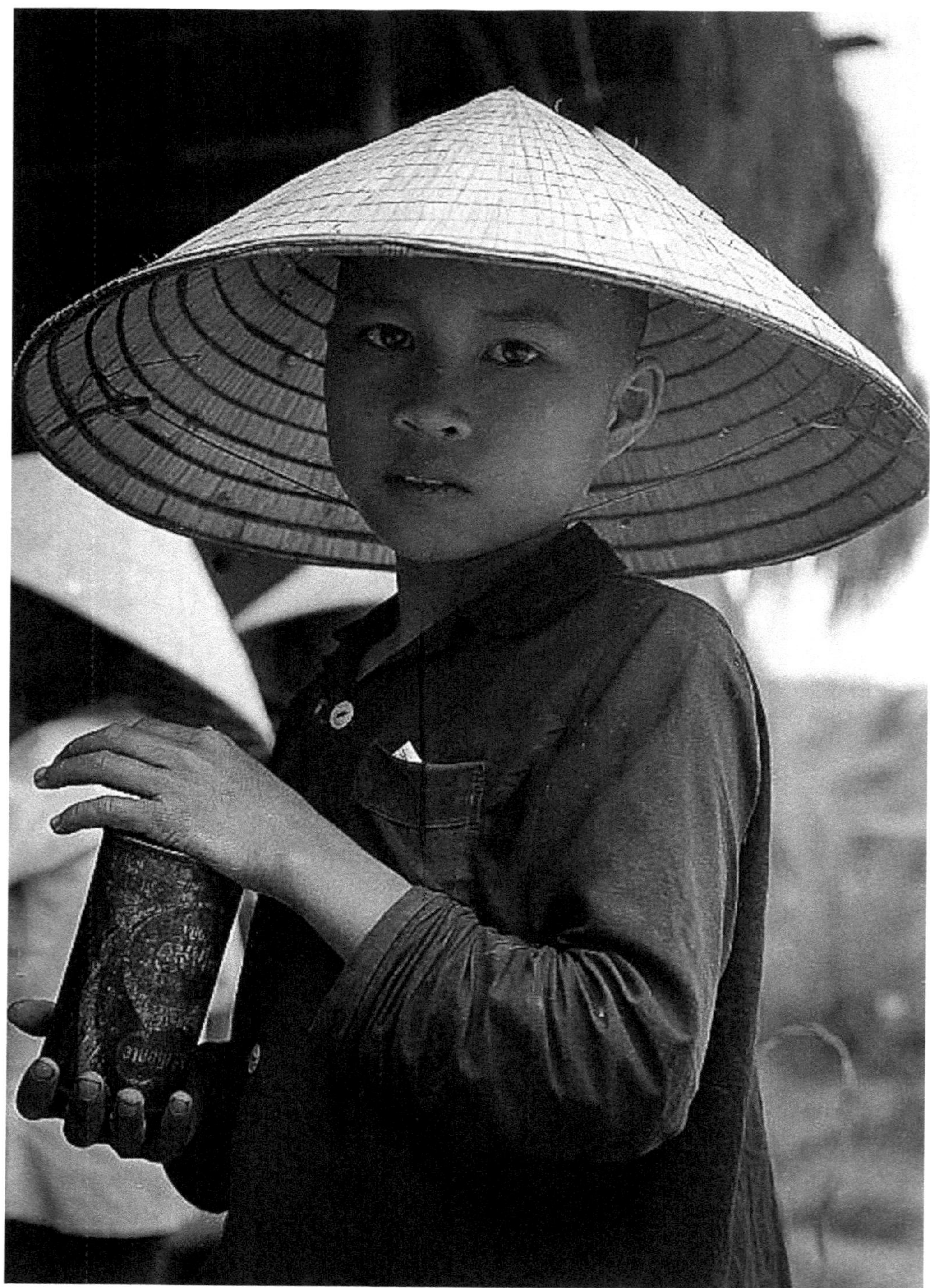

Happy Valley

Duc Duc Resettlement Camp

Phu Da

The Duc Duc Resettlement Camp was established in 1966 by the South Vietnamese government for refugees fleeing the Viet Cong from west of the Song Thu Bon (river). The area west of the river, known as Arizona Territory, was a Viet Cong and NVA (North Vietnamese Army/ PAVN) stronghold and was declared a free-fire zone. Vietnamese civilians within the area either supported or had been terrorized and subjugated by the VC for years.

Duc Duc Massacre

In the early morning hours of March 29, 1971, two battalions of the North Vietnamese Army and two Viet Cong sapper battalions, swept over the Duc Duc camp under the cover of a rocket and mortar barrage. The Viet Cong systematically burned and destroyed 1,500 homes and killed 108 civilians including children. It is likely a number of the children in these photographs were murdered in that tragedy.

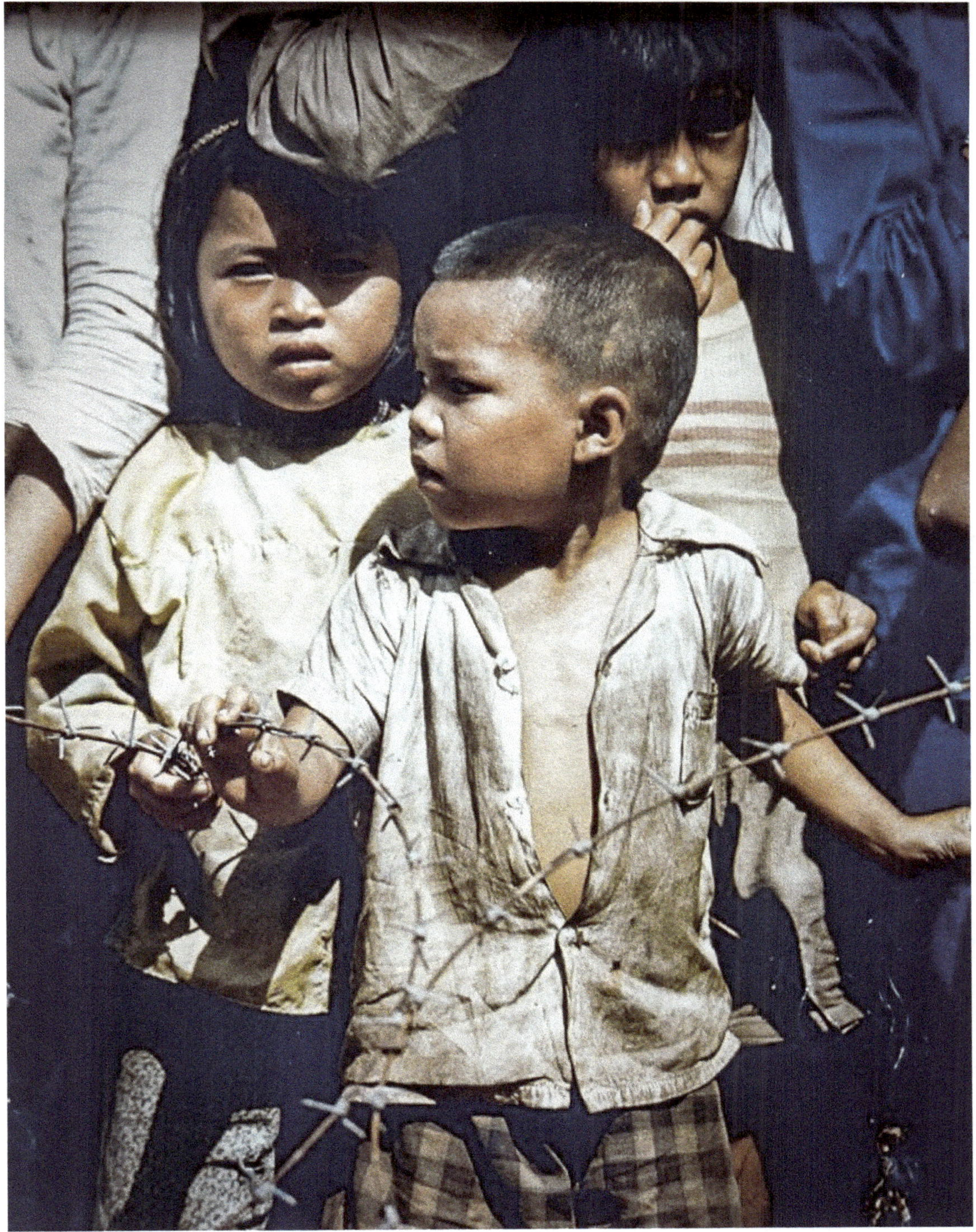

Newly arrived children at Duc Duc.

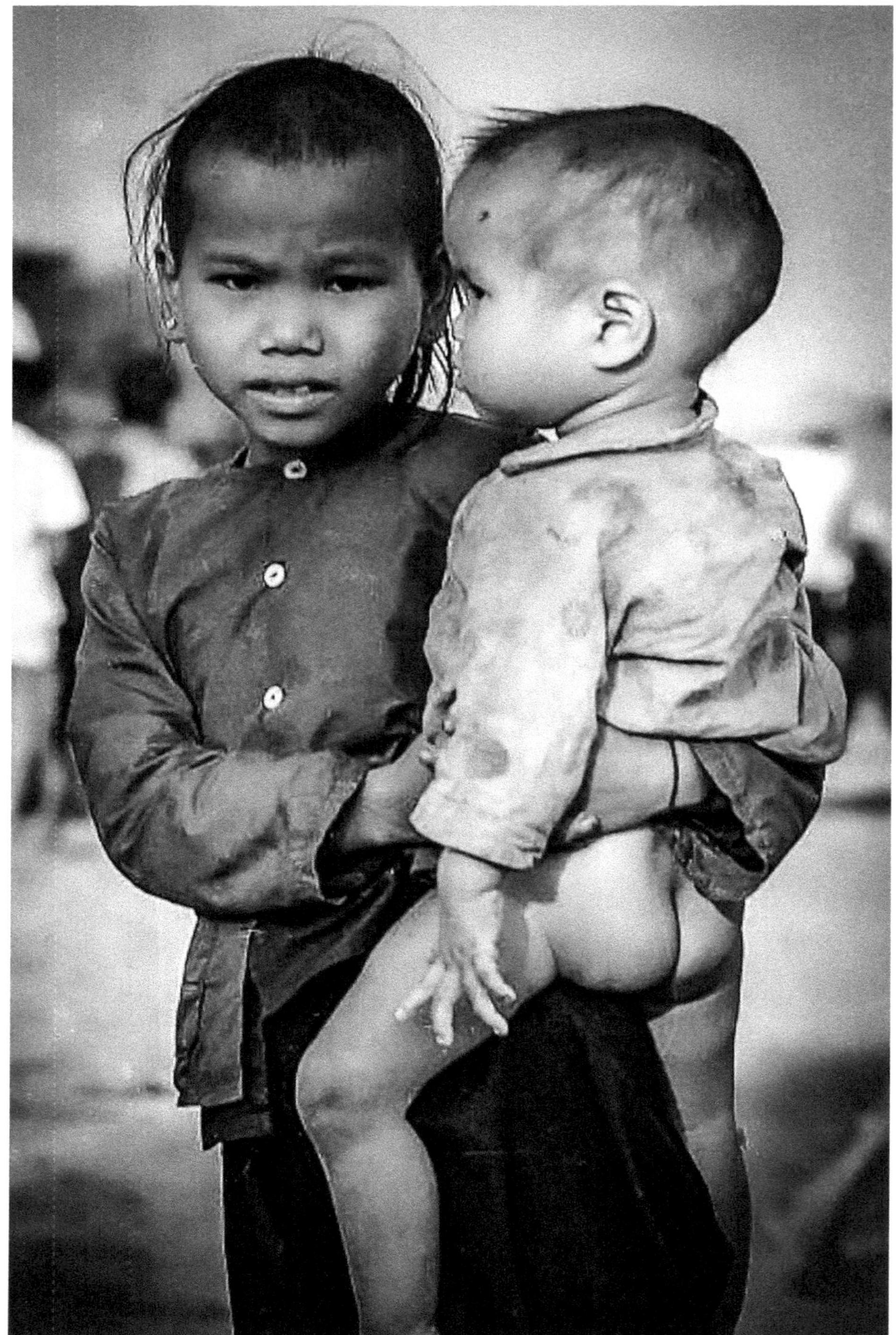

Care Taker of the Brother

Young girls care for their younger brothers and sisters as the parents work in rice paddies and fields. This girl and boy arrived at the Duc Duc Camp possibly without their parents.

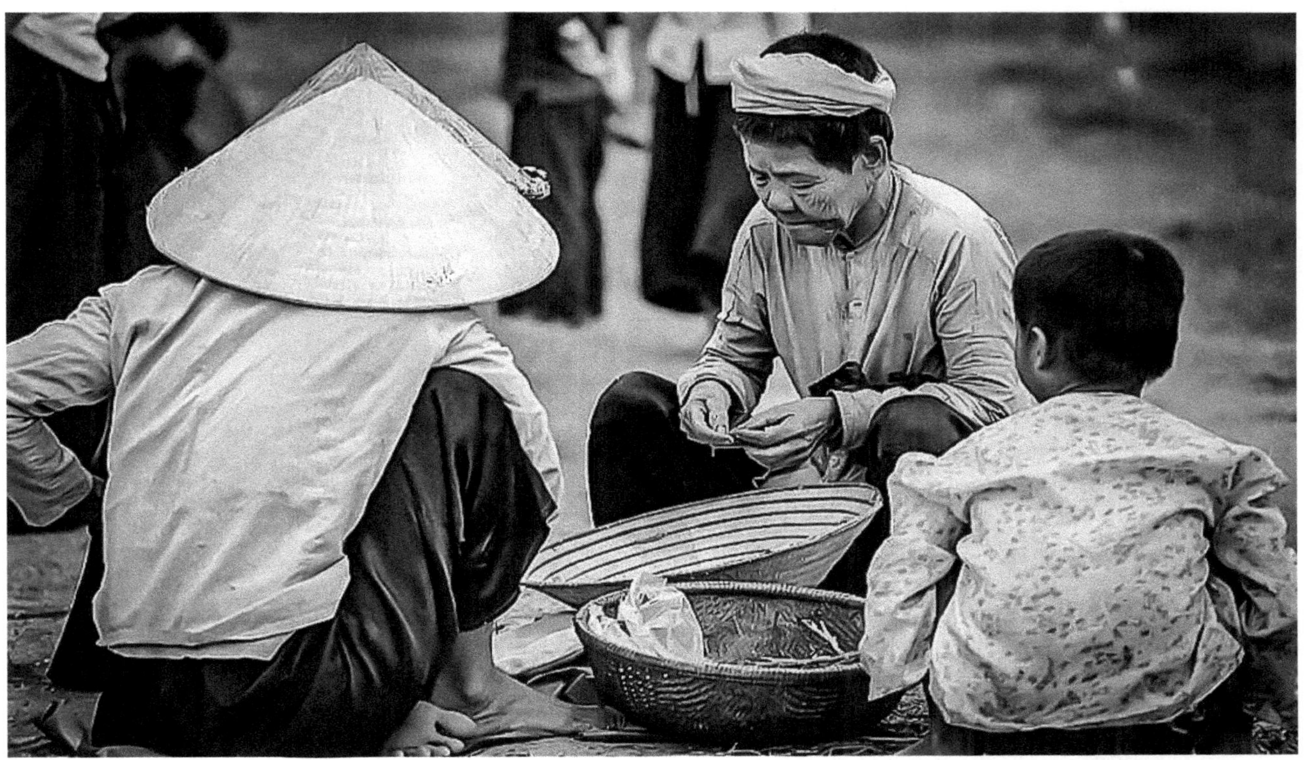

A family just arrived from across the Song Thu Bon River in the An Hoa River Basin (Arizona Territory). They have been removed from their centuries old ancestral home to deny the Viet Cong and PAVN (People's Army of Viet Nam or NVA) food and human resources. The Viet Cong routinely placed a rice tax on the local population as well as requiring the people to provide labor and other material support for their insurgency, often using threats of violence against family members or other methods of terror to obtain cooperation.

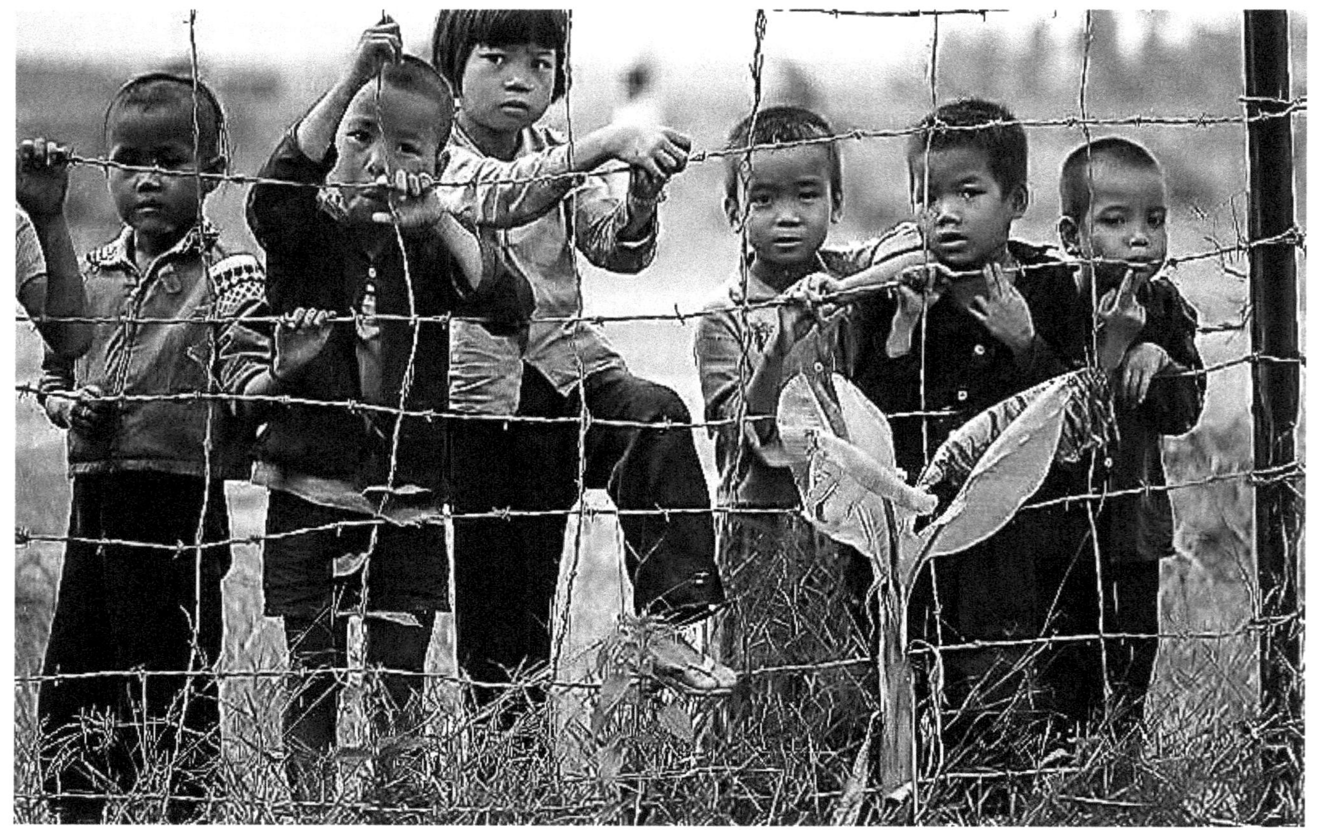

Waiting outside the wire patiently, the children are wary, but curious.

Duc Duc.

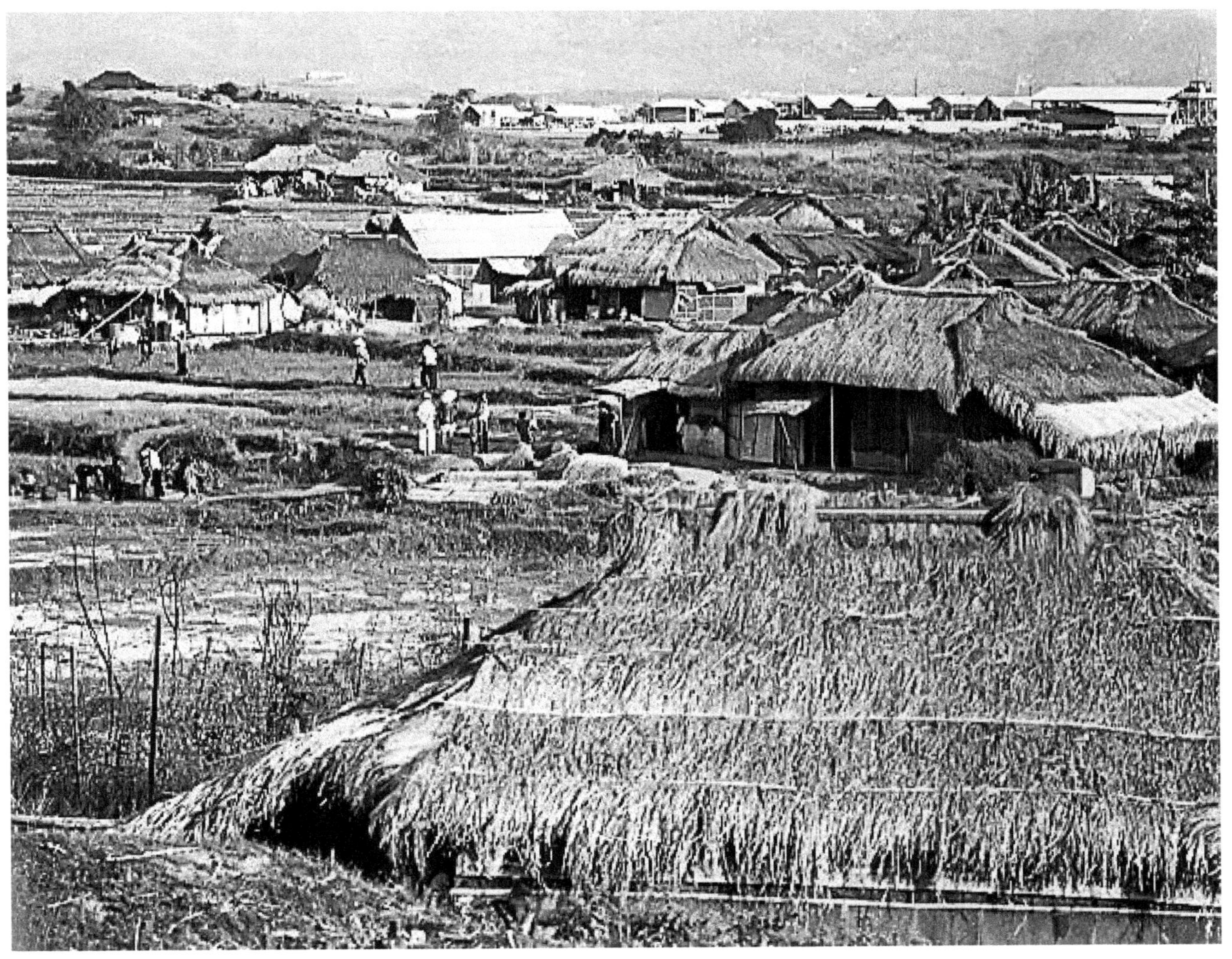

Duc Duc Resettlement Camp

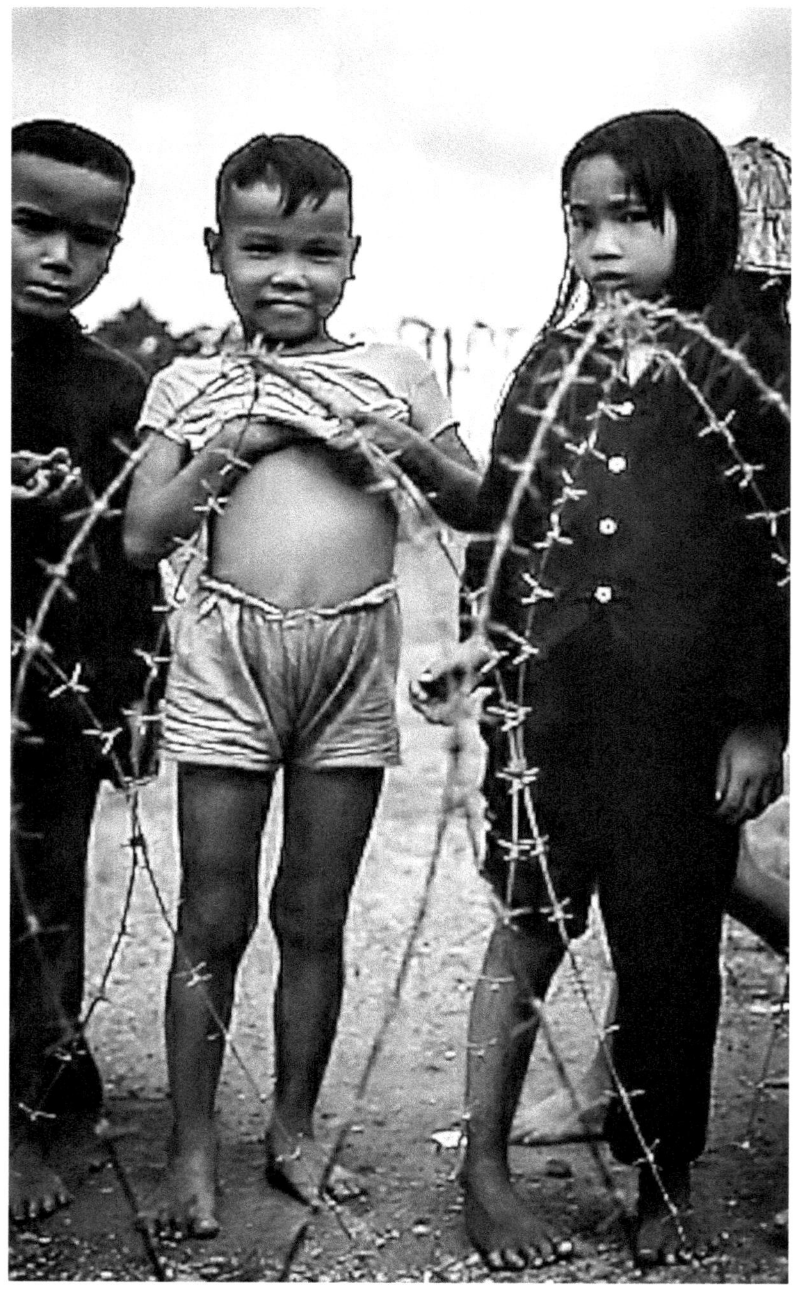

Concertina wire is

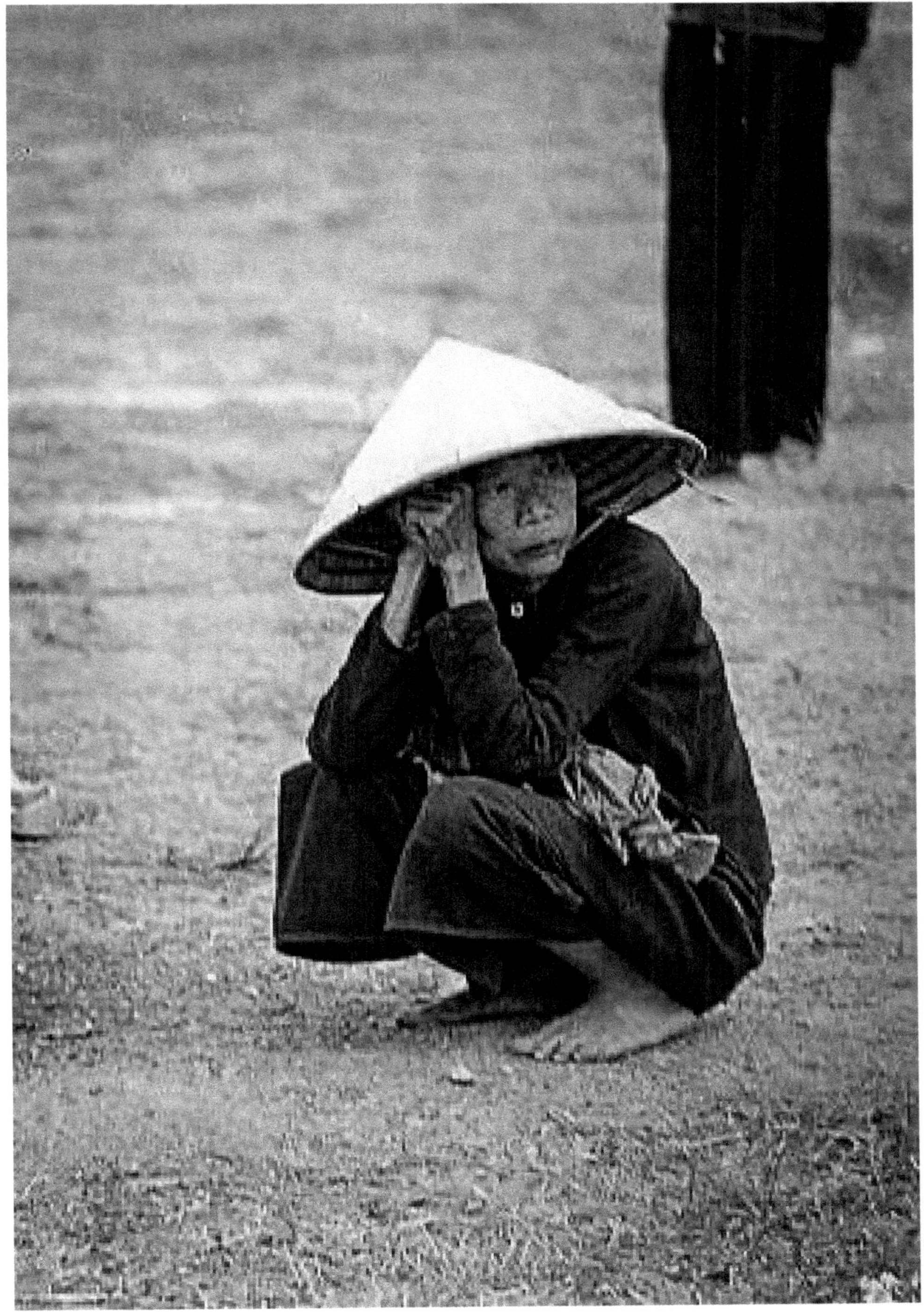

Forlorn elder displaced from Viet Cong territory across the Song Thu Bon River. 1966

Duc Duc

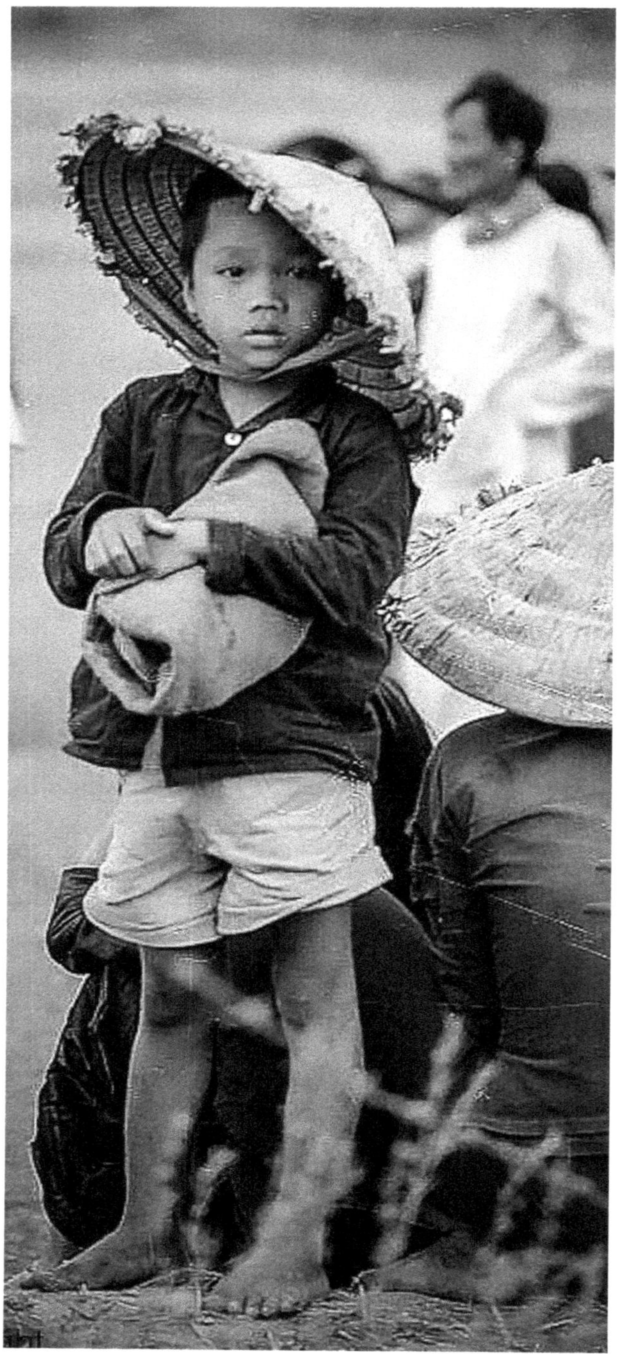

Alone after arriving at the Duc Duc Resettlement Camp without his family.

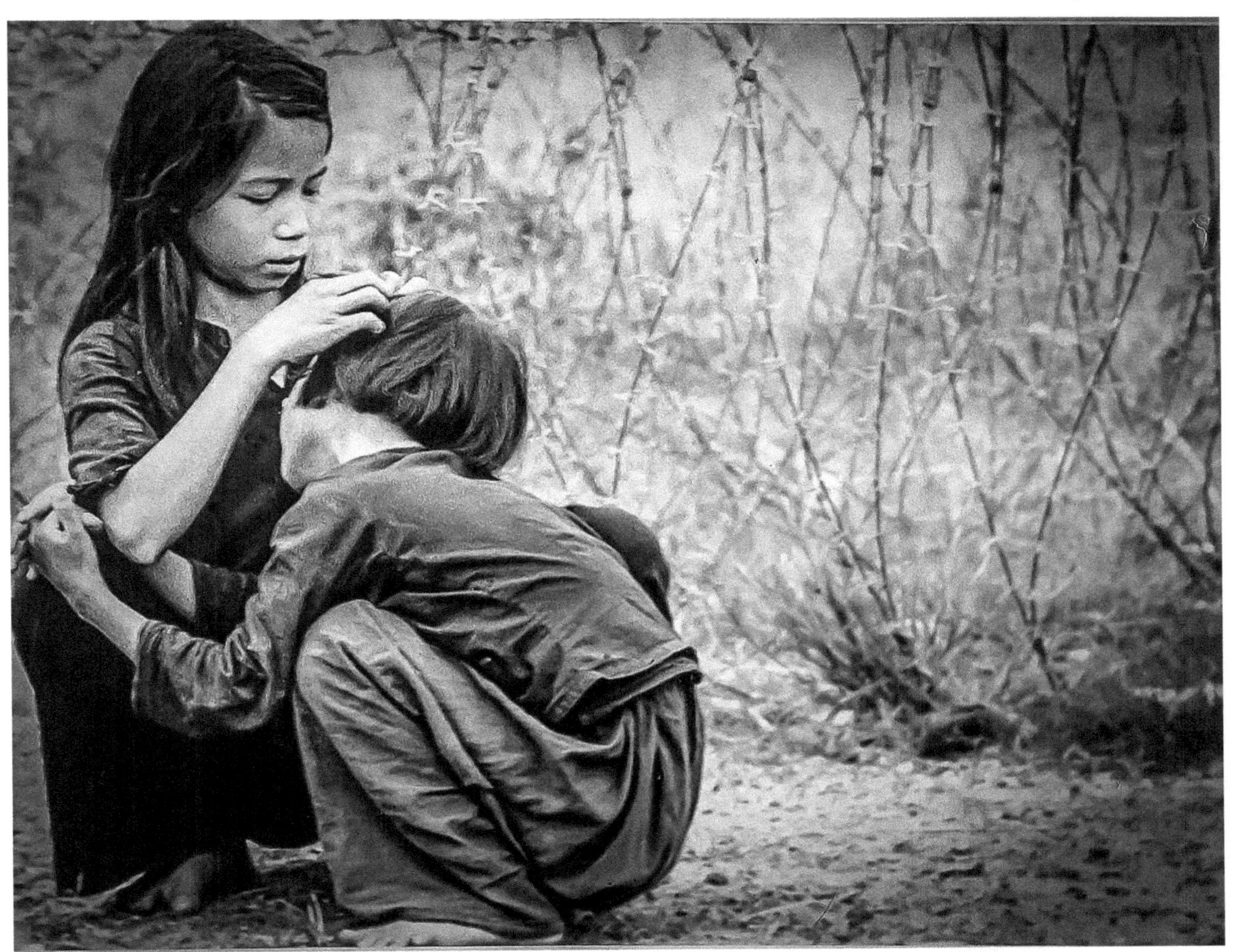

A fundamental and common element of life...lice removal. Tuberculosis, malaria, intestinal parasites, severe skin infections, malnutrition, congenitally acquired hepatitis B infection, and a host of other diseases, which contributed to a shortened life span...all were exacerbated by conditions created by the war...and there was the ever-present risk of a precipitous death as the war incessantly engulfed their ancestral land. 1966

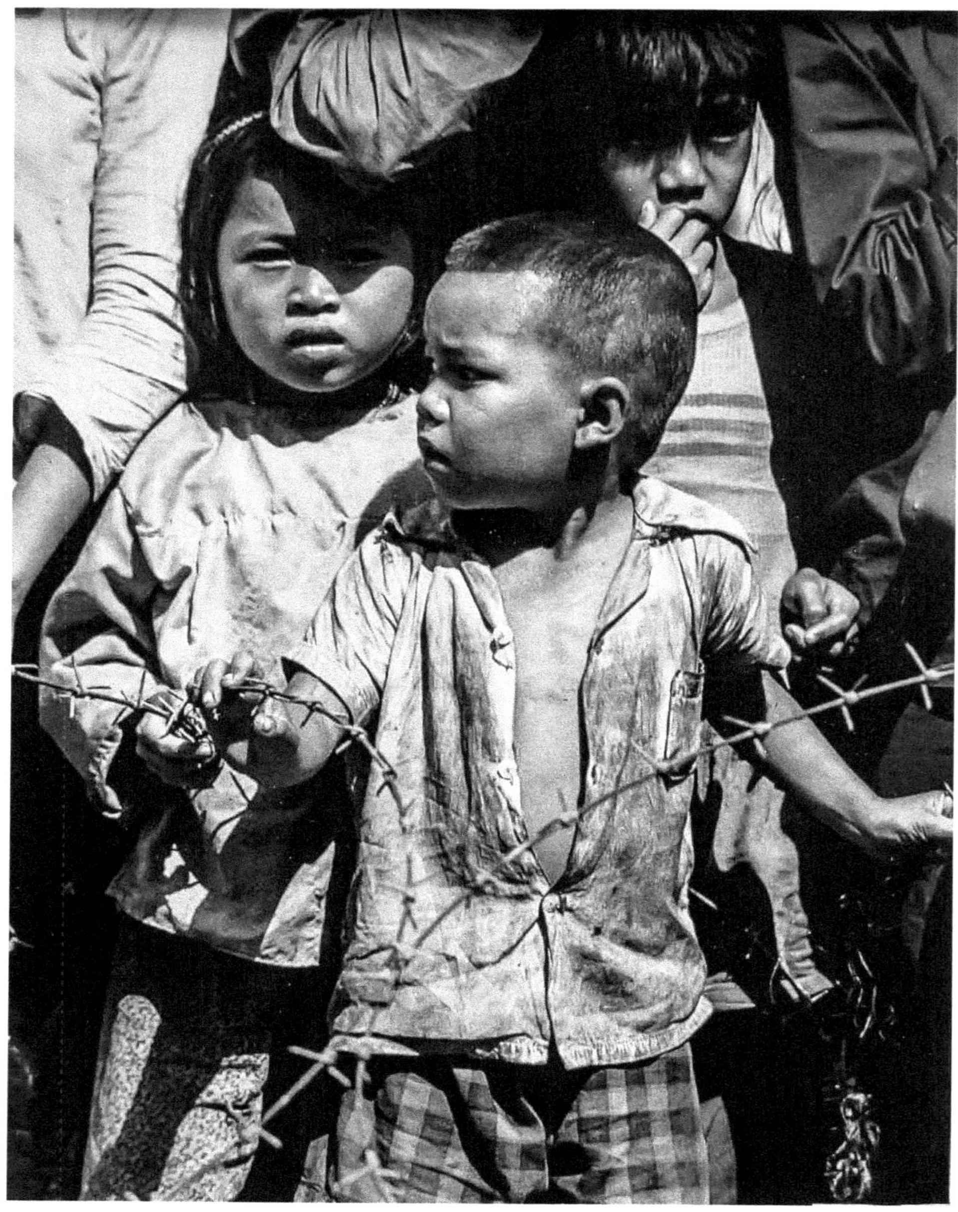

Duc Duc

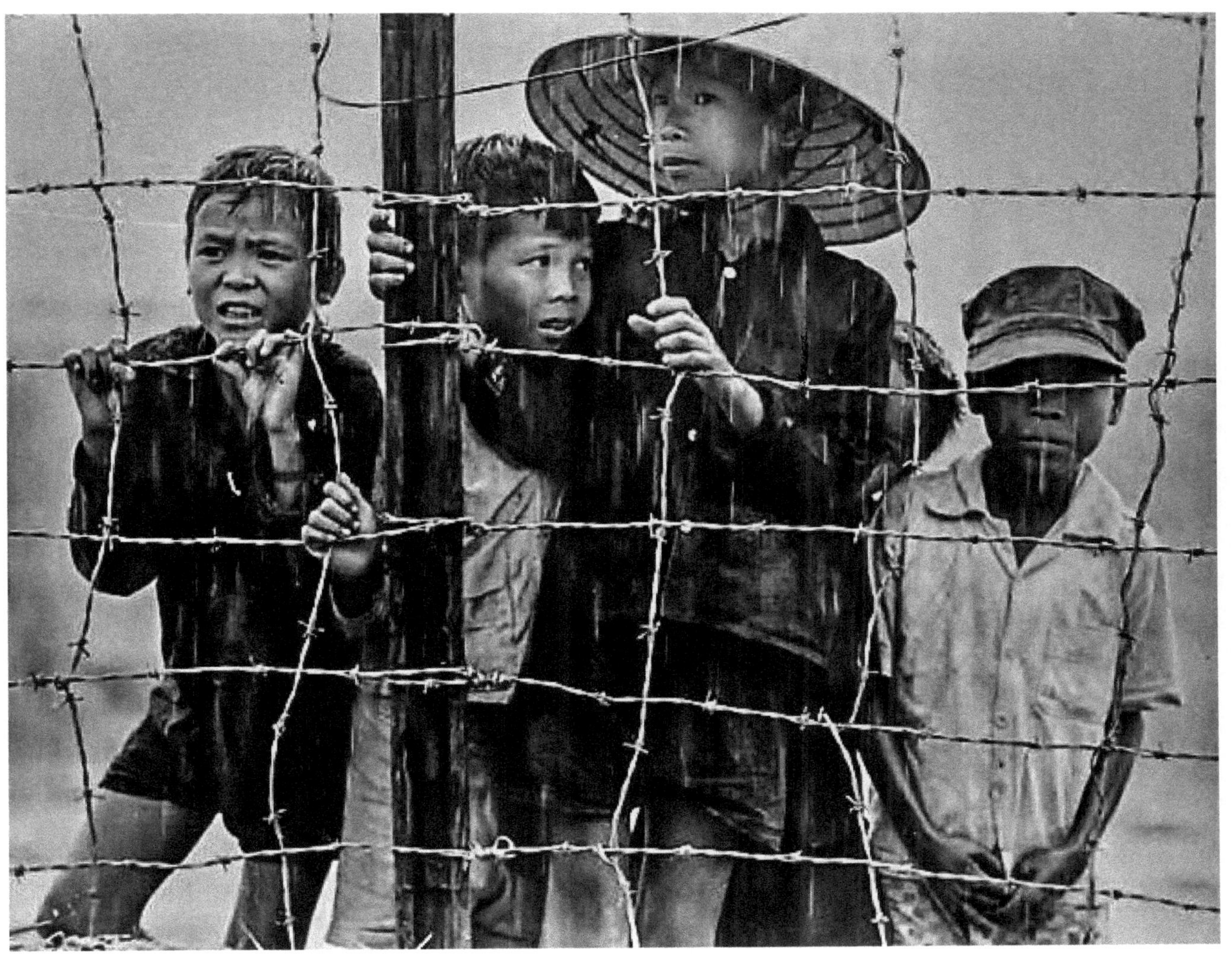

Like all of the children...the boys waited in the rain outside the wire. Duc Duc Camp 1966

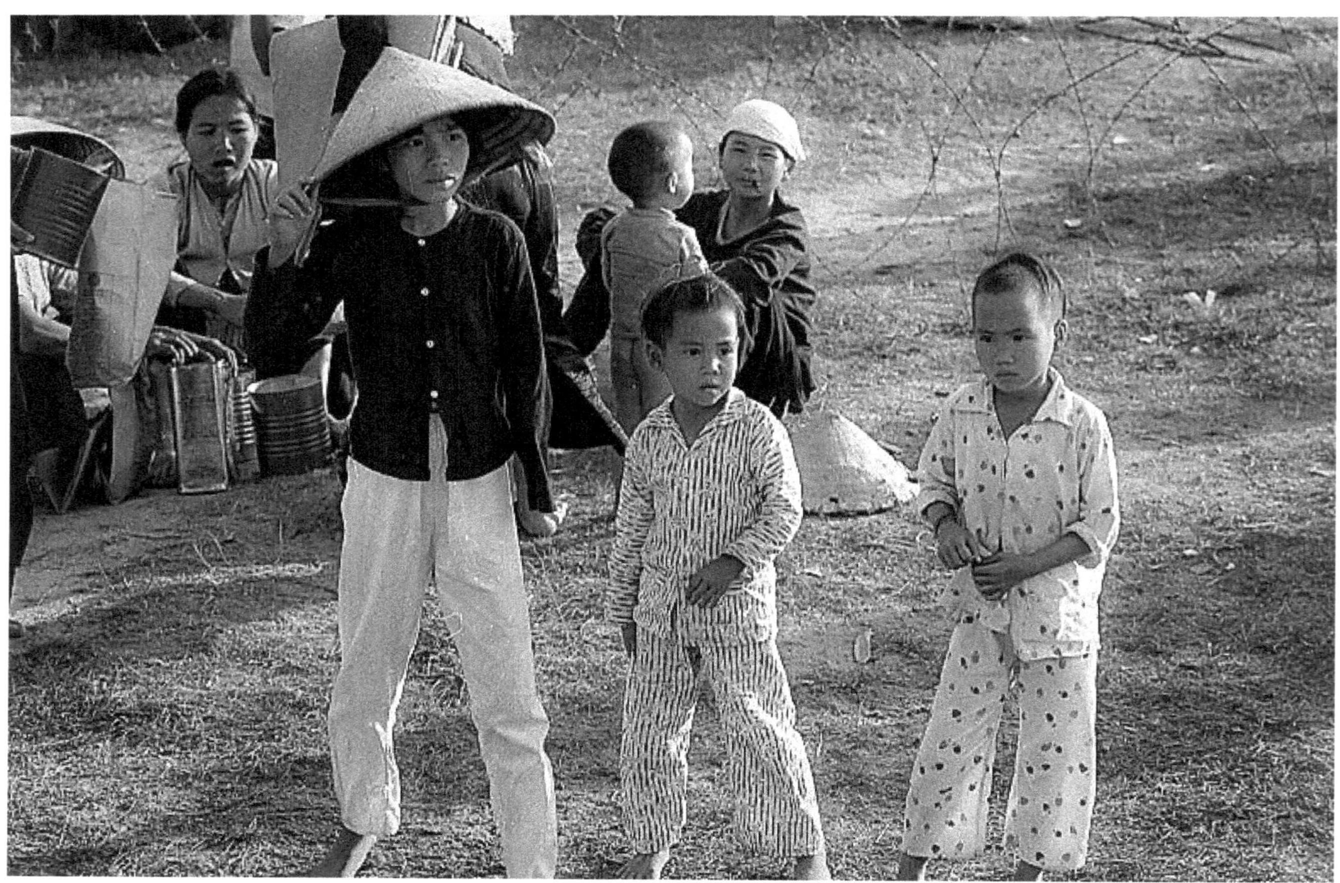

A Mother and two daughters from across the Song Thu Bon River, wear newly acquired clothing. The husband or older boys were notably absent, perhaps fighting with the Viet Cong. The ARVN (Army of the Republic of Viet Nam), or killed. Duc Duc, 1966.

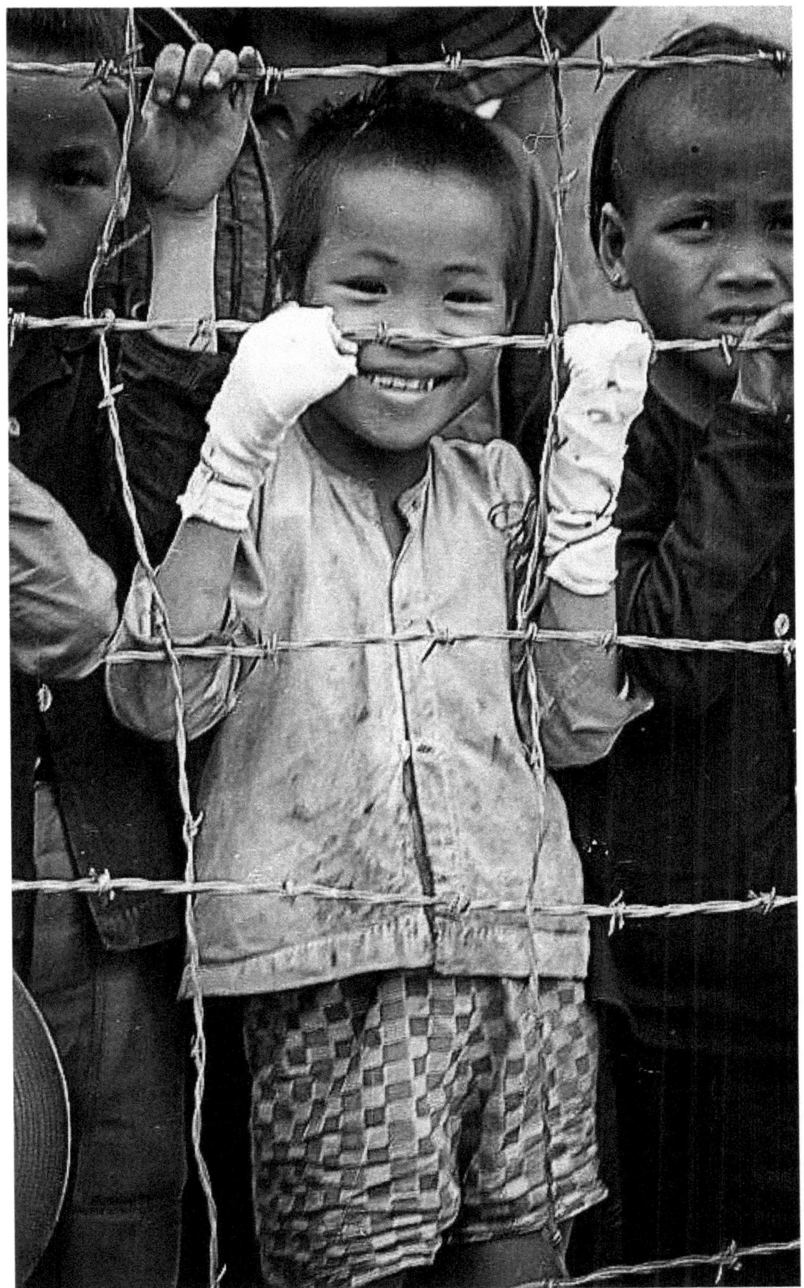

This young girl's serious hand infections required daily dressing changes and the administration of antibiotic injections before improvement occurred. Duc Duc.

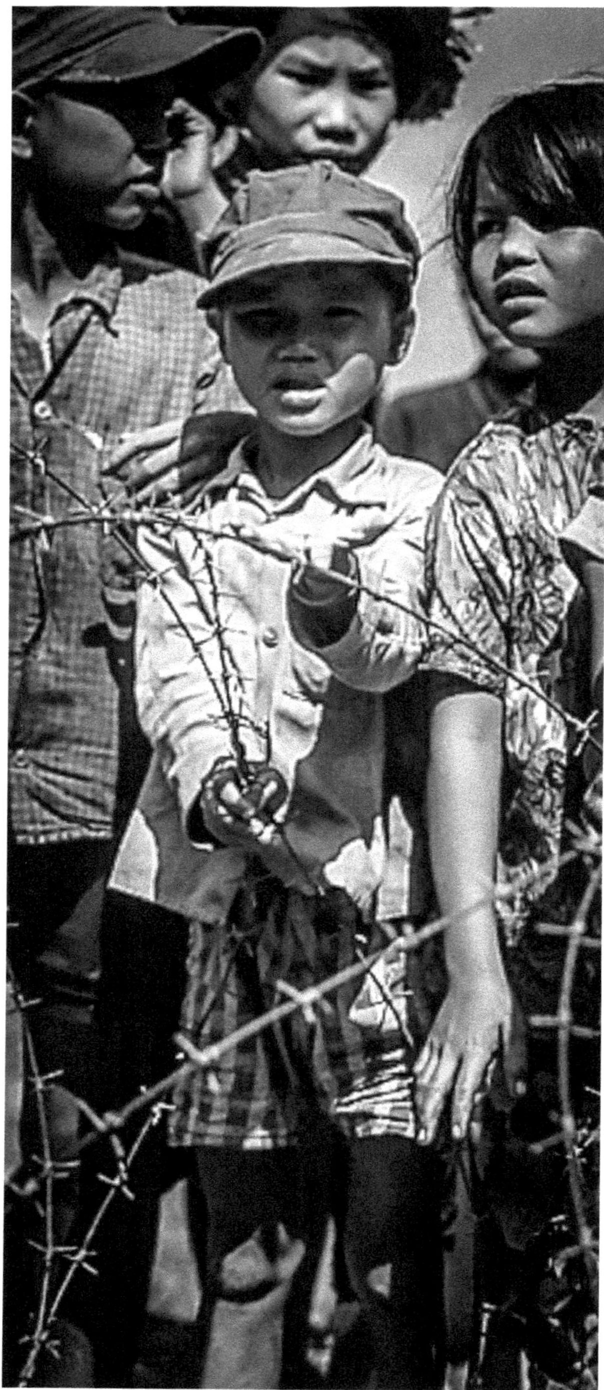

Duc Duc

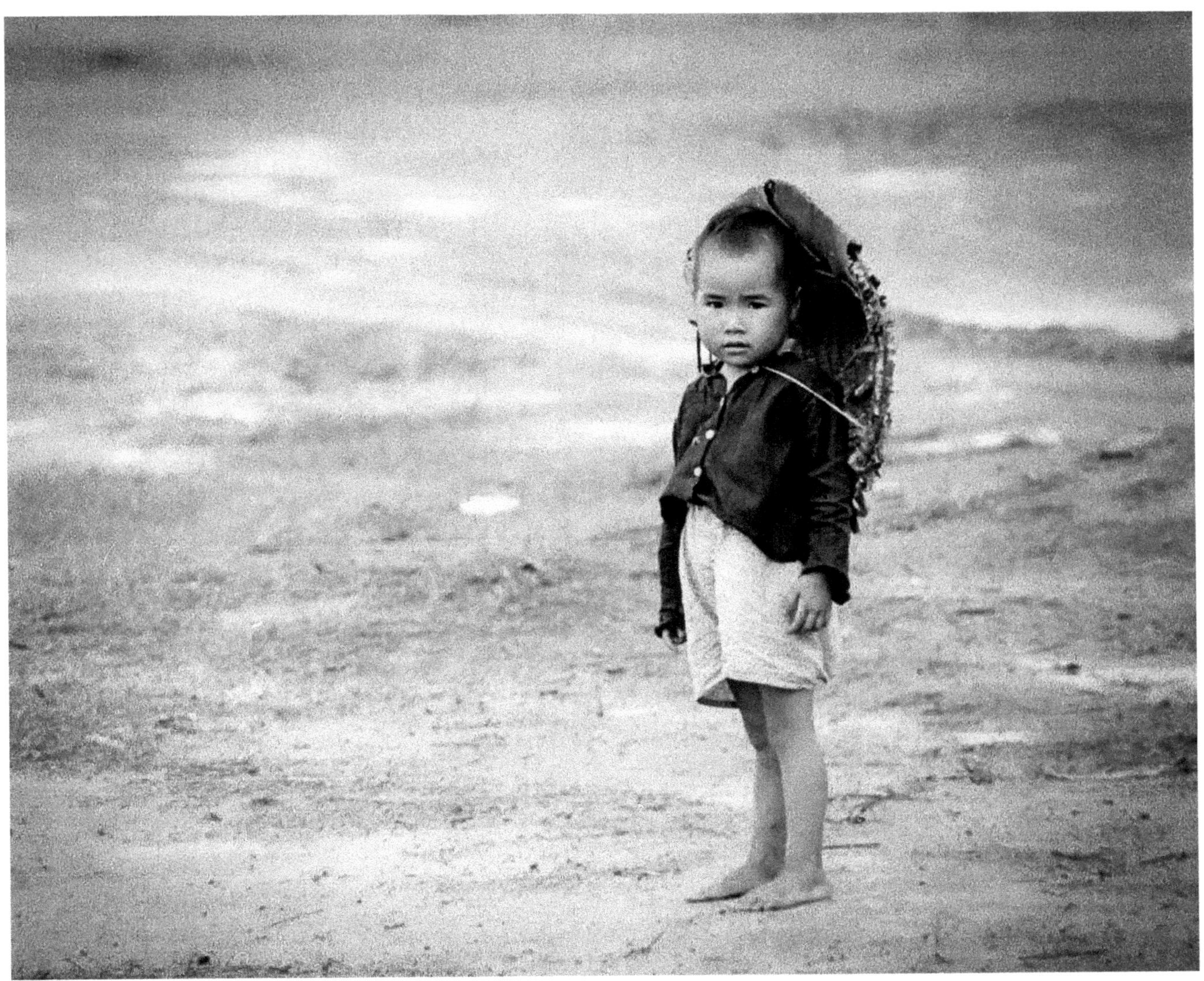

Duc Duc Camp Alone...removed from across the Song Thu Bon River from Viet Cong and NVA (North Vietnamese Army) territory...with whomever in his family survived years of warfare in their ancestral homeland. 1966

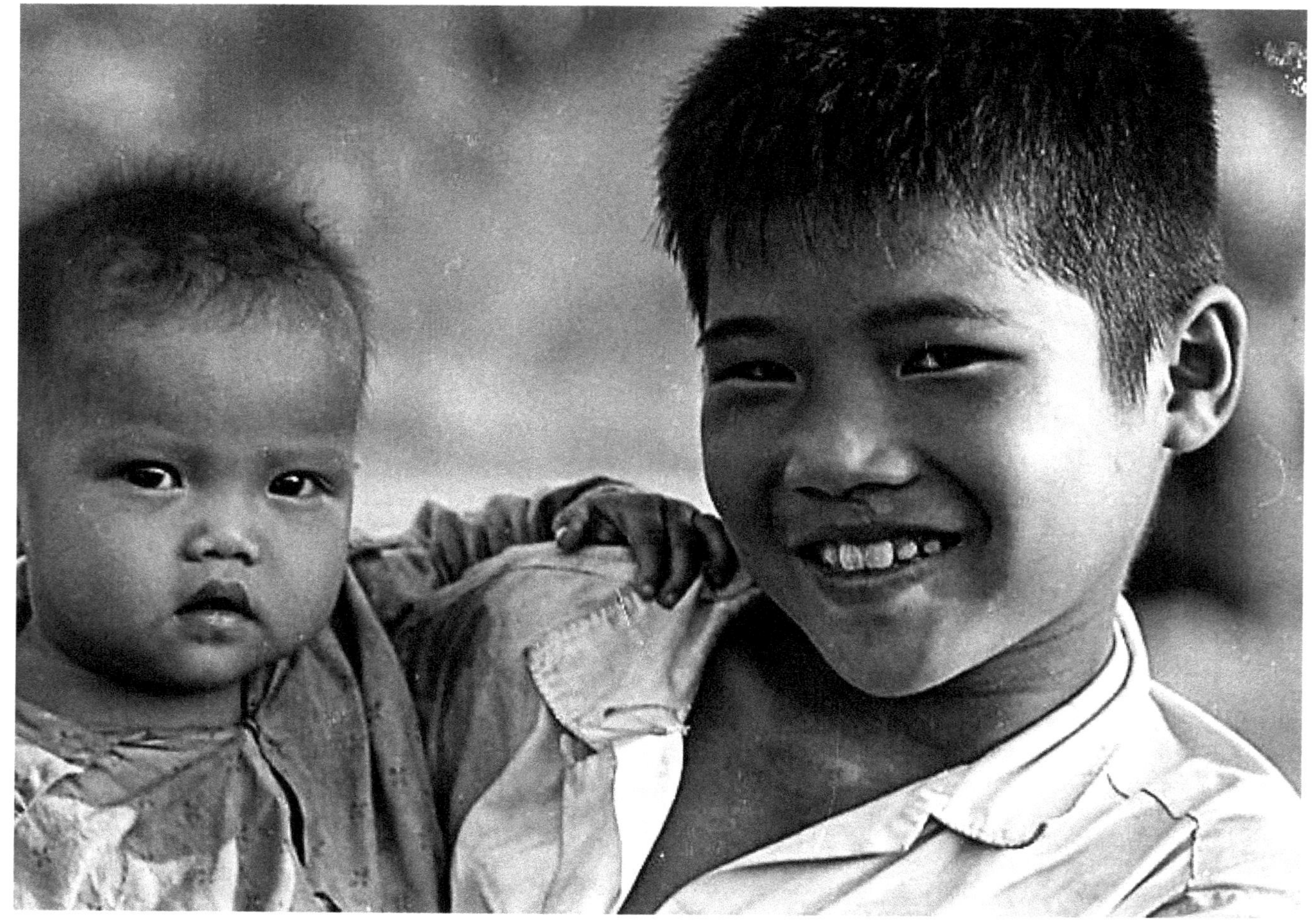

Brothers together in the Duc Duc Resettlement Camp.

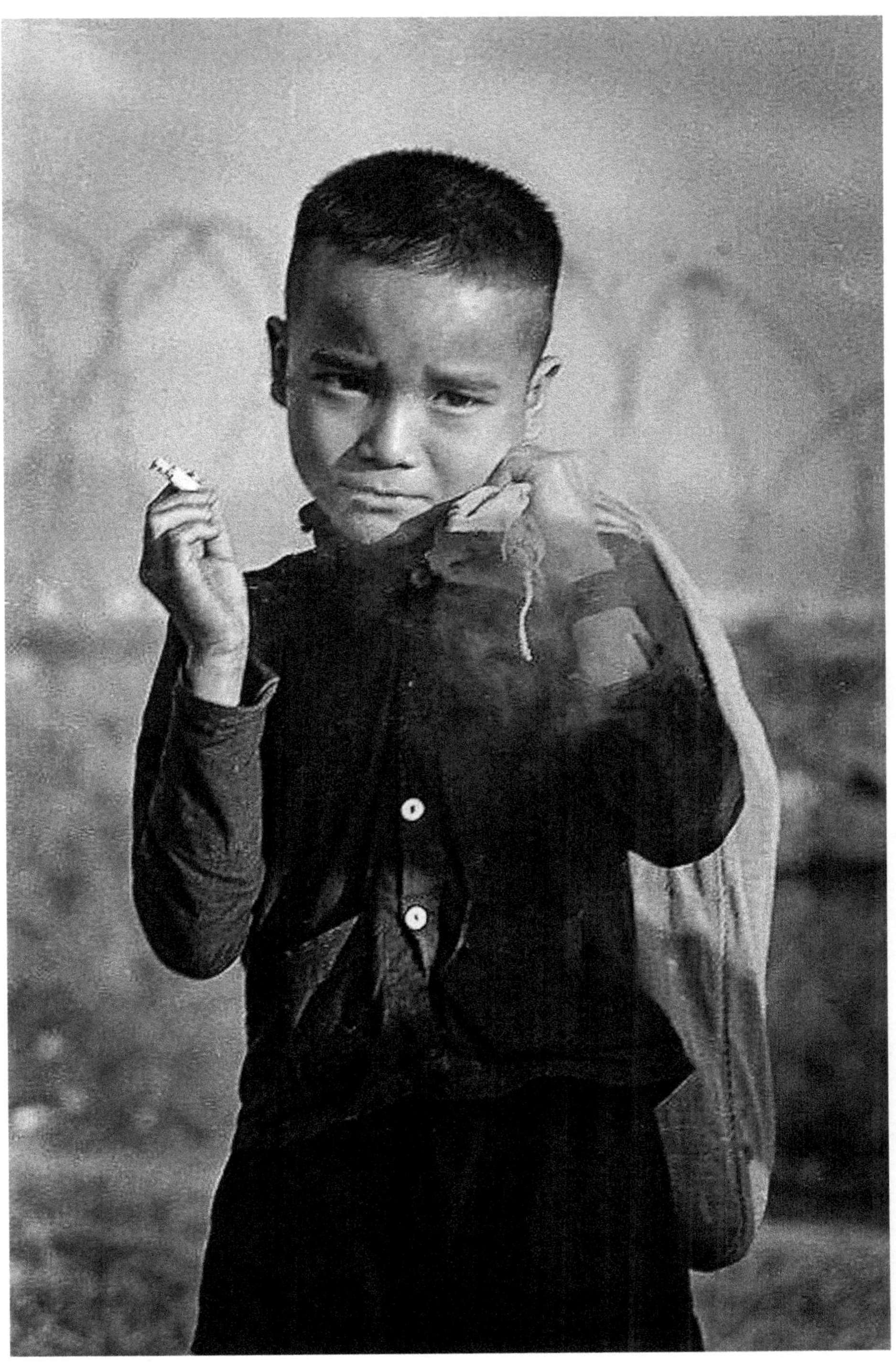

The behavior and conduct of young children reflected requirements and exposures that life handed to them long before they attained adulthood. Children worked in the fields and cared for their siblings. They witnessed and experienced the horrors that destroyed their homes and family members. In Viet Cong controlled areas they were often forcibly recruited by the communist insurgency, in whose service they served as combatants, intelligence gatherers, or laborers. This young boy was removed from across the Viet Cong controlled area west of the Song Thu Bon River in an effort to prevent that from happening to him. Duc Duc Camp.

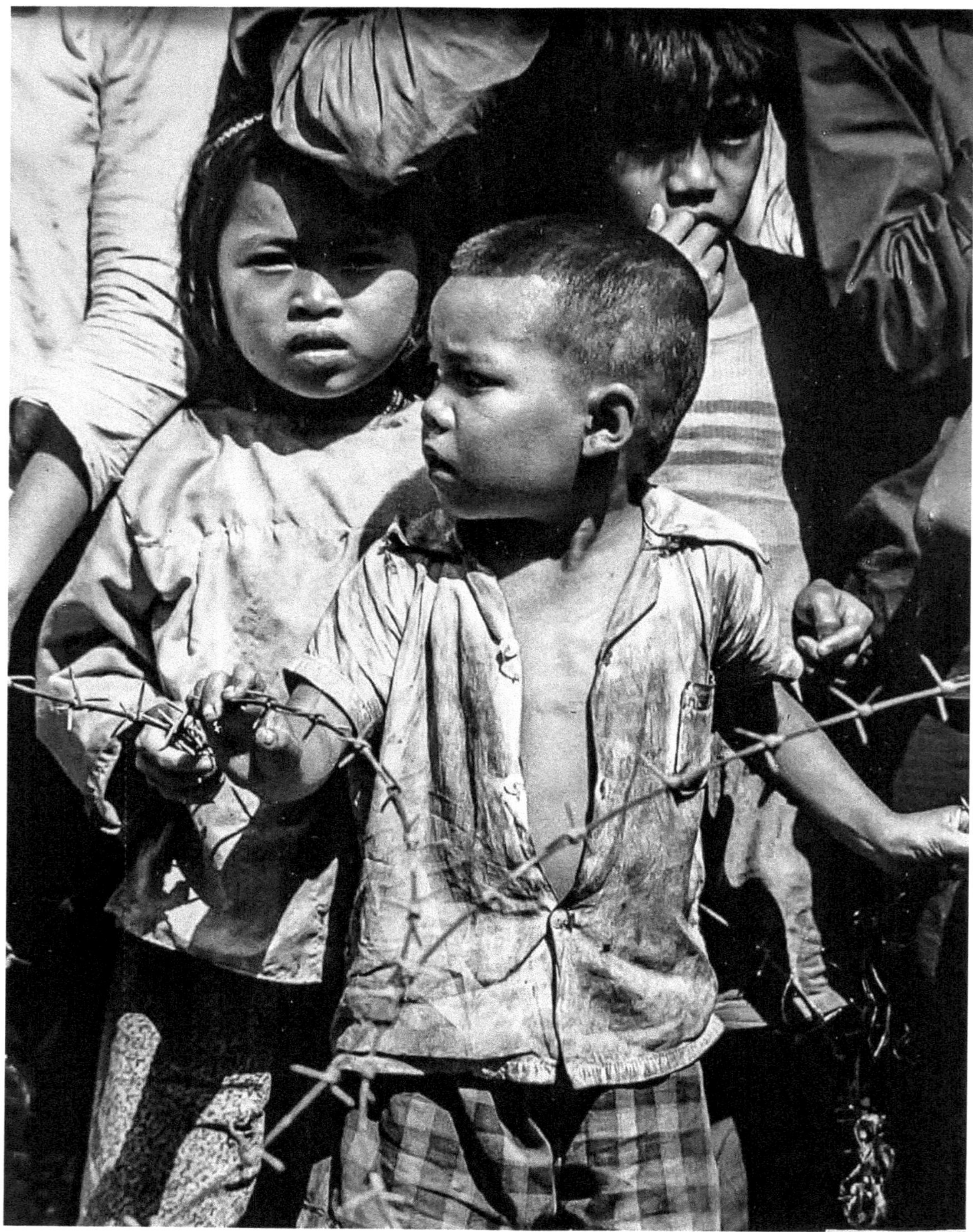

Children and adult women crowd the perimeter entanglement of barbed wire that was placed around our medical tent. Before the barrier was placed, we were unable to provide medical care in an organized manner because of crowd surge.

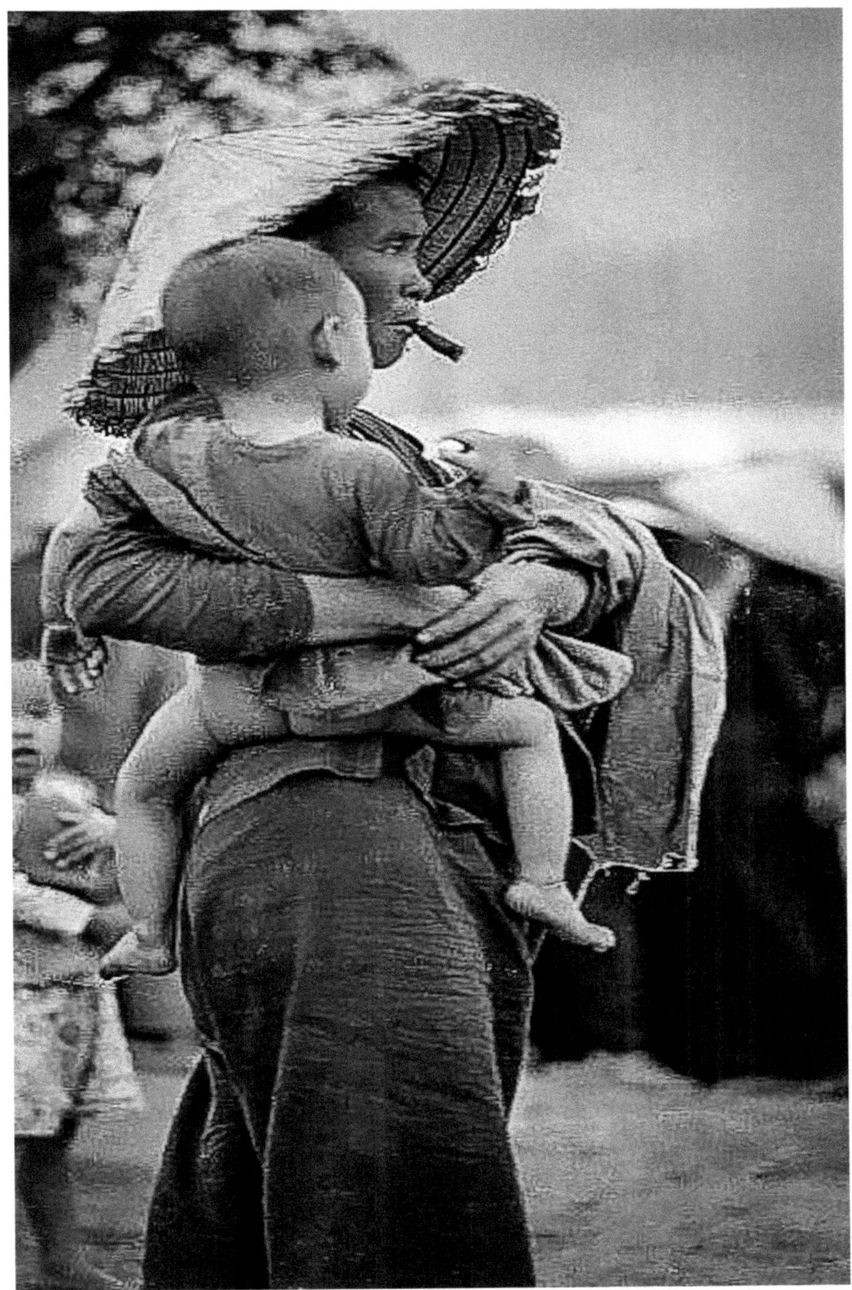

Clutching blanket and child....

a mother, just arrived from Arizona territory west of the Song Thu Bon (river), casts a stern gaze. She and her child, and the surviving members of her family, continued to be innocent victims of warring belligerents.

Duc Duc. 1966.

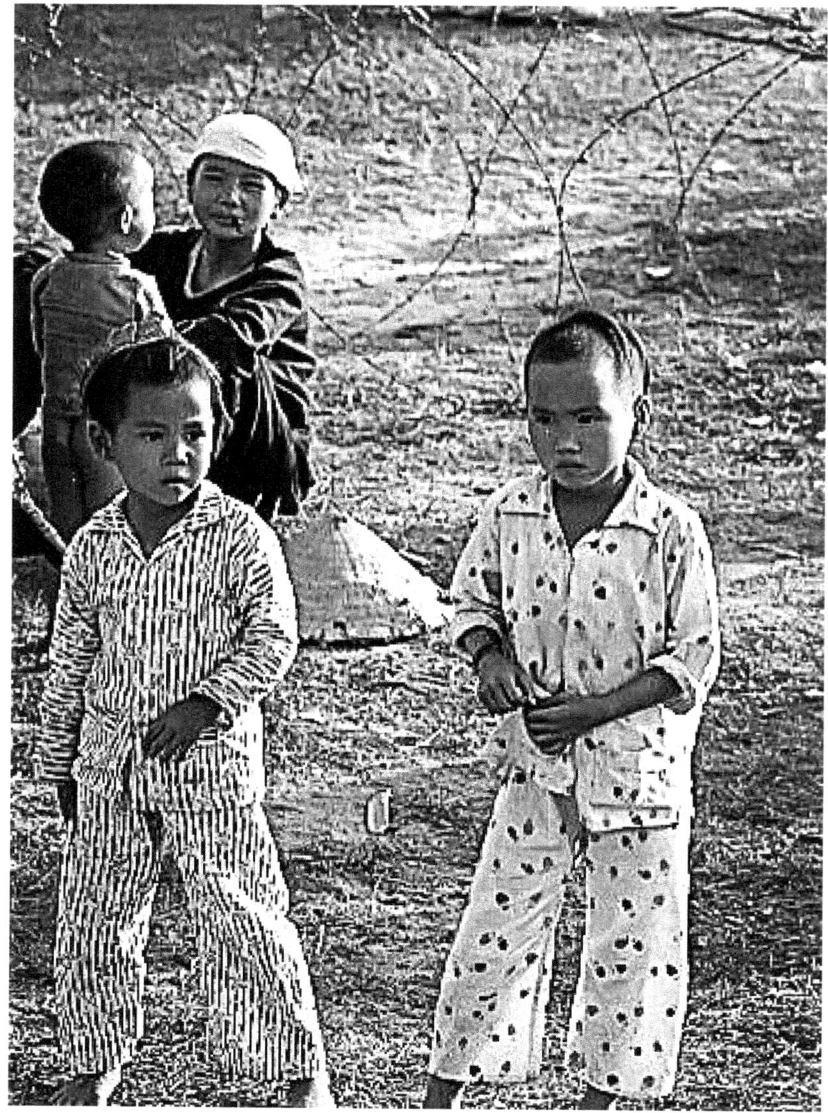

Displaced children from Viet Cong territory across the Song Thu Bon River received new clothing.

Duc Duc1966

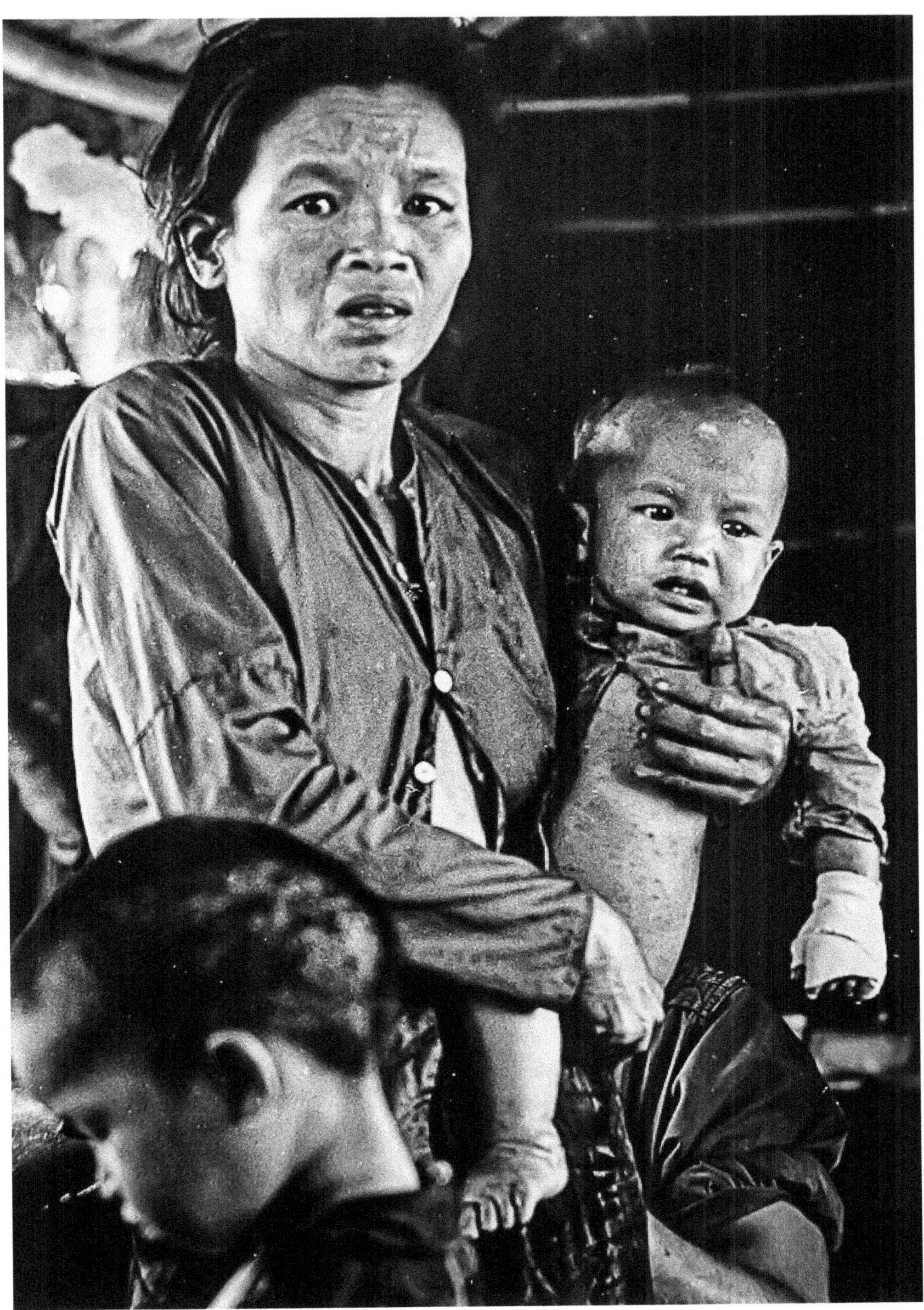

The reflection of fear... in a mother and her child penetrates deeply. In rural areas the Viet Cong instilled a sense of fear of Americans. She may have also witnessed American conduct or military tactics that precipitated this fear. The infant was treated for a severe skin infection after their arrival at the resettlement camp.

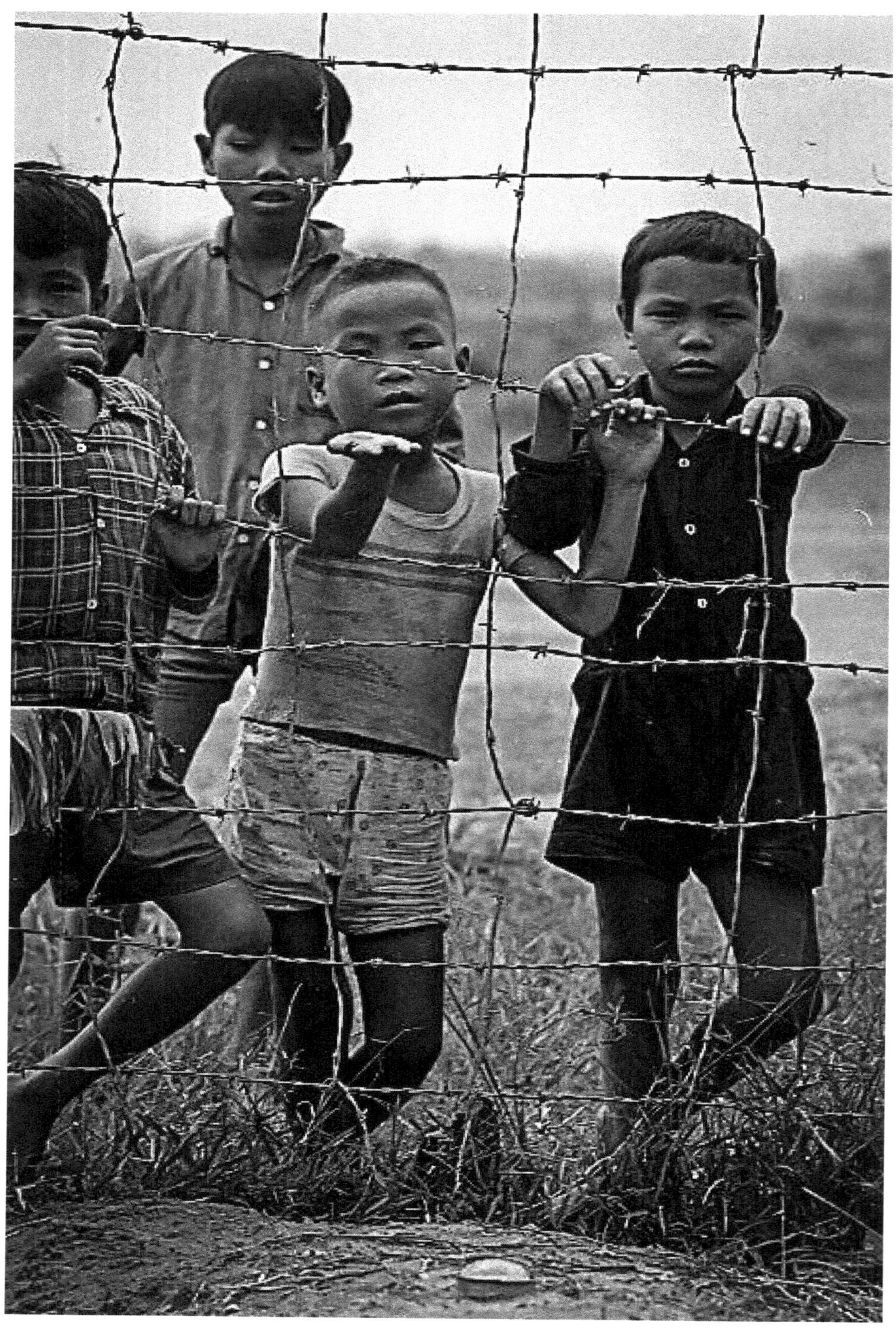

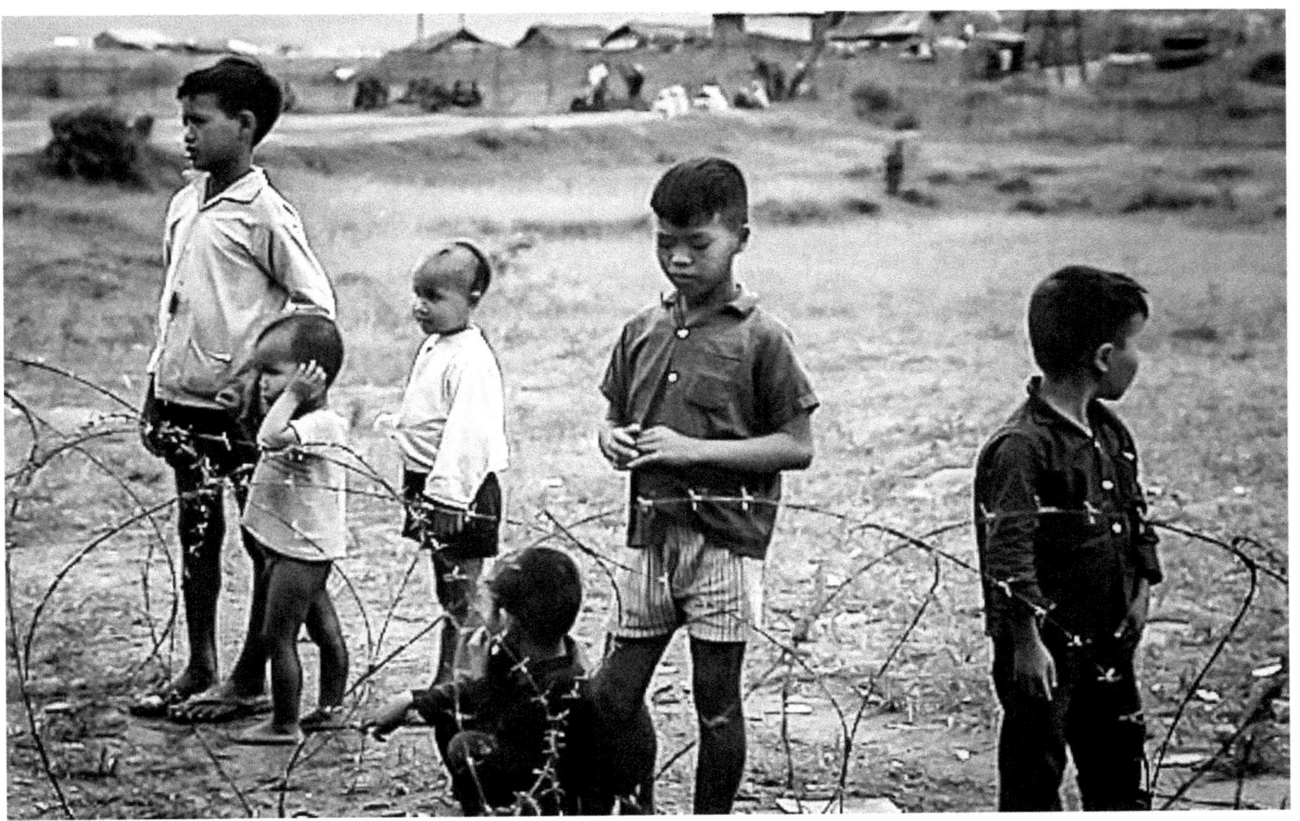

Waiting outside the wire. Duc Duc

Epilogue

The war continued to victimize children and their families for 6 years after I departed Viet Nam in 1969. Innocents would continue to die because of terrorist activities, artillery, aerial bombing, use of various armaments during military operations, landmines and booby traps. Many rural areas, had been declared or were de-facto free-fire zones, resulting in the destruction of property and the killing and wounding of innocent non-combatants. On 29 March 1972, The North Vietnamese Army (People's Army of Viet Nam/PAVN) launched a major conventional military invasion of the 2 northern most provinces, Quang Tri and Hue-Thua Thien, which resulted in the death of 25, 000 civilians and one million refugees. In 1975, South Viet Nam was again invaded by the north causing widespread civilian casualties and a massive refugee exodus.

Our efforts to provide medical care, repair and build wells and schools were successful, but the drawdown and eventual withdrawal of US forces resulted in a cessation of those efforts.

Chemical defoliation resulted in over 500,000 birth defects, and has continued to affect newborn children, and will affect yet unborn generations because of perpetuated genetic defects caused by chemical defoliants used during the war. The unborn became and will continue to be, victims of the war.

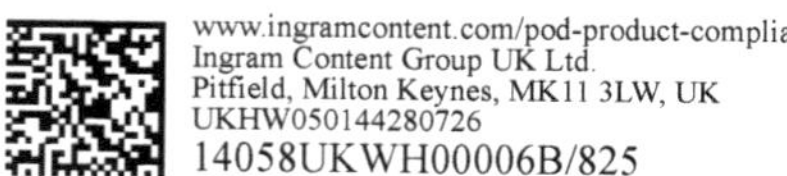
www.ingramcontent.com/pod-product-compliance
Ingram Content Group UK Ltd.
Pitfield, Milton Keynes, MK11 3LW, UK
UKHW050144280726
14058UKWH00006B/825